the complete
trail food
cookbook

Jennifer MacKenzie, Jay Nutt & Don Mercer

Robert
ROSE

The Complete Trail Food Cookbook
Text copyright © 2010 Jennifer MacKenzie, Jay Nutt and Don Mercer
Photographs copyright © 2010 Robert Rose Inc.
Cover and text design copyright © 2010 Robert Rose Inc.

Some of the recipes and information in this book were previously published in *The Dehydrator Bible*, published in 2009 by Robert Rose Inc.

For complete cataloguing information, see page 249.

Disclaimer

The recipes in this book have been carefully tested by our kitchen and our tasters. To the best of our knowledge, they are safe and nutritious for ordinary use and users. For those people with food or other allergies, or who have special food requirements or health issues, please read the suggested contents of each recipe carefully and determine whether or not they may create a problem for you. All recipes are used at the risk of the consumer. Consumers should always consult their dehydrator manufacturer's manual for recommended procedures and drying times.

We cannot be responsible for any hazards, loss or damage that may occur as a result of any recipe use.

For those with special needs, allergies, requirements or health problems, in the event of any doubt, please contact your medical adviser prior to the use of any recipe.

Design and Production: Daniella Zanchetta/PageWave Graphics Inc.
Editor: Sue Sumeraj
Proofreader: Sheila Wawanash
Indexer: Gillian Watts
Photography: Colin Erricson
Food Styling: Kathryn Robertson
Prop Styling: Charlene Erricson

Cover image: Orange and Sweet Pepper Chicken (page 149) with Cheese and Herb Skillet Biscuits (page 187)

We acknowledge the financial support of the Government of Canada through the Book Publishing Industry Development Program (BPIDP) for our publishing activities.

Published by Robert Rose Inc.
120 Eglinton Avenue East, Suite 800, Toronto, Ontario, Canada M4P 1E2
Tel: (416) 322-6552 Fax: (416) 322-6936

Printed and bound in Canada

1 2 3 4 5 6 7 8 9 TCP 18 17 16 15 14 13 12 11 10

Mixed Sources
Product group from well-managed forests, controlled sources and recycled wood or fiber
www.fsc.org Cert no. SW-COC-000952
© 1996 Forest Stewardship Council
FSC

Contents

Introduction

Long before there was a refrigerator (or two) in every home, a deep-freezer in the basement and supermarkets full of pretty much anything in a box, package or jar, making food last between harvest seasons required a great deal of ingenuity. Early civilizations discovered that food left out in the sun was still edible after it was dry. With the advent of fire, drying and smoking became useful tools for food preservation between successful hunts and sustained ancient civilizations by providing a more consistent source of food. At home today, we have the benefit of refrigeration, globalized food production and shipping and commercial processing, so we don't have to preserve our own food at all.

Of course, that all changes when you're heading out on the trail, in a canoe, to a campground or even in an RV. It's as though you're going back in time and those wonders of technology for storing food don't apply. Preparing food is more of a challenge, too. Making meals without the convenience of a four-burner stove, a convection oven, a microwave, a two-door fridge with a water and crushed ice dispenser, a mixer, a panini maker, a slow cooker (and so on!) is a little trickier, but that doesn't mean you have to sacrifice great taste, variety and good nutrition. Enter dehydrated food.

With a little advance planning, making your own camp food is really easy. There are many packaged products on the market, and you can buy a wide array of ready-mixed dried foods at outdoor stores. Of course, the quality varies greatly between brands, and so does the price. As with anything you make from scratch, by preparing camp food with your own dried products, you can control exactly what ingredients you add and be sure you'll like the flavor. With these recipes, you don't have to sacrifice quality and taste for convenience. You can have it all!

We've integrated the latest food safety information into our techniques (we've learned a few things since the earliest days of dehydrating), and have provided easy-to-follow drying instructions and time guidelines to give you the tools you need to preserve your own food safely at home. Rather than drying prepared cooked dishes, we've chosen to use individually dried ingredients, then combine them into meals you can prepare with ease regardless of where you are. This not only keeps the food as safe as possible, it allows you to customize the flavors, pack different meals for different people (allowing for those fussy ones — "no onions in mine!") and dry foods as they come into season or when you happen to have them on hand. We've included recipes that use primarily home-dried ingredients with a few store-bought items that just aren't practical to dry at home (powdered eggs, for instance), and we've given some options for fresh additions for times when you do have fresh ingredients available.

Another bonus of dehydrated food is cost. Whether you grow your own food, buy it locally from farmers' markets or farm stands, hunt for your own meat or even buy your food from a regular supermarket, seasonality still affects the price and abundance. It just makes sense to take advantage of food when it's readily available (and less expensive) and preserve it for times when it's not as plentiful, or not available at all. Drying it is a wonderful way to do this.

Modern appliances designed for food dehydration make this ancient preserving technique faster, more efficient, reliable and easy. We no longer have to worry about wild animals stealing food set out to dry or a sudden downpour ruining days of drying. A simple appliance with trays, a heat source and a fan takes away the element of surprise and essentially allows you to put fresh food in and take dried food out. Of course, drying food does take some know-how and a little trial and error at times.

Cooking is a blend of science and art. Dehydrating food and turning it into delicious meals is an excellent example of that, and our team of authors has combined their expertise to maximize both aspects. Don Mercer is a professional engineer specializing in food science, with years of experience perfecting the technique of drying food in a lab and in practical settings (including his own backyard). Don teaches around the world, helping developing communities implement the science of dehydration to sustain their food supply. Don has taken the guesswork out of drying foods so you can jump right in. Jennifer MacKenzie is a professional home economist with a bachelor of science in Foods and Nutrition. Through her expertise in recipe development, testing and writing, she knows both the science of how food works and the art of making it taste good — and how to write her techniques down so you can get the same results. Jay Nutt is a chef with years of experience cooking in restaurants and teaching cooking classes. He once rode his bicycle from Vancouver, British Columbia, to Mexico and truly learned to appreciate the importance of flavor, variety and convenience when it comes to trail food. He and Jennifer co-own their own café. Jay's flair for creating fabulous food that dazzles customers and keeps them coming back for more is incorporated into the recipes in this book, so you'll get the most out of your dried foods while making tasty dishes you'll love.

We hope you'll enjoy incorporating the age-old practice of food dehydration into your modern life and taking advantage of what nature provides while enjoying wholesome "home-cooked" food. So before you head out on your next adventure, load up your dehydrator and prep your favorite recipes. You'll be thrilled to enjoy your own food wherever the trail takes you!

Happy camping!

Acknowledgments

It takes quite a team to turn an idea into the book you're holding in your hands. From our team of authors, our thanks goes to the team at Robert Rose: our publisher, Bob Dees, for your vision and determination; Marian Jarkovich, for your marketing expertise; and Nina McCreath. To our editor, Sue Sumeraj, we could never have done this without your patience, attention to detail and wonderful way with words — and especially for deciphering what we were trying to say when we couldn't say it clearly ourselves.

The design and creative team took our recipes and instructions and created a lovely and useful book. Special thanks to Daniella Zanchetta and the PageWave Graphics team: Joseph Gisini, Andrew Smith and Kevin Cockburn. Thanks to photographer Colin Erricson, food stylist Kathryn Robertson and props stylist Charlene Erricson — making dried food look fantastic is no easy feat, but you did it. Thanks also to proofreader Sheila Wawanash and indexer Gillian Watts for adding that extra, important polish.

From Jennifer
To Mom, Brent, Alicia, John and Ryder, I realize more and more each day just how lucky I am to have such a supportive, loving family. Thank you!

Jay, thank you for not running the other way when I suggested you co-author another cookbook with me (in your other spare time) and for being there for me — always.

To Don, thank you for guiding us through the science of food drying. You helped us understand the "why?" so we could better apply the "how."

To Sue, I'll never forget your patience and support as an editor and friend, which helped get me through a rough patch.

Thank you to our family and friends who tasted our creations, offered ideas and suggestions and even picked up groceries for us (Ted, Shelly and Sami!).

To my dad, Ken, even though you're no longer here with me, I know your enthusiasm for life, love of travel and nature, and indefatigable encouragement will be with me always, regardless of how tough the trail might get.

From Jay
As with anyone who works with food, there are far more people who have influenced and shaped my career than can be mentioned here in these few words, so I extend my thanks to everyone I've worked with over the last 20 years in the restaurant and food service industry. They have collectively taught me more than I can possibly ever put to use.

Thanks to my family for all the camping trips, both fun and not so fun, and to those who joined me in my assorted wilderness adventures over the years.

Our staff and clientele at Nuttshell Next Door Café deserve special thanks for humoring my whims, frustrations and idiosyncrasies during the formation of this book.

None of the above could have been accomplished without the support of my mother-in-law, Pat MacKenzie, and my late father-in-law, Ken. I offer my love and gratitude for all you have done.

continued...

And finally, I must offer my love and thanks to my wife, Jennifer, whose passion for and knowledge of food and cooking help turn the gunpowder of my ideas from random explosions into orchestrated fireworks.

From Don

It has been a real joy for me to work with such creative individuals as Jennifer and Jay. As an Associate Professor in the Food Science Department at the University of Guelph, I tend to deal more with the scientific or mathematical aspects of drying and drying applications. Working on this book has been a refreshing and interesting experience.

I would like to thank my wife, Jane, for her abundant patience and understanding as I do solar drying experiments in the backyard, run various dehydrators in the garage, and sit down in the evening to enter data from laboratory experiments into spreadsheet programs on my laptop. It's also important to acknowledge the support of other family members: sincere thanks to our son Darren and his wife, Karren; to our son Geoffrey; and to our daughters, Andrea and Destiny. I would also like to welcome the newest addition to our family — our first grandchild, Ethan Douglas Mercer — who was born in April 2008. Of all the important things in this world, there is none as important as family.

To those of you reading this book, I hope you find pleasure and satisfaction as you dry your own products and enjoy using them to prepare the recipes presented here. Happy drying!

Part 1
Dehydrating Foods

Everything You Need to Know About Dehydrating Foods

What is Food Dehydration?

Basically, dehydration — or drying, as it is also called — is the process of removing water from a material. All food is composed of solids (starches, proteins, fiber, etc.) and a significant amount of water. In this book, we will look at the use of dried foods and explain how best to remove moisture from a wide variety of fruits, vegetables and herbs, as well as some prepared dishes, including meat.

The term "dehydration" is often used interchangeably with the term "drying." For our purposes, both words should be considered to mean the same thing.

The History of Drying Food

The origins of food drying predate recorded history. It is not hard to imagine primitive humans finding dried berries clinging to vines long after fresh berries had disappeared. These sweet, nutritious, sun-dried berries would have been a welcome food source during times of the year when other food was scarce. Natural drying processes were then duplicated by spreading fresh foods on the ground or on racks in the sun to dry. By preserving food in this way, early humans were not as vulnerable to food shortages as they had been. Almost every ancient culture developed some form of drying technology to preserve various foods, including fish and meat obtained from hunting. This is particularly true of those who lived in hot, dry regions of the world, where the abundant heat made drying relatively easy.

Not all drying relied on the sun's energy, however. Heat from fires was also an efficient and effective way to remove moisture — especially from meat, where smoke added to the preservation process.

Today, food dehydration is a science. We now understand the complexities of drying. Huge quantities of food can be dried in large commercial dryers, under highly controlled conditions, to produce shelf-stable products of uniformly high quality. One has only to walk through the supermarkets and look at the products on the shelves to see the impact of dried foods on our lives.

Advantages of Food Dehydration

By removing a major portion of the water from a food, we are able to reduce spoilage and increase the food's storage life. Without water, which is essential for their growth, many spoilage microorganisms cannot survive. Dried foods generally have little or no specialized storage requirements, but it is always best to keep them in a cool, dry location, out of direct sunlight, to maximize their shelf life.

Moisture removal also reduces weight and makes food easier to transport. This is of great importance to hikers and campers who have to carry their food supplies. Most of us are familiar with instant potatoes, which are simply potatoes with most of the water removed. Potatoes consist of about 80% water and 20% solids (mostly starches) when they are fresh. By removing most of the water, 5 pounds (2.5 kg) of fresh potatoes can be reduced to about 1 pound (0.5 kg) of dried potato flakes. Such a significant weight reduction is not only a boon to campers and hikers, but it also makes long-term storage more convenient, even in the comfort of home.

Some foods take on entirely different properties when dried. When dried under proper conditions, grapes become raisins, plums become prunes, fruit purées become fruit leathers and so on.

In addition, drying allows us to preserve the food we grow in our gardens so that we can enjoy it throughout the year. There is something immensely satisfying about being able to cook with homegrown fruits and vegetables long after they have been harvested. We can also take advantage of the bounty of locally grown foods from farm stands and farmers' markets or a Community Supported Agriculture (CSA) program; by preserving these foods for when they are out of season, we can reduce our "food miles" while knowing exactly where our food came from.

Do-It-Yourself Food Dehydration

The do-it-yourself approach has become increasingly popular and has worked its way into many aspects of our everyday lives. Food dehydration is no exception. With recent developments in equipment designed for home use, even the most inexperienced person can easily produce safe, high-quality dried foods. Easy-to-follow instructions are provided with most commercial home dehydrators to help you get started.

When you begin to dehydrate food, be prepared to make a few mistakes along the way. Remember, it is better to overdry a product than to underdry it. If you don't remove enough moisture, your product may spoil while in storage. An overly dried product, on the other hand, will not have enough moisture to support microbial growth, which means it will be "safer" than if too little moisture was removed. More liquid can always be added when you rehydrate the food, if necessary.

Always keep accurate records of what you have done. Important things to record are drying times, temperatures, details about the amount of product and how you prepared it, and the date on which the food was dried. It is a good idea to keep a notebook listing this information for future reference, and for possible improvements in future drying applications. All dried products should be properly labeled and dated so that you can refer to your notes at a later time, if the need arises. If you are ever in doubt about the safety of a product, throw it out.

One mistake you may make early in your home food-drying work is comparing your results to those from large-scale commercial drying operations. Commercial products are prepared under conditions that meet exacting standards for which the dryer has been specifically designed. Home dehydrators cannot meet such rigorous standards. They are designed to provide flexibility and versatility for drying a wide range of products that would not normally be encountered in a commercial food processing facility. As well, many commercially dried foods have added sugar, sulphites and oil to further preserve the texture and color, making them softer and brighter-colored than home-dried foods. Home drying allows you to dry food without any additives, and you certainly know exactly what you're eating.

Equipment
Home Food Dehydrators

Drying can be accomplished in a variety of ways, using different forms of equipment. Some people might like to build their own food dryer, but the easiest and safest approach is to purchase one of the many models of home dehydrators that are now commercially available. An Internet search will turn up a wide variety of dehydrators, one of which may appeal to you.

When you're choosing a dehydrator, there are a few considerations that must be taken into account. First and foremost among these is whether the dehydrator has a fan to circulate heated air throughout the dryer and across all food surfaces. Units without a fan will take longer to dry the food to its final desired moisture content than a similarly sized unit equipped with a fan. There may also be an unevenness in the drying. In this book, times given for drying are based on tests conducted using food dehydrators with circulating fans. Some dehydrators have the fan mounted on the top of the machine, some at the back and some at the bottom. Each performs slightly differently, making the drying pattern different between the machines, but the final results are very similar.

Another factor in selecting a home food dehydrator is its heating capacity. A dehydrator with a 500-watt heater may be satisfactory for those who intend to dry only small amounts of product. Those who are drying larger volumes of product, or who might want to in the future, should consider a more powerful heater (e.g., 1 kilowatt).

Other considerations include the size of the machine (and how it will fit into the space you have available) and how easy it is to clean. Some people may want to look for features such as a digital temperature display and a timer that will automatically shut off the dryer after a desired time period.

Whatever your needs or desires, there is probably a dryer available to meet them. If you're new to drying, you may be tempted to buy a small machine, but once you embrace the idea of having your pantry stocked with home-dried foods, you'll likely want a dehydrator with a larger capacity. Many models come with the option to expand the capacity with additional trays; these are certainly something to consider when making your initial purchase.

After selecting a food dehydrator, you will have to experiment to identify the best conditions for the products you wish to dry. Do not become discouraged by any failures or setbacks you may encounter; this is all part of the learning process. Once you get over your initial apprehension about doing your own food drying, you will begin to enjoy the opportunities it offers. We have made every effort to provide you with the information you need to successfully prepare each of the dried ingredients for the recipes presented here.

Other Essential Equipment

- **Airtight containers:** Glass jars or metal canisters with a tight-sealing lid or plastic containers designed for food storage provide the best protection to preserve dried foods.

- **Colander:** This should be sturdy and made of a heat-resistant material, such as stainless steel, enameled steel or silicone, for draining blanched or checked foods (the term "checking" is explained on page 22).

- **Fine-mesh tray liners (e.g., Clean-A-Screen):** Some dehydrators have trays with a fairly open mesh or rungs. For food that gets very small when dried, such as asparagus or grains, and for those that are higher in sugar and may stick, such as strawberries, the more flexible fine-mesh liners are essential for successful drying.

- **Heatproof metal strainer:** A long-handled mesh strainer made of stainless steel is useful when you're blanching and checking fruits and vegetables before drying. By using a strainer to lift the food out of the water, rather than dumping the pot of water and food into a colander, you can blanch multiple batches of produce in the same pot of water. After removing the food from the water, transfer it to a colander to continue draining.

- **Parchment paper:** Parchment paper has many uses in cooking and food preparation. It can be used in place of specialized leather sheets, to protect bakeware and to prevent foods from sticking to trays or pans when you're drying and cooking. It is available with other food wraps at most supermarkets.

- **Ruler:** A plastic or metal ruler that can be washed is best. Unless you're very experienced at gauging size by eye, use the ruler to make sure food slices and cubes are as close to exact as possible for even drying. We find it helpful to use a permanent marker to highlight the $1/4$-inch (0.5 cm) and $1/2$-inch (1 cm) marks for easy viewing while chopping.

- **Sharp knives:** A good-quality chef's (or French) knife, paring knives and a serrated knife make preparation of foods much easier than poor-quality or dull knives.

- **Timer:** Look for electronic timers that can be set for up to 24 hours to remind you to check the foods in the dehydrator. It's easy to lose track of time, especially when you're adding items to the dryer at different times. We like to have a few timers on hand and stick a note on each timer that says what item it's for. Be sure to record what time you started drying as well, in case you need to add more time to the timer.

- **Vegetable peeler:** A sturdy, sharp vegetable peeler makes food preparation much easier. We prefer the Y-shaped peelers over the traditional straight style, because they tend to remove thinner peelings and are easier on the hands when you're peeling large amounts of produce. Peelers don't last forever; if you're not getting thin, cleanly cut pieces of peel, it's likely the blade is getting dull. It's worth investing in a new peeler.

Optional (But Helpful) Equipment

- **Immersion blender, mini chopper, food processor or blender:** An immersion blender (or hand blender) with a mini chopper attachment is the most versatile option. The wand attachment works well for puréeing foods for leathers and snacks, and the mini chopper attachment is the best tool for making powders from dried ingredients. A food processor or blender is useful for puréeing foods for leathers and snacks, but doesn't work as well for making powders.

- **Jerky gun:** This specially designed press for squeezing a ground meat mixture into thin strips is a terrific tool to have if you plan to make jerky with ground meats, as it makes shaping the strips fast and efficient.

- **Kitchen scissors:** Sharp scissors reserved for food are very handy for snipping dried foods into smaller pieces.

- **Leather, or "fruit roll," sheets:** These dehydrator accessories are handy when you're making fruit and vegetable leathers or snacks. They are available through dehydrator manufacturers or where dehydrators are sold. For most purposes, though, you can use parchment paper if you don't have leather sheets specifically designed for your machine.

- **Mandoline:** This manual slicing tool is ideal for cutting fruits and vegetables into thin, uniform slices. Mandolines range in price dramatically (from $20 to $200) and vary as much in quality. Seek out one that suits your needs and budget. If you frequently slice hard root vegetables, for example, a sturdy stainless steel model will be worth the investment. The Benriner mandoline, available at kitchenware stores and some Asian grocery stores, is our particular favorite for its economical price, effectiveness and compact size.
- **Salad spinner:** After you've washed herbs and other leafy greens, a salad spinner is an easy way to remove excess surface water without bruising the leaves.

Foods to Dehydrate

Most common foods are reasonably well suited to home dehydration. That being said, some are more easily dried than others, and there are some that you may wish to avoid altogether. Sliced apples are a wonderful starting point. Avocados and some meats and fish are not suited to home dehydration because they contain high levels of fat. High-fat products tend to spoil through a process known as oxidative rancidity: oxygen in the air reacts with the fats and oils to produce off-flavors and other undesirable traits. Because water is not a major factor in the spoilage of high-fat foods, removing it doesn't preserve the food.

Certain foods benefit from blanching, followed by quenching (see the definitions of these terms on pages 22 and 23), or from being fully cooked; these heat treatments improve the speed of drying and the final dried product. Foods that typically require heat treatment before drying include harder vegetables and those you don't generally eat raw; the blanching or cooking method is spelled out in the individual drying instructions when such treatment is needed.

Meat, poultry and fish must be fully cooked before they are dried. This was not considered necessary in the past, but we now have more knowledge about the risks of food-borne illnesses. Taking this extra precaution ensures that you'll have a good, safe dried product.

Some berries may be difficult to dry in your home dehydrator, but with a little perseverance and planning, most can be dried with a reasonable level of success. Fleshy berries, such as strawberries, are not generally a problem. They can be sliced and placed in the dryer. However, cranberries, blueberries and other fruits with a naturally occurring waxy coating and thick skin can take an extremely long time to dry unless certain pretreatment steps are followed. Drying rates can be greatly increased by disrupting the waxy surface coating, or by cutting the berries in half to expose a non-coated surface. Keep in mind that a waxy skin, and the peel on many fruits, is designed to prevent the loss of moisture so that the seeds have nourishment to develop once the fruit is ripe. You are working against nature when you try to remove moisture from a berry or other thick-skinned fruit. Therefore, you must take special pretreatment measures, such as piercing the skin, cutting the berry or "checking" the berry's surface to create pathways for moisture removal (the term "checking" is explained on page 22).

Other berries, such as blackberries, are composed of many small segments or seed compartments. They do not dry well in their whole form and must be mashed to a purée to remove their moisture. (Although raspberries have the same composition, their surface is not as waxy as that of blackberries and they are easier to dry.)

Certain fruits and vegetables brown when exposed to air. Commercially dried fruits are often treated with sulfites to preserve the color; however, we prefer not to use this type of additive. To prevent browning, you can use a commercial ascorbic acid product (such as Fruit-Fresh), prepared according to package directions, or a mixture of $\frac{1}{4}$ cup (50 mL) lemon juice and 4 cups (1 L) water. As you slice the food, place it in the solution and leave it for about 10 minutes. Drain and shake off excess moisture, then place the sliced food on the drying trays. Whether you pretreat food this way is up to you: some pretreated foods stay much brighter in color; with others, pretreatment doesn't make much of a difference to the final product.

Drying Techniques

There are four key factors that will affect the success you have with food dehydration. These are:

1. Time
2. Temperature
3. Air speed, or velocity
4. Raw material preparation

We have provided instructions on drying a wide variety of foods, explaining how best to prepare each food for dehydration and at what temperature to do the drying. We've included representative times, based on an average of tests conducted using several home dehydrators. Your drying times may vary, depending on the type of dryer you have and the properties of the food you are drying.

Even though it is the final item on our list, discussing raw material preparation first will allow us to examine the drying process in a more straightforward manner. The best way to begin is to visualize what water must do to escape from the food being dried. In most cases, moisture at the center of the food must travel to the surface by a process called diffusion. Once at the surface, this moisture is removed by the warm air in the dryer. Fruits such as apples can be cut into uniform slices of appropriate thickness to improve their drying. If the slices are too thick, they will take longer to dry. If they are too thin, the slices may not remain intact and will crumble or break easily. Based on our experience, we have found that $\frac{1}{4}$-inch (0.5 cm) thickness is suitable for most drying applications.

Generally, the more surface area exposed to the air in the dryer, the faster the drying will proceed. Just as cutting a turnip into small cubes speeds its cooking (compared to cooking a whole turnip), small cubes of turnip will dry far more quickly than thick slices.

In the home dehydrator, food to be dried is spread on trays or racks. These are then stacked on top of one another or inserted into a specially designed drying chamber. It is important to spread the food as evenly as possible to expose its entire surface to the heated air. In units equipped with a circulating fan, air is brought into the dryer by the fan and passed over a heating coil, where it is heated to the desired temperature (which you indicate by setting the thermostat on the dryer). The heated air then passes across the surface of the wet material, where it picks up moisture and exhausts it from the dryer. When you use open-mesh racks or trays, both the top and bottom surfaces of the food are exposed to the drying air. To ensure that all surfaces are exposed to the heated air and enhance the rate of drying, you may want to flip the food slices periodically during the drying process (or gently stir the bed of small food pieces if you are drying something like kernel corn or peas).

Some dryers may not have a completely uniform distribution of air throughout. There may be variations between the left and right sides of the trays, or between the front and back. This problem can be easily overcome by rotating the trays every few hours. Similarly, some dryers may have variable air circulation depending on whether the tray is located at the top, bottom or middle of the machine. By changing the order of the trays every few hours, this unevenness can be minimized. You may want to number the trays in your dryer so that you can keep track of the order in which they started and how you have rotated them.

Time is probably the most important factor in any drying process, but drying time is closely linked with temperature and air velocity, so we must consider some basic interactions of the three factors. The most common mistake in food drying is thinking you can rush the process by increasing the temperature, thereby reducing the time it takes to satisfactorily remove the desired amount of water. Don't give in to this temptation. The recommended temperature for drying most products is 130°F (55°C). For heat-sensitive products, such as herbs, 110°F (43°C) is appropriate. Meats are dried at a higher temperature, 155°F (68°C), to minimize bacterial growth. Some instructions for dehydrating suggest using a slightly higher temperature during the first several hours of drying, when the moisture content of the food is at its highest, but for simplicity and uniformity, we recommend using the same temperature settings throughout the drying process. A higher initial temperature does not significantly reduce drying time, and if you forget to lower the temperature, you may reduce the quality of your finished product.

Excessively high temperatures may, in fact, actually slow the drying process. When exposed to very high heat, the surface of the food may dry to a leathery texture, creating a barrier to further water removal. This is known as case hardening. By maintaining lower drying temperatures, case hardening can be avoided and you'll get a better dried product in the end.

The speed at which heated air flows through the dryer is determined by the speed of the circulating fan on those units so equipped. On most dryers, the fan speed has been preset by the manufacturer and no adjustments are possible during use. It is important to have adequate movement of air across the surface of the food being dried. Where airflow is limited, moist air can stagnate at the surface of the food in the dryer and prevent the removal of additional moisture. With proper airflow, this stagnant layer of air is swept away and fresh heated air is brought in to replace it, thereby encouraging the removal of water from the food itself. In dehydrators not equipped with fans, drying times can be significantly increased due to air stagnation inside the drying chamber.

Laboratory tests have shown that air movement is a major factor in successful food drying. Combining adequate air movement with a suitable drying temperature is much better than trying to use high temperatures with poor air circulation.

Throughout the drying process, time is a critical factor. When fresh food is first placed in the dryer, there is often a great deal of moisture on its surface that is easily removed by the heated air moving through the dryer. This is where we see a rapid loss in moisture and a correspondingly rapid decrease in the weight of the material. Once the surface moisture is removed, moisture must then diffuse from the inner portions of the product to the surface. Moisture diffusion takes time and cannot be rushed. Even though the surface of the food may feel dry, there may still be moisture within the product that must be given time to reach the surface and be picked up by the heated air. Increasing the temperature of the air will not speed the process. Slicing your food to a suitable thickness (in general, $1/4$ inch/0.5 cm) is one of the few ways in which you can speed up moisture diffusion. Moisture has less distance to travel in thinner slices and can reach the surface more quickly.

You cannot simply touch the surface of the food to determine if it is completely dry, but you will learn to recognize the distinct signs that a product is dry enough to be removed from the dryer and packaged for storing. Some products, such as sliced apples, are firm and leathery when suitably dried. Other products, such as grated carrots, may be brittle. Some fruits that are high in sugar, such as grapes, will be soft and pliable even when completely dried; however, they won't feel juicy. This is something you'll get a feel for as you experiment with your dehydrator.

If you're not sure whether the food is dry inside, break or tear a piece open and squeeze the flesh. No liquid should come to the surface of the tear. If there is moisture inside, return the food to the dryer. Again, it is better to overdry than risk underdrying, which will lead to premature spoilage.

Storing Dehydrated Foods

Once you have dried your food, it is important to store it properly for future use. Take care to select appropriate storage containers that meet the needs of the product. In all cases, the containers should be completely clean and dry.

Factors that have a negative impact on the quality and storage life of dried foods include:

1. Exposure to moisture
2. Exposure to air
3. Exposure to heat
4. Exposure to sunlight
5. Time

During the drying process, every effort was made to remove moisture from the product. If the dried product is exposed to moisture during storage, it will pick up this moisture. If it picks up enough moisture, the food may begin to spoil or develop off-flavors and change in texture, in much the same way soda crackers diminish in quality during humid periods of the year. Therefore, we must protect dried foods from sources of moisture in the air. Although plastic bags with zip-lock or tie closures are convenient, they may allow air and moisture into the product over prolonged periods of time. For this reason, you may want to seal small quantities of dried foods in plastic bags and then place them in rigid airtight containers such as glass jars or metal canisters with tightly sealing lids. Larger quantities may simply be stored in these glass or metal containers.

If you are storing different dried foods in plastic bags and placing them in the same large container, be careful to include only foods that are compatible with each other. You do not want to risk a flavor or aroma transfer from strong spices or seasonings to blander products (from onions to strawberries, for instance). You should also label each bag appropriately with a tag. Do not write on the plastic surface with a black ink marker, as this may affect the food inside the bag.

Air is another potential enemy of dried foods. Not only does air carry moisture, but about 20% of air is oxygen. Oxygen can react with various components in dried foods to produce off-flavors or promote other undesirable reactions, including color changes. To reduce the chance of air getting to your dried product, it is best to store it in tightly sealed glass or metal containers, just as you did to protect it from moisture. You can minimize the amount of air (and oxygen) in the headspace between the surface of the product and the lid of the container by completely filling your storage containers. If you use plastic bags, squeeze out as much air as possible before sealing the bag.

It is a good idea to let dried food cool before placing it in a sealed container for storage. Warm food products have a tendency to sweat, even though their moisture content is quite low. Any moisture that is given off can collect on the inside walls of the container and may lead to localized pockets of mold.

Once filled, storage containers should be placed in a cool, dry area. Most reactions within food products that ultimately lead to spoilage are sped up by heat. Keeping your dried product cool will help it retain its quality for a longer time. A cool pantry, lower cupboard or a storage bin placed well away from heat vents, water pipes, the stove or other sources of heat are good choices. Some people even place their dried product in the freezer to lengthen its storage life. Although freezing (or refrigeration) is not necessary, it does help preserve quality and is useful as extra insurance for meats, fish and dairy products.

Exposure to sunlight can have a negative effect on the flavor and color of dried foods. Even household lighting may reduce food quality over a prolonged time period. It is best to store your products in a dark area.

No matter how careful you are in storing your dried foods, there is always a limit to how long a food will retain its quality, though there are no definitive "best before" dates for each type of dried food. You can maximize storage life by properly drying the food and storing it under the best possible conditions. By comparing the quality of a dried food with the record you kept about its preparation and storage, you may be able to determine an appropriate expectation for its shelf life.

Rehydrating Dried Foods

Some dried foods are typically eaten in their dry form. Fruit purée made into leather is a perfect example of dried food meant to be eaten as is. Dried berries and pieces of fruit may be eaten as a snack or in a trail mix. Dried cucumber slices can be used with dips. However, many other foods must be rehydrated before they are consumed. Rehydration is the process of putting water back into a dried product and is really the reverse of the dehydration process.

Methods of food rehydration can be quite varied, but they are never very complicated. Some products can be rehydrated simply by soaking them in water at room temperature until they have absorbed as much water as possible. Others, such as dried tomatoes, rehydrate best when placed in heated liquid. This makes them ideal for stews: you can add dried tomatoes to the mixture and, as the mixture simmers, the tomatoes will absorb the necessary moisture. (Since the tomatoes are taking moisture from the stew, you must adjust your recipe to compensate for their water uptake). When rehydrating a dried product, you should not expect it to regain the moisture level and texture of the original fresh product — it will be slightly different but should be tender and palatable.

You may want to rehydrate certain dried foods with liquid other than water. For example, you can substitute fruit juices for water if you wish. By experimenting, you may be able to create some interesting and flavorful rehydrated products.

Many foods need to be rehydrated separately before they are added to recipes that call for fresh foods. It may take some trial and error before you get a feel for using home-dried foods in your favorite recipes. In Parts 2 and 3, we have included recipes developed specifically for home-dried foods, using the rehydration method that works best for those foods. These recipes will help you learn how to enjoy using your dried foods. From there, you can dry and cook away!

Troubleshooting

If the necessary precautions are taken during drying and storage, you should not have to worry about problems occurring later on. Most potential problems can be resolved before you finish drying the food — the key is to recognize the signs of these difficulties early enough to correct them.

Uneven drying is one of the most commonly observed problems. As mentioned above, food at one side of the dryer may dry more slowly than food on the other side of the same tray or rack. If you have a dehydrator with the fan mounted on the rear, you may notice that food near the back of the rack or tray dries faster than the food near the front. By rotating the trays every few hours, you can minimize uneven drying. In other cases, you may observe signs of uneven drying between trays or racks at the top and those in the middle or at the bottom of the dryer. By periodically moving the trays from one position to another, this unevenness can be successfully overcome.

There may be times when you notice that the outer surfaces of the food are dry and leathery but the inner portions are still soft and slightly moist. In all likelihood, the temperature of the air in the dryer was too high, causing case hardening. There is no easy fix for case hardening after the fact, but you may be able to continue drying the food at a lower temperature, recognizing that the drying process will be significantly slower than normal for this batch of product. If you suspect that the centers of your food pieces are still moist, do not package them for storage — they will probably spoil. You can either eat the food or use it in a recipe right away, or refrigerate it in an airtight container and use it within a few days.

If foods you have sliced and placed in the dryer are taking a long time to dry, check the temperature settings on the dryer and make sure that air is circulating inside. You'll know it is if you can feel air leaving the dryer through the vents. Consult the manufacturer's instructions if the air isn't flowing or the heat isn't working. If the dryer is functioning properly, the trouble may be caused by the food slices being too thick, or you may not have pretreated the food appropriately before putting it in the dryer.

Some products may change color during drying or storage when naturally occurring enzymes within them create undesirable pigments as the product ages. Uncooked dried cauliflower, for example, may turn a dark purple and then blacken. Proper blanching of the food before drying will destroy these enzymes.

If your storage containers are not airtight, off-flavors can develop as oxygen reacts with compounds in the food. You can reduce this problem by filling containers to the top and minimizing the amount of air trapped inside at the time of packaging.

It can be incredibly disheartening when your food visibly spoils after all your efforts to dry and store it. If the drying process has not removed enough moisture from the food, mold may grow, usually appearing as a fuzzy or furry gray patch on the surface of the food. You might also see molds of other colors. Regardless of the color, food showing signs of mold should be thrown away. You may be tempted to simply cut off the moldy portion of the food, but it is likely that there is more mold inside that you cannot see. Mold growth occurs where there is sufficient moisture to support it, so make every effort to minimize moisture by adequately drying the food, cooling it to prevent sweating and using thoroughly dried containers.

Some Definitions

Certain terms that you may not be familiar with will be used frequently throughout this book. Here's a brief explanation of what each term means:

Blanching: Blanching is a process that is carried out with many fresh vegetables to prepare them for drying or freezing. It is done by subjecting the vegetables to high temperatures for an appropriate length of time. The time depends on the vegetable itself and the size of the pieces that are being blanched. Blanching can be done by immersing the cut vegetables in boiling water or by exposing them to steam. The scalding action of the hot water destroys naturally occurring enzymes that contribute to flavor loss, texture changes and color changes during storage.

For water blanching, you can place the food directly into the boiling water and remove it with a strainer at the end of the blanching period. Alternatively, you can keep the food in the strainer during the blanching process, as long as you keep the boiling water moving through the strainer and across the surface of the food pieces.

For steam blanching, you need to place the cut food in a basket, which is then set inside a pot containing a shallow layer of boiling water. Cover the pot with a tight-fitting lid to trap the steam.

Timing is important for blanching, as under-blanching will not destroy the enzymes and may even accelerate their activity. Over-blanching can begin to cook the fruits or vegetables and soften them excessively. You should only blanch small amounts of food at a time so that the temperature of the water does not fall too low below its boiling point. Start timing when the water comes back up to the boil. Steam blanching generally takes longer than water blanching and is not as easy to do as water blanching. For that reason, we recommend water blanching where applicable in our recipes.

Checking: Checking is a technique applied to berries with a waxy coating on their outer skin, such as grapes and blueberries. In the checking process, you are trying to create small disruptions in the waxy layer. These disruptions will appear as small cracks and may have a checkered appearance. Without these small breaks in their skin, many berries will not easily give up their moisture in the drying process.

To "check" berries, place a small batch in a heatproof strainer and dip them into a pot of boiling water for the recommended time. You must be careful not to heat them long enough to split the skins if you want the berries to maintain their shape and appearance. With a little trial and error, you will be able to determine the proper checking time for particular berries. The times given in this book are meant as guidelines only and are for representative berry samples. Your times may vary depending on the size and nature of the berries you are using.

If you find that checking does not work well for you, you may pierce the outer skin of each berry numerous times with a toothpick or the tines of a fork. This approach is particularly effective with grapes, which are large enough to easily pierce with a fork. We did notice some flavor loss in berries that were checked compared with those that were pierced with a toothpick. However, piercing individual berries is time-consuming, so you may decide that the slight flavor loss caused by checking is a minor sacrifice.

Quenching: After blanching or checking, it is necessary to stop the action of the heat on the food. Excessive exposure to heat can soften the outer portions of the food or cause the skin of berries to rupture. By plunging the hot food into a sink or basin of cold water, its temperature is lowered rapidly enough to stop the effects of heating in a very short time. Some sources refer to this process as "refreshing."

Cooking: Cooking also involves heating food and should not be confused with blanching or checking. Even though it is a word we routinely use in everyday conversation, defining the term "cooking" is not that easy to do, as it has different meanings to different people and can have different implications depending on the context in which it is used. Cooking is a very complex process that has various effects on food, ranging from altering its texture and appearance to rendering it safe from disease-causing microorganisms. While blanching and checking are generally short-term exposures to heat, cooking usually takes significantly longer and involves thoroughly heating the food until it reaches a relatively high temperature right through to its core.

Tips and Tricks

- As a general rule, when preparing vegetables for drying, if you wouldn't normally eat the vegetables raw (e.g., potatoes), you should blanch or precook them before drying. Blanching and cooking tenderize the cells and deactivate enzymes, which improves the quality of the dried product and makes vegetables more palatable once they're rehydrated.

- When drying foods that naturally vary in size, such as blueberries and asparagus, sort them into similar-sized pieces and place smaller or thinner ones on one drying tray, medium on another and larger or thicker ones on a third tray. This will make checking for doneness easier and more efficient.

- Strong foods such as garlic and onions can taint the plastic of the mesh trays or leather sheets, so you may prefer to use parchment paper or reserve some trays or sheets just for those foods by marking them with a heatproof permanent marker.

- When you're drying very small food items, such as rice, grains or peas, they may fall through the mesh — even fine mesh — to the bottom of the dryer. You have two options to help reduce this: line the tray with two mesh liners, slightly offset from each other to make the holes smaller; or line a drying tray with a leather sheet or parchment paper and place it below the mesh racks to catch any pieces that fall through. You can also dry small pieces directly on leather sheets, though this does slow the drying process considerably.

- If drying items that might drip, such as very juicy fruits or meats, place them on racks below other foods and place an empty tray lined with a leather sheet or parchment paper below the racks to keep the bottom of the dryer clean.

- When dehydrating pungent items, be sure there is good ventilation in the room or you'll be smelling the aroma for days. If the weather is moderate (60°F to 78°F/16°C to 26°C), you can use your dryer in the garage. Don't attempt this on particularly humid or wet days or days that are too hot or cold, as drying won't be very efficient. Never use an electric dehydrator outdoors.

- If using parchment paper to line trays for leathers or other puréed or small foods, secure the paper to the mesh tray with metal paper clips to prevent the paper from blowing and lifting in the dryer. Let paper clips cool before handling.

- Number your trays with a heatproof permanent marker on the outside edge so you can keep track of them easily when loading trays at different times or rearranging trays within the dryer.

- Think efficiency when you're using your dryer. Plan to fill the dryer with foods that require the same drying temperature. If drying different foods, start those that take the longest first, then add foods that require less time, timing it so everything is dry at approximately the same time.

- If you have a dryer with removable stacking trays, remove any trays that are not loaded with food. The air circulation and heat will be more concentrated, and drying will be faster.

- If using plastic storage bags to store dried foods, seal the bag almost completely, squeezing out air with your hands, then insert a straw in the small opening and suck out as much of the remaining air as possible. Quickly remove the straw and seal the opening. It's best to then place bags in an airtight container in case of small leaks.

- If you've packed your pantry full of dried foods, it's easy to forget what you've got on hand. Compile an inventory list of the items you have, as well as approximate amounts, and keep it somewhere handy, such as inside a kitchen cupboard, taped to the inside cover of this book or right in the pantry. When you're planning to cook, you can quickly glance at the list to see if you have the ingredients on hand. Don't forget to update the list each time you use some of your stores.

Dehydrating Fresh Produce

continued...

Vegetables

HERBS AND SEASONINGS

Basil

Preparation: Remove leaves from large stems. Small terminal leaf clusters can be left on thin stems.

Drying: Place on mesh drying trays. Dry at 110°F (43°C).

Time: 16 to 18 hours.

Doneness test: Leaves should be brittle and should crumble easily.

Tip
- Store dried basil leaves whole to preserve the most flavor. Crumble just before using.

Bay Leaves

Preparation: Cut leaves from branches, discarding branches.

Drying: Place on mesh drying trays. Dry at 110°F (43°C).

Time: 5 to 7 hours.

Doneness test: Leaves should be very crisp and should break easily when bent.

Tip
- Fresh bay leaves can be found with the other fresh herbs in some supermarkets, or you can grow your own bay laurel tree indoors.

Chives

Preparation: Trim off tough ends.

Drying: Place on mesh drying trays. Dry at 130°F (55°C).

Time: 5 to 6 hours.

Doneness test: Chives should be very crisp and should break easily when bent.

Tip
- It is easiest to dry chives whole and then snip them with scissors into small pieces to store and use.

Cilantro

Preparation: Remove leaves from large stems. Small terminal leaf clusters can be left on thin stems.

Drying: Place on mesh drying trays. Dry at 110°F (43°C).

Time: 8 to 10 hours.

Doneness test: Leaves should be brittle and should crumble easily.

Tip
- Store dried cilantro leaves whole to preserve the most flavor. Crumble just before using.

Curry Leaves

Preparation: Cut small sprigs of leaves from branches, discarding branches. Trim sprigs to lengths that fit easily on drying trays.

Drying: Place on mesh drying trays, overlapping as little as possible. Dry at 110°F (43°C).

Time: 5 to 7 hours.

Doneness test: Leaves should be very crisp and should break easily when bent.

Tip
- Strip dried leaves from stems before storing, discarding stems. The stems may hold some moisture that can lead to spoilage even though leaves are thoroughly dry.

Dill

Preparation: Cut long coarse stems off sprigs.

Drying: Place on mesh drying trays, overlapping as little as possible. Dry at 110°F (43°C).

Time: 7 to 8 hours.

Special instructions: Rearrange any overlapped sprigs as necessary to ensure even drying.

Doneness test: Sprigs should be dry and crisp, with no evidence of moisture inside.

Tip

- Store dried dill sprigs whole to preserve the most flavor. Crumble just before using.

Garlic

Slices

Preparation: Peel cloves and cut lengthwise into slices about 1/8 inch (0.25 cm) thick.

Drying: Place on mesh drying trays. Dry at 130°F (55°C).

Time: 10 to 12 hours.

Doneness test: Slices should be dry, leathery and still pliable, with no evidence of moisture inside.

Tip

- You may want to dry garlic in the garage — or at least in a well-ventilated room — as the drying process is quite aromatic.

Roasted

Preparation: Wrap peeled garlic cloves in a large piece of foil. Roast in 350°F (180°C) oven for about 1 hour or until very soft. Let cool. Transfer to a food processor or use an immersion blender and purée until smooth.

Drying: Spread out to 1/4-inch (0.5 cm) thickness, as evenly as possible, on leather sheets or on mesh drying trays lined with parchment paper, leaving it slightly thicker around the edges. Dry at 130°F (55°C).

Time: 14 to 18 hours.

Special instructions: Check after 10 hours. When top is very firm and edges start to lift, carefully peel leather from sheet, flip over and continue drying.

Doneness test: Garlic sheet should be dry, very firm and just slightly pliable.

Tip

- You can store roasted garlic as a sheet or, once cooled, transfer to a food processor or mini chopper and chop into small pieces.

Gingerroot

Slices

Preparation: Peel ginger and cut crosswise into slices about 1/8 inch (0.25 cm) thick, cutting any slices that are larger than a quarter in half.

Drying: Place on mesh drying trays. Dry at 130°F (55°C).

Time: 3 to 4 hours.

Doneness test: Slices should be dry, leathery and still pliable, with no evidence of moisture inside.

Tips

- Use a sharp Y-shaped vegetable peeler to peel the gingerroot.
- Store dried ginger slices whole to preserve the most flavor. Chop or mince just before using.

Grated

Preparation: Peel gingerroot and grate the flesh on the coarse side of a box grater.

Drying: Spread on leather sheets or on mesh drying trays lined with parchment paper. Dry at 110°F (43°C).

Time: 6 to 8 hours.

Special instructions: Stir occasionally to break up any clumps and ensure even drying.

Doneness test: Pieces should be dry, leathery and still pliable, with no evidence of moisture inside.

Tip
- Fresh gingerroot has a taut, shiny skin and juicy flesh. Avoid wrinkled or moldy roots.

Lavender

Preparation: Cut any thick stems off sprigs so they fit easily on drying trays.

Drying: Place on mesh drying trays. Dry at 110°F (43°C).

Time: 8 to 10 hours.

Doneness test: Flowers and stems should be dry and crisp, and stems should break easily when bent.

Tips
- Cut fresh lavender just as the flowers are fully formed and colored but have not started to open.
- If you plan to use the flowers for cooking, strip them from the stems before storing, discarding stems or using for potpourri.

Mint

Preparation: Remove leaves from large stems. Small terminal leaf clusters can be left on thin stems.

Drying: Place on mesh drying trays. Dry at 110°F (43°C).

Time: 18 to 20 hours.

Special instructions: Be careful not to remove the mint leaves from the dryer too early. Even though they may feel dry

to the touch after 10 hours or so, the leaves may not yet be adequately dried.

Doneness test: Leaves should be brittle and should crumble easily.

Tip
- Store dried mint leaves whole to preserve the most flavor. Crumble just before using.

Oregano and Marjoram

Preparation: Remove leaves from large stems. Small terminal leaf clusters can be left on thin stems.

Drying: Place on mesh drying trays. Dry at 110°F (43°C).

Time: 10 to 12 hours.

Doneness test: Leaves should be brittle and should crumble easily.

Tips
- For the best flavor, cut fresh oregano and marjoram when the leaves are fully formed but before flowers start to develop.
- Store dried oregano leaves whole to preserve the most flavor. Crumble just before using.

Parsley

Preparation: Cut long coarse stems off sprigs.

Drying: Place on mesh drying trays, overlapping as little as possible. Dry at 110°F (43°C).

Time: 6 to 8 hours.

Doneness test: Leaves should be brittle and should crumble easily, and stems should break when bent.

Tips
- Strip the dry leaf clusters from the stems for more space-efficient storage and just in case there is any moisture left in the

stems that could spoil the leaves. Stems can be added to flavor stocks (freeze them for later use).

- Store dried parsley leaves whole to preserve the most flavor. Crumble just before using.

Rosemary

Preparation: Trim off any thick woody stems below the line of the leaves. Do not remove the leaves from the stems.

Drying: Place on mesh drying trays. Dry at 110°F (43°C).

Time: 10 to 12 hours.

Doneness test: The rosemary should be brittle, and the "leaves" should break away from the stem easily.

Tip

- Strip the dry leaves from the stems for more space-efficient storage and just in case there is any moisture left in the stems that could spoil the leaves. Stems can be added to flavor stocks (freeze them for later use).

Sage

Preparation: Remove leaves from large stems. Small terminal leaf clusters can be left on thin stems.

Drying: Place on mesh drying trays. Dry at 110°F (43°C).

Time: 12 to 14 hours.

Doneness test: Leaves should be brittle and should crumble easily.

Tip

- Store dried sage leaves whole to preserve the most flavor. Crumble just before using.

Savory

Preparation: Trim off thick ends of stems.

Drying: Place on fine-mesh drying trays (e.g., Clean-A-Screen). Dry at 110°F (43°C).

Time: 12 to 14 hours.

Doneness test: Leaves should be brittle and should crumble easily, and stems should break easily when bent.

Tip

- Strip the dry leaves from the stems for more space-efficient storage and just in case there is any moisture left in the stems that could spoil the leaves. Stems can be added to flavor stocks (freeze them for later use).

Tarragon

Preparation: Trim off thick ends of stems.

Drying: Place on mesh drying trays, overlapping as little as possible. Dry at 110°F (43°C).

Time: 10 to 12 hours.

Special instructions: Rearrange any overlapped sprigs as necessary to ensure even drying.

Doneness test: Leaves should be brittle and should crumble easily, and stems should break easily when bent.

Tips

- Strip the dry leaves from the stems for more space-efficient storage and just in case there is any moisture left in the stems that could spoil the leaves. Stems can be added to flavor stocks (freeze them for later use).
- Store dried tarragon leaves whole to preserve the most flavor. Crumble just before using.

Thyme

Preparation: Trim off thick woody stems below the leaves.

Drying: Place on mesh drying trays. Dry at 110°F (43°C).

Time: 12 to 14 hours.

Doneness test: Leaves should be brittle and should crumble easily, and stems should break easily when bent.

Tip

- Strip the dry leaves from the stems for more space-efficient storage and just in case there is any moisture left in the stems that could spoil the leaves. Stems can be added to flavor stocks (freeze them for later use).

FRUIT

Apples

Rings

Preparation: Peel apples, if desired, and remove core. Cut crosswise into rings about ¼ inch (0.5 cm) thick.

Pretreatment (optional): To prevent browning, dip apple rings in lemon juice or an ascorbic acid solution (see page 17) as you slice them. Drain well.

Drying: Place on mesh drying trays. Dry at 130°F (55°C).

Time: 5 to 6 hours.

Doneness test: Rings should feel dry and leathery and be spongy and still flexible.

Tips

- Choose apples that have a good flavor once heated, such as Granny Smith, McIntosh, Crispin, Cortland or Northern Spy. Apple varieties that are more suited to fresh eating, such as Royal Gala, don't have much flavor once dried.
- A mechanical apple peeler works well. It will peel, core and slice the apple all at once. They are available at hardware stores.

Slices

Preparation: Peel apples, if desired, and remove core. Cut lengthwise into slices about ¼ inch (0.5 cm) thick at the widest part.

Pretreatment (optional): To prevent browning, dip apple slices in lemon juice or an ascorbic acid solution (see page 17) as you slice them. Drain well.

Drying: Place on mesh drying trays. Dry at 130°F (55°C).

Time: 4 to 6 hours.

Doneness test: Slices should feel dry and leathery and be spongy and still flexible.

Tips

- Choose apples that have a good flavor once heated, such as Granny Smith, McIntosh, Crispin, Cortland or Northern Spy. Apple varieties that are more suited to fresh eating, such as Royal Gala, don't have much flavor once dried.
- Apple skin does toughen slightly when dried. If you're planning to rehydrate and cook the apples, you may wish to peel them before drying. If you're eating them as snacks, leave the skin on for extra fiber.

Apricots

Preparation: Cut lengthwise into quarters or wedges about ¼ inch (0.5 cm) thick at the widest part.

Pretreatment (optional): To prevent browning, dip apricots in lemon juice or an ascorbic acid solution (see page 17) as you slice them. Drain well.

Drying: Place on mesh drying trays. Dry at 130°F (55°C).

Time: 20 to 24 hours.

Doneness test: Slices should feel dry and leathery and still be flexible.

Tip

- Home-dried apricots will have a much dryer texture than those that are commercially dried.

Bananas

Preparation: Peel bananas and cut crosswise into slices about ¼ inch (0.5 cm) thick.

Pretreatment (optional): To prevent browning, dip banana slices in lemon juice or an ascorbic acid solution (see page 17) as you slice them. Drain well.

Drying: Place on mesh drying trays. Dry at 130°F (55°C).

Time: 8 to 10 hours.

Doneness test: Slices should feel dry and leathery and still be flexible.

Tip

- The bananas will be a bit sticky when fully dried. Peel them from the mesh drying trays as soon as you remove them from the dryer (while they're still warm) to prevent sticking.

Blueberries

Preparation: Check berries (see page 22) or, using a toothpick, pierce berries several times.

Drying: Spread on mesh drying trays. Dry at 130°F (55°C).

Time: 18 to 22 hours.

Doneness test: Berries should be slightly shriveled, firm and no longer juicy inside.

Tips

- Checking the berries is faster and easier than piercing, but there will be a slight loss in flavor.
- Sort the berries on the trays according to approximate size to make it easier to remove those that are done earlier.

Cantaloupe

Slices

Preparation: Using a serrated knife, cut skin and underlying green flesh from cantaloupe. Cut in half lengthwise and scoop out seeds and loose flesh. For larger melons, cut each half lengthwise into two or three wedges. Cut each wedge crosswise into slices about ¼ inch (0.5 cm) thick.

Drying: Place on mesh drying trays. Dry at 130°F (55°C).

Time: 12 to 14 hours.

Doneness test: Slices should feel dry and leathery and still be flexible.

Tips

- Use ripe, but not overripe cantaloupe. Ripe cantaloupe has a sweet aroma at the stem end, and the skin under the mesh will have turned from green to beige.
- Store slices whole to preserve the most flavor and best texture. Use scissors to snip into smaller pieces just before using.

Cubes

Preparation: Using a serrated knife, cut skin and underlying green flesh from cantaloupe. Cut in half lengthwise and scoop out seeds and loose flesh. For larger melons, cut each half lengthwise into two or three wedges. Cut each wedge crosswise into slices about ¼ inch (0.5 cm) thick. Cut slices into ¼-inch (0.5 cm) cubes.

Drying: Place on mesh drying trays. Dry at 130°F (55°C).

Time: 8 to 10 hours.

Doneness test: Cubes should feel dry and leathery, with no evidence of moisture inside.

Tip

- Use ripe, but not overripe cantaloupe. Ripe cantaloupe has a sweet aroma at the stem end, and the skin under the mesh will have turned from green to beige.

Cherries, Sweet or Sour (Tart)

Preparation: Cut cherries in half lengthwise around the pit and remove pit. Using a toothpick, pierce skin several times.

Drying: Place skin side down on mesh drying trays. Dry at 130°F (55°C).

Time: 14 to 24 hours.

Doneness test: Cherries should be leathery and pliable but no longer juicy inside.

Tips

- If cherries are very large, cut them into quarters to speed drying.
- Cherries can vary greatly in moisture level; therefore, the time range for drying is quite wide.

Citrus Fruits

Zest

Preparation: Using the coarse side of a box grater, scrape colored zest from the fruit. Alternatively, use a sharp Y-shaped vegetable peeler to remove thin strips of the colored zest. Be sure not to scrape through to the bitter white pith.

Drying: Spread on leather sheets. Dry at 130°F (55°C).

Time: 3 to 4 hours.

Special instructions: Stir occasionally to break up any clumps and ensure even drying.

Doneness test: Pieces should be firm, brittle and just slightly pliable.

Tip

- Store dried zest in larger pieces to preserve the most flavor. Using a sharp knife, chop finely just before using.

Slices

Preparation: Cut fruit crosswise into slices about ¼ inch (0.5 cm) thick.

Drying: Place on mesh drying trays. Dry at 130°F (55°C).

Time: Limes and oranges: 16 to 18 hours; lemons: 18 to 20 hours; grapefruit: 22 to 24 hours.

Special instructions: If possible, flip the slices several times so they dry evenly.

Doneness test: Slices should be firm, brittle and no longer pliable.

Tips

- The flesh may pull away from the center of the slices as they dry.
- Even though the fruit slices may feel dry, moisture from within the juice sacs can diffuse outwards upon cooling and make previously firm slices feel pliable. You may have to put slices back in the dryer after they have been stored overnight to finish the drying process.

Coconut

Preparation: Drill a hole in the end of the coconut shell and drain the liquid (or collect it for another use). Using a hammer, break the shell into pieces. Using the blunt point of a butter knife, pry the meat from the shell. Rinse coconut meat to remove shell debris and pat dry. Cut chunks into slices about ¼ inch (0.5 cm) thick.

Drying: Spread on mesh drying trays. Dry at 130°F (55°C).

Time: 6 to 8 hours.

Doneness test: Slices should be firm, brittle and just slightly pliable, with no evidence of moisture inside.

Tips

- If desired, use a vegetable peeler to peel off brown skin before cutting coconut meat into slices.
- Store dried coconut in larger pieces to preserve the most flavor. Using scissors or a sharp knife, snip or finely chop just before using.

Cranberries

Preparation: If using frozen berries, let thaw and drain off any excess liquid. Cut berries in half crosswise.

Drying: Place skin side down on mesh drying trays. Dry at 130°F (55°C).

Time: 10 to 14 hours.

Doneness test: Berries should be slightly shriveled, firm and no longer juicy inside.

Tips

- Berries that have been frozen and thawed will dry faster than fresh berries.
- Cutting berries crosswise, rather than lengthwise from the stem, exposes more surface area in the interior of the berry and speeds up the drying process.

Figs

Preparation: Cut figs lengthwise into wedges about ½ inch (1 cm) thick at the widest part.

Drying: Place skin side down on mesh drying trays. Dry at 130°F (55°C).

Time: 16 to 20 hours.

Doneness test: Wedges should feel dry and leathery and still be flexible.

Tip

- Home-dried figs will have a much firmer, dryer texture than those that are commercially dried. Don't attempt to dry them whole — it will take an extremely long time.

Grapes

Whole

Preparation: Check grapes (see page 22) or, using a toothpick, pierce grapes all over.

Drying: Place on mesh drying trays. Dry at 130°F (55°C).

Time: 20 to 36 hours.

Doneness test: Grapes should be leathery and pliable but no longer juicy inside.

Tips

- The high sugar content and pulpy texture of grapes make them feel much softer when dried than other home-dried fruits; just make sure they're not juicy inside.
- Home-dried raisins may feel a little crispy on the outside when first dried but will become leathery upon cooling and storage.

Halves

Preparation: Cut grapes in half.

Drying: Place skin side down on mesh drying trays. Dry at 130°F (55°C).

Time: 18 to 20 hours.

Doneness test: Grapes should be leathery and pliable but no longer juicy inside.

Tip

- Halved grapes will produce unconventionally shaped raisins, but halving them does speed up drying.

Honeydew Melon

Preparation: Using a serrated knife, cut skin and underlying thick flesh from melon. Cut in half lengthwise and scoop out seeds and loose flesh. Cut each half lengthwise into three or four wedges. Cut each wedge crosswise into slices about $\frac{1}{4}$ inch (0.5 cm) thick.

Drying: Place on mesh drying trays. Dry at 130°F (55°C).

Time: 16 to 18 hours.

Doneness test: Slices should feel dry and leathery and still be flexible.

Tip
- Choose a melon that feels heavy for its size to avoid buying one that is dry and pulpy.

Kiwifruit

Preparation: Peel kiwis and cut crosswise into slices about $\frac{1}{4}$ inch (0.5 cm) thick.

Pretreatment (optional): To prevent browning, dip kiwi slices in lemon juice or an ascorbic acid solution (see page 17) as you slice them. Drain well.

Drying: Place on mesh drying trays. Dry at 130°F (55°C).

Time: 8 to 10 hours.

Doneness test: Slices should feel dry and leathery and still be flexible.

Tip
- Use a sharp Y-shaped vegetable peeler to peel the thin brown skin from kiwis.

Mangos

Preparation: Peel mangos. Holding the mango vertically, with the stem on the cutting board, cut lengthwise along both sides of the pit to make two "cheeks." Place cheeks cut side down and cut into slices about $\frac{1}{4}$ inch (0.5 cm) thick. Using a paring knife, cut remaining flesh from around the pit and cut into pieces about $\frac{1}{4}$ inch (0.5 cm) thick.

Drying: Place on mesh drying trays. Dry at 130°F (55°C).

Time: 10 to 12 hours.

Doneness test: Slices should feel dry and leathery and still be flexible.

Tips
- Choose firm, ripe mangos for drying. They should be fragrant, and the skin should yield lightly when pressed, but the flesh shouldn't be very soft or the slices will fall apart.
- Use a sharp Y-shaped vegetable peeler to peel the skin from mangos.

Papayas

Preparation: Using a serrated knife, cut skin and underlying green or yellow flesh from papayas. Cut in half lengthwise and scoop out seeds and loose flesh. Cut each half crosswise into slices about $\frac{1}{4}$ inch (0.5 cm) thick.

Drying: Place on mesh drying trays. Dry at 130°F (55°C).

Time: 12 to 14 hours.

Doneness test: Slices should feel dry and leathery and still be flexible.

Tip
- Use ripe, but not overripe papaya. The skin of ripe papaya yields slightly when pressed and there is a faint sweet aroma at the stem end. Signs of overripeness are dimpled or wrinkled skin or soft spots and a strong aroma.

Peaches and Nectarines

Preparation: If desired, peel peaches by blanching for 30 seconds. Using a slotted spoon, remove from boiling water and immediately plunge into cold water; let stand until cold. Drain well. Peel off skin. Cut lengthwise into wedges about $\frac{1}{4}$ inch (0.5 cm) thick at the widest part, or cut in half lengthwise around the pit, place cut side down on cutting board and cut into slices about $\frac{1}{4}$ inch (0.5 cm) thick.

Pretreatment (optional): To prevent browning, dip peach slices in lemon juice or an ascorbic acid solution (see page 17) as you slice them. Drain well.

Drying: Place on mesh drying trays. Dry at 130°F (55°C).

Time: 10 to 12 hours.

Doneness test: Wedges or slices should feel dry and leathery and still be flexible.

Tip
- The skin on peaches isn't too tough when dried and is perfectly fine for peaches that will be used dry. If you're planning to rehydrate and cook the peaches, you may wish to peel them before drying.

Pears

Preparation: Peel pears, if desired. Cut in half lengthwise, scoop out core and remove strings. Place cut side down on cutting board and cut into slices about $\frac{1}{4}$ inch (0.5 cm) thick at the widest part.

Pretreatment (optional): To prevent browning, dip pear slices in lemon juice or an ascorbic acid solution (see page 17) as you slice them. Drain well.

Drying: Place on mesh drying trays. Dry at 130°F (55°C).

Time: 12 to 14 hours.

Doneness test: Slices should feel dry and leathery and still be flexible.

Tip
- Pear skin is generally fairly tender but does toughen slightly when dried. If you're planning to rehydrate and cook the pears, you may wish to peel them before drying.

Pineapple

Rings

Preparation: Using a large serrated knife, cut skin from pineapple. Remove eyes with a paring knife. Cut pineapple crosswise into slices about $\frac{1}{4}$ inch (0.5 cm) thick. Cut out core.

Drying: Place on mesh drying trays. Dry at 130°F (55°C).

Time: 14 to 16 hours.

Doneness test: Rings should feel dry and leathery and still be flexible.

Tip
- If you plan to dry pineapple often, purchase a specially designed pineapple corer/peeler/slicer.

Quarter Rings

Preparation: Using a large serrated knife, cut skin from pineapple. Remove eyes with a paring knife. Cut pineapple lengthwise into quarters and cut off core. Cut quarters crosswise into slices about $\frac{1}{4}$ inch (0.5 cm) thick.

Drying: Place on mesh drying trays. Dry at 130°F (55°C).

Time: 14 to 16 hours.

Doneness test: Quarter rings should feel dry and leathery and still be flexible.

Tip
- To make cutting simple, purchase a peeled, cored pineapple, available at many supermarkets.

Pieces

Preparation: Using a large serrated knife, cut skin from pineapple. Remove eyes with a paring knife. Cut pineapple lengthwise into 8 wedges (if small) or 12 wedges (if large) and cut off core. Cut wedges crosswise into slices about $\frac{1}{4}$ inch (0.5 cm) thick.

Drying: Place on mesh drying trays. Dry at 130°F (55°C).

Time: 12 to 14 hours.

Doneness test: Pieces should feel dry and leathery and still be flexible.

Tip

- Peel pieces from the mesh drying trays as soon as you remove them from the dryer (while they're still warm) to prevent sticking.

Plums

Preparation: Cut plums lengthwise into quarters or wedges about $\frac{1}{2}$ inch (1 cm) thick at the widest part. Small plums can be cut in half; pierce the skin several times with a toothpick.

Drying: Place skin side down on mesh drying trays. Dry at 130°F (55°C).

Time: 18 to 20 hours.

Doneness test: Plums should feel dry and leathery and still be flexible.

Tip

- Firmer prune-style (blue, Italian) plums give the nicest texture when dried and have a flavor more like commercial prunes.

Raspberries

Preparation: None.

Drying: Place hollow side down on mesh drying trays. Dry at 130°F (55°C).

Time: 20 to 24 hours.

Doneness test: Berries should feel dry and crisp, with no evidence of moisture inside.

Tips

- Use fine-mesh tray liners (e.g., Clean-A-Screen) if necessary to prevent berries from sticking to tray. When removing dried berries, slide a dull metal spatula underneath to loosen and avoid crushing the berries.
- Locally grown, fresh-picked berries dry faster than varieties grown for shipping and a long shelf life.

Strawberries

Preparation: Hull strawberries and cut lengthwise into slices about $\frac{1}{4}$ inch (0.5 cm) thick.

Drying: Place cut side up on mesh drying trays. Dry at 130°F (55°C).

Time: 8 to 16 hours.

Doneness test: Slices should feel dry, leathery and no longer juicy but still slightly flexible.

Tips

- Use fine-mesh tray liners (e.g., Clean-A-Screen) if necessary to prevent berries from sticking to tray.
- Locally grown, fresh-picked berries dry faster than varieties grown for shipping and a long shelf life.

VEGETABLES

Asparagus

Preparation: Remove tough ends and any large scales. Cut spears into 1-inch (2.5 cm) sections.

Pretreatment: In a pot of boiling water, blanch asparagus for 3 minutes. Using a strainer, remove from boiling water and immediately plunge into cold water; let stand until cold. Drain well.

Drying: Place on mesh drying trays. Dry at 130°F (55°C).

Time: 12 to 14 hours.

Doneness test: Asparagus should feel dry and crisp and have no sign of moisture inside when broken open.

Tips

- Use fine-mesh tray liners (e.g., Clean-A-Screen) if necessary to prevent small pieces from falling through trays.
- Sort stalks on trays according to approximate thickness to make it easier to remove those that are done earlier.

Beans, Green and Yellow Wax

Preparation: Slice beans into 1-inch (2.5 cm) sections.

Pretreatment: In a pot of boiling water, blanch beans for 2 minutes. Using a strainer, remove from boiling water and immediately plunge into cold water; let stand until cold. Drain well.

Drying: Place on mesh drying trays. Dry at 130°F (55°C).

Time: 10 to 12 hours.

Doneness test: Beans should feel dry and crisp and have no sign of moisture inside when broken open.

Tip

- Use fine-mesh tray liners (e.g., Clean-A-Screen) if necessary to prevent small pieces from falling through trays.

Beans, Lima

Preparation: For fresh lima beans, remove beans from pods, discarding pods. For frozen lima beans, let thaw and drain off any excess liquid. For canned lima beans, drain and rinse beans.

Pretreatment: For fresh beans only, in a pot of boiling water, cook beans for 5 to 10 minutes (depending on size), or until tender. Using a strainer, remove from boiling water and immediately plunge into cold water; let stand until cold. Drain well.

Drying: Spread on mesh drying trays. Dry at 130°F (55°C).

Time: 5 to 12 hours.

Doneness test: Beans should feel dry and crisp and have no sign of moisture inside when broken open.

Tip

- The drying time will depend on what size beans you use; baby lima beans will dry in 5 to 6 hours; large lima beans will take 10 to 12 hours.

Beets

Preparation: Remove leaves, leaving 1 inch (2.5 cm) of stem on the beet. In a pot of boiling water, boil beets for 30 minutes, or until fork-tender. Using a strainer, remove from boiling water and immediately plunge into cold water; let stand until cold. Drain well. Cut off tops and remove skins. Cut into slices ⅛ to ¼ inch (0.25 to 0.5 cm) thick.

Drying: Place on mesh drying trays. Dry at 130°F (55°C).

Time: 10 to 12 hours.

Doneness test: Slices should feel firm and leathery and still be flexible.

Tip
- Completely cooking the beets speeds up drying and provides a better texture once they're rehydrated.

Broccoli

Preparation: Break into 1-inch (2.5 cm) florets. Discard stems or reserve for another use.

Pretreatment: In a pot of boiling water, blanch broccoli for 2 minutes. Using a strainer, remove from boiling water and immediately plunge into cold water; let stand until cold. Drain well.

Drying: Place on mesh drying trays. Dry at 130°F (55°C).

Time: 6 to 8 hours.

Doneness test: Florets should feel dry and crisp and have no sign of moisture inside when broken open.

Tip
- Stems tend to remain tough after drying and rehydrating, so it's best to use just the florets. The stalks can be added to soups or peeled and cut up to serve with dip.

Carrots and Parsnips

Slices

Preparation: Peel carrots or parsnips and cut crosswise into slices about ¼ inch (0.5 cm) thick.

Pretreatment: In a pot of boiling water, blanch carrots for 3 minutes. Using a strainer, remove from boiling water and immediately plunge into cold water; let stand until cold. Drain well.

Drying: Place on mesh drying trays. Dry at 130°F (55°C).

Time: 6 to 8 hours.

Doneness test: Slices should feel dry and crisp but still be slightly flexible.

Tip
- The edges of sliced carrots will ripple when dried.

Thin Slices

Preparation: Peel carrots or parsnips and cut crosswise into slices about ⅛ inch (0.25 cm) thick.

Pretreatment (optional): In a pot of boiling water, blanch carrots for 1 minute. Using a strainer, remove from boiling water and immediately plunge into cold water; let stand until cold. Drain well.

Drying: Place on mesh drying trays. Dry at 130°F (55°C).

Time: 4 to 6 hours.

Doneness test: Slices should feel dry and crisp but still be slightly flexible.

Tip
- Thin carrot slices will curl up when dried. Use fine-mesh tray liners (e.g., Clean-A-Screen) to prevent small pieces from falling through trays.

Pieces

Preparation: Peel carrots or parsnips and cut crosswise into large sections. Cut each section in half lengthwise. Cut thicker ends in half lengthwise again to make quarters. Cut crosswise into ¼-inch (0.5 cm) pieces.

Pretreatment (optional): In a pot of boiling water, blanch carrots for 3 minutes. Using a strainer, remove from boiling water and immediately plunge into cold water; let stand until cold. Drain well.

Drying: Place on mesh drying trays. Dry at 130°F (55°C).

Time: 4 to 5 hours.

Doneness test: Pieces should feel dry and crisp but still be slightly flexible.

Tips

- This is a more efficient way to cut carrots for drying than a conventional diced shape. True cubes will take considerably longer to dry.
- Use fine-mesh tray liners (e.g., Clean-A-Screen) to prevent small pieces from falling through trays.

Grated

Preparation: Grate carrots or parsnips on the coarse side of a box grater or using the shredding plate of a food processor.

Drying: Spread on fine-mesh drying trays (e.g., Clean-A-Screen). Dry at 130°F (55°C).

Time: 3 to 4 hours.

Special instructions: Stir occasionally to break up any clumps and ensure even drying.

Doneness test: Carrots should be shriveled, leathery and just slightly pliable.

Tip

- Remove carrots from the trays when warm and let cool in a shallow dish. If left to cool on the trays, they tend to stick.

Cauliflower

Preparation: Break cauliflower into 1-inch (2.5 cm) florets.

Pretreatment: In a pot of boiling water, blanch cauliflower for 4 minutes. Using a strainer, remove from boiling water and immediately plunge into cold water; let stand until cold. Drain well.

Drying: Place on mesh drying trays. Dry at 130°F (55°C).

Time: 8 to 10 hours.

Doneness test: Florets should feel dry and crisp and have no sign of moisture inside when broken open.

Tip

- Cauliflower florets will darken considerably as they dry, ending up an orangey-brown color, but will lighten up again when rehydrated.

Celery

Preparation: Trim ends and cut stalks crosswise into slices about $\frac{1}{4}$ inch (0.5 cm) thick.

Pretreatment (optional): In a pot of boiling water, blanch celery for 1 minute. Using a strainer, remove from boiling water and immediately plunge into cold water; let stand until cold. Drain well.

Drying: Place on mesh drying trays. Dry at 130°F (55°C).

Time: 6 to 8 hours.

Doneness test: Slices should feel dry and crisp and have no sign of moisture inside when broken open.

Tip

- Celery will shrink a lot as it dries. Use fine-mesh tray liners (e.g., Clean-A-Screen) to prevent small pieces from falling through trays.

Corn

Preparation: If using fresh corn, cook cobs in boiling water for 5 minutes. Let cool slightly and cut kernels from the cob. Let frozen corn thaw and drain off any excess liquid.

Drying: Spread on mesh drying trays. Dry at 130°F (55°C).

Time: 10 to 12 hours.

Doneness test: Corn should be shriveled, firm and brittle.

- To cut kernels from cobs, hold the wide end of the cob in your hand, placing the narrow end in a deep bowl, and use a small, flexible serrated knife to gently saw the kernels off the cob into the bowl.

Cucumbers, English and Field

Preparation: Trim ends and cut cucumbers crosswise into slices about ¼ inch (0.5 cm) thick. (Do not peel.)

Drying: Place on mesh drying trays. Dry at 130°F (55°C).

Time: 6 to 8 hours.

Doneness test: Slices should feel dry and crisp and have no sign of moisture inside when broken open.

Tip

- Some field cucumbers have very thick skins and tough seeds. Those with thinner skins and smaller seeds are better suited to drying.

Dandelion Greens

Preparation: Remove leaves from stalks.

Drying: Place on mesh drying trays. Dry at 110°F (43°C).

Time: 6 to 8 hours.

Special instructions: Rearrange leaves and flip over as necessary to ensure even drying.

Doneness test: Leaves should be crisp and brittle.

Tips

- If picking wild dandelion greens, be sure to use only those that haven't been sprayed with a pesticide.
- Dried greens add a boost of color and flavor to soups and stews.

Eggplant

Preparation: Peel eggplant and cut crosswise into slices about ¼ inch (0.5 cm) thick.

Pretreatment (optional): In a pot of boiling water, blanch eggplant for 1 minute. Using a strainer, remove from boiling water and immediately plunge into cold water; let stand until cold. Drain well.

Drying: Place on mesh drying trays. Dry at 130°F (55°C).

Time: 8 to 10 hours.

Doneness test: Slices should feel firm and leathery and still be flexible.

Tips

- Choose smaller eggplants, which tend to have fewer, smaller and less bitter seeds than larger eggplants.
- Use kitchen scissors to snip dried eggplant into smaller pieces before using.

Fennel

Preparation: Trim off root end and any tough outer layers. Cut crosswise into slices about ¼ inch (0.5 cm) thick. Cut slices into ½-inch (1 cm) pieces.

Pretreatment: In a pot of boiling water, blanch fennel for 1 minute. Using a strainer, remove from boiling water and immediately plunge into cold water; let stand until cold. Drain well.

Drying: Place on mesh drying trays. Dry at 130°F (55°C).

Time: 6 to 8 hours.

Doneness test: Pieces should be dry, leathery and just slightly pliable, with no sign of moisture inside.

Tip

- The thick outer layers of fennel get quite stringy when dried. To avoid waste and use up the layers you've cut from the fresh fennel bulb, slice them very thinly and sauté or add to stock or soup.

Leeks

Slices

Preparation: Trim off roots and tough green tops of leeks. Cut in half lengthwise and rinse thoroughly between layers. Place cut side down and cut crosswise into $\frac{1}{4}$-inch (0.5 cm) slices.

Drying: Place on mesh drying trays. Dry at 130°F (55°C).

Time: 6 to 8 hours.

Doneness test: Slices should feel dry and crisp and have no sign of moisture inside when broken open.

Tip

• Be sure to rinse between the layers well, as there is often sand trapped deep inside.

Pieces

Preparation: Trim off roots and tough green tops of leeks. Cut in half lengthwise and rinse thoroughly between layers. Place cut side down and cut lengthwise, then crosswise into $\frac{1}{4}$- to $\frac{1}{2}$-inch (0.5 to 1 cm) pieces.

Drying: Place on mesh drying trays. Dry at 130°F (55°C).

Time: 6 to 8 hours.

Doneness test: Pieces should feel dry and crisp and have no sign of moisture inside when broken open.

Tip

• The green tops of leeks are very tough and stringy, so they are not suited to drying or regular cooking. You can wash them well and use them to flavor stocks.

Mushrooms

Preparation: Cut mushrooms lengthwise into slices about $\frac{1}{4}$ inch (0.5 cm) thick.

Drying: Place on mesh drying trays. Dry at 130°F (55°C).

Time: 8 to 14 hours.

Doneness test: Slices should feel dry and crisp and have no sign of moisture inside when broken open.

Tips

• These instructions will work for all types of mushrooms. If stems are thick and chewy, such as those on shiitake or portobello mushrooms, trim them off and dry only the caps. Stems can be used to flavor stocks.

• Mushrooms are easiest to dry in slices. For smaller mushroom pieces, crumble dried slices just before using.

Onions

Slices

Preparation: Remove the outer skin and first layer of the onion flesh. Cut into rings about $\frac{1}{4}$ inch (0.5 cm) thick, separating rings.

Drying: Place on mesh drying trays. Dry at 130°F (55°C).

Time: 6 to 8 hours.

Doneness test: Slices should feel dry and crisp and have no sign of moisture inside when broken open.

Tips

• Nest small rings inside larger rings to conserve space in the dryer.

• You may want to dry onions in the garage — or at least in a well-ventilated room — as the drying process is quite aromatic.

Pieces

Preparation: Remove the outer skin and first layer of the onion flesh. Cut into $\frac{1}{4}$- to $\frac{1}{2}$-inch (0.5 to 1 cm) pieces, separating layers.

Drying: Place on mesh drying trays. Dry at 130°F (55°C).

Time: 6 to 8 hours.

Doneness test: Pieces should feel dry and

crisp and have no sign of moisture inside when broken open.

Tips

- To ensure even drying, stir periodically and separate any layers of onions that are stuck together.
- You may want to dry onions in the garage — or at least in a well-ventilated room — as the drying process is quite aromatic.

Roasted

Preparation: Remove the outer skin and first layer of the onion flesh. Cut into $1/2$-inch (1 cm) pieces, separating layers. For each $1 1/2$ lbs (750 g) onions, add 2 tbsp (25 mL) balsamic, red wine, white wine or cider vinegar and salt and pepper to taste; toss to coat. Spread out on a baking sheet lined with parchment paper. Bake in a 350°F (180°C) oven for about 1 hour, stirring once, until browned and very tender.

Drying: Spread on fine-mesh drying trays (e.g., Clean-A-Screen). Dry at 130°F (55°C).

Time: 4 to 6 hours.

Doneness test: Onions should be shriveled, leathery and just slightly pliable.

Tip

- To ensure even drying, stir periodically and separate any layers of onions that are stuck together.

Peas, Green

Preparation: Remove fresh peas from pods, discarding pods. Let frozen peas thaw and drain off any excess liquid.

Pretreatment: If using fresh peas, blanch in a pot of boiling water for 3 minutes. Using a strainer, remove from boiling water and immediately plunge into cold water; let stand until cold. Drain well.

Drying: Spread on mesh drying trays. Dry at 130°F (55°C).

Time: 8 to 10 hours.

Doneness test: Peas should be shriveled, firm and brittle.

Peppers, Bell

Slices

Preparation: Cut peppers in half lengthwise. Cut out stem, core and seeds. Cut lengthwise or crosswise into $1/4$- to $1/2$-inch (0.5 to 1 cm) strips.

Drying: Place cut side down on mesh drying trays. Dry at 130°F (55°C).

Time: 14 to 18 hours.

Doneness test: Slices should feel dry and crisp and have no sign of moisture inside when broken open.

Tip

- Peppers vary quite a bit in the thickness of the flesh. Thicker, meatier peppers will take longer to dry. Thinner peppers may dry more quickly than the time specified.

Pieces

Preparation: Cut peppers in half lengthwise. Cut out stem, core and seeds. Cut lengthwise into $1/4$- to $1/2$-inch (0.5 to 1 cm) strips. Cut strips crosswise into $1/4$- to $1/2$-inch (0.5 to 1 cm) pieces.

Drying: Place skin side down on mesh drying trays. Dry at 130°F (55°C).

Time: 12 to 16 hours.

Doneness test: Pieces should feel dry and crisp and have no sign of moisture inside when broken open.

Peppers, Chile

Preparation: Cut peppers in half lengthwise. Cut out stem, core and seeds. Cut crosswise into slices about ¼ inch (0.5 cm) thick.

Drying: Place on mesh drying trays. Dry at 130°F (55°C).

Time: 12 to 18 hours.

Doneness test: Slices should feel dry and crisp and have no sign of moisture inside when broken open.

Tips

- When handling hot peppers, wear gloves to protect your hands from the peppers' oils and be careful not to touch your eyes.
- Use fine-mesh tray liners (e.g., Clean-A-Screen) if necessary to prevent peppers from falling through trays.

Potatoes

Slices

Preparation: Peel potatoes and cut crosswise into slices ⅛ to ¼ inch (0.25 to 0.5 cm) thick.

Pretreatment: In a pot of boiling water, blanch potatoes for 5 minutes. Using a strainer, remove from boiling water and immediately plunge into cold water; let stand until cold. Drain well.

Drying: Place on mesh drying trays. Dry at 130°F (55°C).

Time: 8 to 10 hours.

Doneness test: Slices should feel dry and crisp and have no sign of moisture inside when broken open.

Tips

- Use a mandoline to make quick work of cutting thin, even slices of potato.
- Dried potato slices can be broken or cut into smaller pieces for rehydrating and cooking.

Cubes

Preparation: Peel potatoes and cut into ½-inch (1 cm) cubes.

Pretreatment: In a pot of boiling water, boil potatoes for 10 minutes. Using a strainer, remove from boiling water and immediately plunge into cold water; let stand until cold. Drain well.

Drying: Place on mesh drying trays. Dry at 130°F (55°C).

Time: 12 to 16 hours.

Doneness test: Cubes should feel dry and crisp and have no sign of moisture inside when broken open.

Tip

- Be sure the potatoes are completely dry inside. They may feel firm on the outside when they still have moisture trapped within. It is better to leave them in the dryer longer to prevent premature spoilage.

Grated

Preparation: Peel potatoes, if desired, and shred on the coarse side of a box grater or using the shredding plate of a food processor.

Pretreatment: Place in a heatproof colander or strainer and check in boiling water (see page 22). Using a strainer, remove from boiling water and immediately plunge into cold water; let stand until cold. Gently press to squeeze out any excess liquid.

Drying: Spread on fine-mesh drying trays (e.g., Clean-A-Screen). Dry at 130°F (55°C).

Time: 2 to 3 hours.

Special instructions: Stir occasionally to break up any clumps and ensure even drying.

Doneness test: Potatoes should be dry, crisp and translucent.

Tip

- Remove potatoes from the trays when warm and let cool in a shallow dish. If left to cool on the screens, they tend to stick.

Pumpkin and Winter Squash

Slices

Preparation: Peel pumpkin or squash, cut in half lengthwise and scrape out seeds and loose flesh. Cut lengthwise into quarters or sixths, if desired. Cut crosswise into slices about $\frac{1}{4}$ inch (0.5 cm) thick.

Pretreatment: In a pot of boiling water, blanch pumpkin for 3 minutes. Using a strainer, remove from boiling water and immediately plunge into cold water; let stand until cold. Drain well.

Drying: Place on mesh drying trays. Dry at 130°F (55°C).

Time: 6 to 8 hours.

Doneness test: Slices should be dry, leathery and still pliable, with no evidence of moisture inside.

Tips

- Use only pie pumpkins or winter squash with firm, dense flesh. Pulpy jack-o'-lantern pumpkins and spaghetti squash, for example, don't dry well.
- Use a sharp Y-shaped vegetable peeler to peel hard pumpkins or squash. For the best texture, make sure to remove the thick layer just under the skin.

Cubes

Preparation: Peel pumpkin or squash and cut into $\frac{1}{4}$- to $\frac{1}{2}$-inch (0.5 to 1 cm) cubes.

Pretreatment: In a pot of boiling water, blanch pumpkin for 3 minutes. Using a strainer, remove from boiling water and immediately plunge into cold water; let stand until cold. Drain well.

Drying: Place on mesh drying trays. Dry at 130°F (55°C).

Time: 6 to 10 hours.

Doneness test: Cubes should feel dry and crisp and have no sign of moisture inside when broken open.

Grated

Preparation: Peel pumpkin or squash, cut in half lengthwise and scrape out seeds and loose flesh. Cut into chunks and shred on the coarse side of a box grater or using the shredding plate of a food processor.

Pretreatment: Place in a heatproof colander or strainer and check in boiling water (see page 22). Using a strainer, remove from boiling water and immediately plunge into cold water; let stand until cold. Gently press to squeeze out any excess liquid.

Drying: Spread on fine-mesh drying trays (e.g., Clean-A-Screen). Dry at 130°F (55°C).

Time: 2 to 3 hours.

Special instructions: Stir occasionally to break up any clumps and ensure even drying.

Doneness test: Pumpkin should be shriveled, leathery and just slightly pliable.

Tips

- Butternut squash is the easiest to use for grating because of its smooth shape and firm flesh.
- Remove pumpkin from the trays when warm and let cool in a shallow dish. If left to cool on the screens, it tends to stick.

Radishes

Preparation: Trim ends and cut radishes crosswise into slices about $\frac{1}{8}$ inch (0.25 cm) thick.

Drying: Place on mesh drying trays. Dry at 130°F (55°C).

Time: 5 to 6 hours.

Doneness test: Slices should feel dry and crisp and have no sign of moisture inside when broken open.

Tip

- Thin radish slices will curl up when dried. Use fine-mesh tray liners (e.g., Clean-A-Screen) to prevent small pieces from falling through trays.

Rhubarb

Thin slices

Preparation: Cut thin (less than $3/4$ inch/2 cm) stalks crosswise on a diagonal into $1/2$-inch (1 cm) slices.

Pretreatment: In a pot of boiling water, blanch rhubarb for 1 minute. Using a strainer, remove from boiling water and immediately plunge into cold water; let stand until cold. Drain well.

Drying: Place on mesh drying trays. Dry at 130°F (55°C).

Time: 8 to 10 hours.

Doneness test: Slices should feel dry and crisp and have no sign of moisture inside when broken open.

Tip

- Use fine-mesh tray liners (e.g., Clean-A-Screen) if necessary to prevent small pieces from falling through trays.

Thick slices

Preparation: Cut thick (larger than $3/4$ inch/2 cm) stalks crosswise on a diagonal into 1-inch (2.5 cm) slices.

Pretreatment: In a pot of boiling water, blanch rhubarb for 5 minutes. Using a strainer, remove from boiling water and immediately plunge into cold water; let stand until cold. Drain well.

Drying: Place on mesh drying trays. Dry at 130°F (55°C).

Time: 12 to 14 hours.

Doneness test: Slices should feel dry and crisp and have no sign of moisture inside when broken open.

Tip

- For best results, do not use rhubarb stalks that are very thick and woody.

Rutabaga and Turnips

Slices

Preparation: Peel rutabaga and cut in half lengthwise. Place cut side down and cut crosswise into slices about $1/4$ inch (0.5 cm) thick.

Pretreatment: In a pot of boiling water, blanch rutabaga for 3 minutes. Using a strainer, remove from boiling water and immediately plunge into cold water; let stand until cold. Drain well.

Drying: Place on mesh drying trays. Dry at 130°F (55°C).

Time: 6 to 8 hours.

Doneness test: Slices should be dry, leathery and still pliable, with no evidence of moisture inside.

Tip

- If rutabaga or turnips are large, you can cut them lengthwise into quarters to make smaller slices. The drying time will be about the same.

Cubes

Preparation: Peel rutabaga and cut into $1/4$- to $1/2$-inch (0.5 to 1 cm) cubes.

Pretreatment: In a pot of boiling water, blanch rutabaga for 3 minutes. Using a strainer, remove from boiling water and immediately plunge into cold water; let stand until cold. Drain well.

Drying: Place on mesh drying trays. Dry at 130°F (55°C).

Time: 6 to 10 hours.

Doneness test: Cubes should feel dry and crisp and have no sign of moisture inside when broken open.

Tip

- Choose rutabaga and turnips that are heavy for their size and have no signs of shriveling, sprouting or mold.

Shallots

Slices

Preparation: Remove the outer skin of the shallots. Cut crosswise into slices about 1/4 inch (0.5 cm) thick, separating rings.

Drying: Place on mesh drying trays. Dry at 130°F (55°C).

Time: 8 to 10 hours.

Doneness test: Shallots should be dry, leathery and just slightly pliable.

Tip

- Shallots are easiest to dry in rings. If you need chopped or finely chopped shallots, use scissors to cut dried rings into smaller pieces just before using.

Roasted

Preparation: Remove the outer skin of the shallots. Cut into 1/2-inch (1 cm) pieces, separating layers. For each 1 lb (500 g) shallots, add 2 tbsp (25 mL) red wine or white wine vinegar and salt and pepper to taste; toss to coat. Spread out on a baking sheet lined with parchment paper. Bake in a 350°F (180°C) oven for about 45 minutes, stirring once, until browned and very tender.

Drying: Spread on fine-mesh drying trays (e.g., Clean-A-Screen). Dry at 130°F (55°C).

Time: 4 to 6 hours.

Doneness test: Shallots should be shriveled, leathery and just slightly pliable.

Tip

- To ensure even drying, stir periodically and separate any layers of shallots that are stuck together.

Sweet Potatoes

Slices

Preparation: Bake sweet potatoes in a 350°F (180°C) oven for 45 minutes. Let rest until cool enough to touch, then remove the skins and cut flesh crosswise into slices about 1/4 inch (0.5 cm) thick.

Drying: Place on mesh drying trays. Dry at 130°F (55°C).

Time: 10 to 12 hours.

Doneness test: Slices should feel firm and leathery and still be flexible.

Tip

- Roasting sweet potatoes before drying them helps maintain the shape much better than blanching and speeds up the drying process.

Cubes

Preparation: Bake sweet potatoes in a 350°F (180°C) oven for 45 minutes. Let rest until cool enough to touch, then remove the skins and cut flesh into 1/2-inch (1 cm) cubes.

Drying: Place on mesh drying trays. Dry at 130°F (55°C).

Time: 12 to 14 hours.

Doneness test: Cubes should be shriveled and hard, with no sign of moisture inside.

Tip

- Roasting sweet potatoes before drying them helps maintain the shape much better than blanching and speeds up the drying process.

Tomatoes, Grape

Preparation: Cut tomatoes in half lengthwise.

Drying: Place on mesh drying trays. Dry at 130°F (55°C).

Time: 20 to 24 hours.

Doneness test: Tomatoes should feel dry, be just slightly pliable and have no sign of moisture inside when broken open.

Tip

- Home-dried tomatoes will be firmer than commercially dried tomatoes. If you don't dry them enough and leave them soft, they will spoil quickly.

Tomatoes, Plum (Roma)

Preparation: Cut smaller tomatoes lengthwise into 8 wedges; cut larger ones into 12 wedges.

Drying: Place skin side down on mesh drying trays. Dry at 130°F (55°C).

Time: 20 to 24 hours.

Doneness test: Wedges should feel dry, be just slightly pliable and have no sign of moisture inside when broken open.

Tips

- Point the thin part of the slices toward the center of the tray so that the air flow across the slices is not impeded by the thicker portion.
- Beefsteak-style tomatoes and juicy cherry tomatoes have a lot of moisture, so there's very little tomato — and thus very little flavor — left after drying. Plum (Roma) or other paste-style tomatoes are better suited to drying.
- Home-dried tomatoes will be firmer than commercially dried tomatoes. If you don't dry them enough and leave them soft, they will spoil quickly.

Zucchini and Summer Squash

Slices

Preparation: Trim zucchini or squash and cut crosswise into slices about $\frac{1}{4}$ inch (0.5 cm) thick. (Do not peel.)

Drying: Place on mesh drying trays. Dry at 130°F (55°C).

Time: 6 to 10 hours.

Doneness test: Slices should feel dry and crisp and have no sign of moisture inside when broken open.

Tip

- Thinner zucchini are better for drying, as they tend to have firmer flesh and smaller seeds than large zucchini.

Grated

Preparation: Shred zucchini or squash on the coarse side of a box grater or using the shredding plate of a food processor. Place in a colander and gently press to squeeze out any excess liquid.

Drying: Spread on fine-mesh drying trays (e.g., Clean-A-Screen). Dry at 130°F (55°C).

Time: 2 to 3 hours.

Special instructions: Stir occasionally to break up any clumps and ensure even drying.

Doneness test: Zucchini should be shriveled, leathery and just slightly pliable.

Tip

- Remove zucchini from the trays when warm and let cool in a shallow dish. If left to cool on the screens, it tends to stick.

Making Fruit and Vegetable Leathers

Leather-Making Techniques and Tips

- A food processor is the best tool for puréeing thicker mixtures such as those used for leathers. If you don't have a food processor, an immersion blender in a tall cup works almost as well. If you only have a regular blender, you may need to add a bit of water to thin it out enough to blend; however, more water in the purée will increase the drying time.

- Use an offset spatula or a straight-edged dough scraper to spread the puréed mixture evenly on the sheet.

- It's best to press, rather than spread, thicker, dryer vegetable purées onto the sheet to help prevent fissures from forming as the purée dries. Some fissures will form in foods without pectin, creating cracked leather, and spreading tends to increase this chance.

- To determine whether the purée is spread to the right thickness, stick a toothpick straight down into the mixture and lift it out, then measure the moisture level on the toothpick.

- The thickness of the purée is more important than covering the entire leather sheet. Because sheets vary in size for different machines, you may need to use more than one, or cover only part of the sheet.

- Be sure not to spread the purée too thin. Even though it will dry faster, it will be difficult to lift off the leather sheet and will likely tear into shreds.

- If you don't have leather sheets, you can use parchment paper. It does tend to wrinkle slightly with very moist purées, and the drying time may be quite a bit shorter, so start checking for dryness earlier. Tuck the edges of the parchment paper underneath the mesh on the drying tray, or use metal paper clips to secure the paper to the tray, to keep it from flying around in the circulating air.

- If you have hard plastic leather sheets or trays, drier mixtures such as vegetable leathers tend to stick. To prevent sticking, cut out a sheet of parchment paper the same size and shape as the sheet and line the sheet before spreading the purée.

- You don't have to flip the leather, but it does speed up drying.

- To make flipping the leather easier, invert the leather sheet onto another mesh drying tray, then carefully peel off the leather sheet. Alternatively, if the leather seems fragile, invert another mesh drying tray on top of the leather on sheet. Slide your hand under the leather sheet and flip both over so the leather is inverted on the mesh tray, then carefully peel off the leather sheet.

- Fruit leather can be sweetened to taste, but keep in mind that sugar will slow the drying process and that adding too much can make for a sticky product that may never get leathery.

- When testing for doneness, keep in mind that the leather will firm up more upon cooling. You want to make sure there are no moist patches, but overdried leather can become crispy.

- As soon as leather is dry, peel it off the sheet or tray while still warm and let cool. Place on a sheet of plastic wrap, parchment paper or waxed paper and roll up jellyroll-style, rolling wrap between layers of the leather to prevent it from sticking to itself. Place in an airtight container or sealable plastic bag and store at room temperature for up to 6 months.

- Vegetable leathers tend to get quite hard and dry, so they work best when turned into powder. Break cooled leather into pieces, chop in a mini chopper or spice grinder and process until finely chopped or to a powder. Add to soups, stews and rice.

FRUIT LEATHERS

Apple Cinnamon Leather

Preparation: In a bowl, combine 2 cups (500 mL) unsweetened applesauce and ½ tsp (2 mL) ground cinnamon.

Drying: Spread out to ¼-inch (0.5 cm) thickness, as evenly as possible, on a leather sheet or a drying tray lined with parchment paper, leaving it slightly thicker around the edges. Dry at 130°F (55°C).

Time: 6 to 9 hours.

Special instructions: Start checking leather after 4 hours. When top is very firm and edges are easy to lift, carefully peel leather from sheet, flip over and continue drying.

Doneness test: Leather should be evenly translucent, with no visible moist spots, and should still be flexible.

Tip
- This works equally well with homemade or store-bought applesauce from a jar. Just be sure to read the label to make sure there's no added sugar. The amount of sugar added to commercial sauces interferes with proper drying.

Apricot Leather

Preparation: In a food processor, purée 2 cups (500 mL) halved apricots, 1 tbsp (15 mL) freshly squeezed lemon juice and 1 tbsp (15 mL) granulated sugar (if desired) until smooth.

Drying: Spread out to ¼-inch (0.5 cm) thickness, as evenly as possible, on a leather sheet or a drying tray lined with parchment paper, leaving it slightly thicker around the edges. Dry at 130°F (55°C).

Time: 5 to 7 hours.

Special instructions: Start checking leather after 3 hours. When top is very firm and edges are easy to lift, carefully peel leather from sheet, flip over and continue drying.

Doneness test: Leather should be evenly translucent, with no visible moist spots, and should still be flexible.

Tip
- Taste your apricots before puréeing them. Some are quite tart and will need some sugar; others are naturally quite sweet.

Strawberry Apple Leather

Preparation: In a food processor, purée 2 cups (500 mL) strawberries and 1 apple, peeled and chopped, until smooth.

Drying: Spread out to ¼-inch (0.5 cm) thickness, as evenly as possible, on a leather sheet or a drying tray lined with parchment paper, leaving it slightly thicker around the edges. Dry at 130°F (55°C).

Time: 6 to 8 hours.

Special instructions: Start checking leather after 5 hours. When top is very firm and edges are easy to lift, carefully peel leather from sheet, flip over and continue drying.

Doneness test: Leather should be evenly translucent, with no visible moist spots, and should still be flexible.

Tip

- Tart cooking apples that hold their flavor when heated, such as Granny Smith, Crispin and McIntosh, work best.

Banana Chocolate Leather

Preparation: In a food processor, purée 4 ripe bananas, broken into chunks, 2 tbsp (25 mL) unsweetened cocoa powder and 1 tbsp (15 mL) granulated sugar until smooth.

Drying: Spread out to ¼-inch (0.5 cm) thickness, as evenly as possible, on a leather sheet or a drying tray lined with parchment paper, leaving it slightly thicker around the edges. Dry at 130°F (55°C).

Time: 9 to 11 hours.

Special instructions: Start checking leather after 8 hours. When top is very firm and edges are easy to lift, carefully peel leather from sheet, flip over and continue drying.

Doneness test: Leather should be evenly firm, with no visible moist spots, and should still be flexible.

Tip

- Use very ripe bananas (with brown spots) for the best flavor. Underripe bananas aren't sweet or moist enough to make a nice leather.

Banana Nut Leather

Preparation: In a food processor, pulse ½ cup (125 mL) nuts (almonds, pecans, peanuts, hazelnuts) until finely chopped. Add 4 bananas, broken into chunks, and purée until fairly smooth.

Drying: Spread out to ¼-inch (0.5 cm) thickness, as evenly as possible, on a leather sheet or a drying tray lined with parchment paper, leaving it slightly thicker around the edges. Dry at 130°F (55°C).

Time: 9 to 11 hours.

Special instructions: Start checking leather after 7 hours. When top is very firm and edges are easy to lift, carefully peel leather from sheet, flip over and continue drying.

Doneness test: Leather should be evenly firm, with no visible moist spots, and should still be flexible.

Tips

- This leather tends to get crispy if overdried. If it does get crispy, break it into pieces and call it Banana Nut Crunch.
- The oil in the nuts reduces the shelf life of this leather. Store it at room temperature for up to 2 months or refrigerate for longer storage.

Cantaloupe Blueberry Leather

Preparation: In a food processor, purée 1½ cups (375 mL) chopped cantaloupe and 1 cup (250 mL) blueberries until smooth.

Drying: Spread out to ¼-inch (0.5 cm) thickness, as evenly as possible, on a leather sheet or a drying tray lined with parchment paper, leaving it slightly thicker around the edges. Dry at 130°F (55°C).

Time: 6 to 9 hours.

Special instructions: Start checking leather after 4 hours. When top is very firm and edges are easy to lift, carefully peel leather from sheet, flip over and continue drying.

Doneness test: Leather should be evenly firm, with no visible moist spots, and should still be flexible.

Tip

- Use a ripe and flavorful cantaloupe, but avoid an overripe melon, which can be pulpy or very juicy and give an unpleasant texture to the leather.

Mango Raspberry Leather

Preparation: In a food processor, purée 1½ cups (375 mL) chopped mango and 1 cup (250 mL) raspberries.

Drying: Spread out to ¼-inch (0.5 cm) thickness, as evenly as possible, on a leather sheet or a drying tray lined with parchment paper, leaving it slightly thicker around the edges. Dry at 130°F (55°C).

Time: 6 to 9 hours.

Special instructions: Start checking leather after 4 hours. When top is very firm and edges are easy to lift, carefully peel leather from sheet, flip over and continue drying.

Doneness test: Leather should be evenly translucent, with no visible moist spots, and should still be flexible.

Tip

- Use very ripe, soft mango for the best flavor and texture.

Peach Vanilla Leather

Preparation: In a food processor, purée 2½ cups (625 mL) chopped peaches, 1 tbsp (15 mL) granulated sugar or liquid honey, 1 tsp (5 mL) freshly squeezed lemon juice and ¼ tsp (1 mL) vanilla extract until smooth.

Drying: Spread out to ¼-inch (0.5 cm) thickness, as evenly as possible, on a leather sheet or a drying tray lined with parchment paper, leaving it slightly thicker around the edges. Dry at 130°F (55°C).

Time: 5 to 7 hours.

Special instructions: Start checking leather after 3½ hours. When top is very firm and edges are easy to lift, carefully peel leather from sheet, flip over and continue drying.

Doneness test: Leather should be evenly firm, with no visible moist spots, and should still be flexible.

Tip

- The peaches don't need to be peeled; just rub off any fuzz under running water before chopping.

Plum Cherry Leather

Preparation: In a food processor, purée 1½ cups (375 mL) chopped plums and 1 cup (250 mL) pitted sweet cherries until smooth.

Drying: Spread out to ¼-inch (0.5 cm) thickness, as evenly as possible, on a leather sheet or a drying tray lined with parchment paper, leaving it slightly thicker around the edges. Dry at 130°F (55°C).

Time: 7 to 9 hours.

Special instructions: Start checking leather after 5 hours. When top is very firm and edges are easy to lift, carefully peel leather from sheet, flip over and continue drying.

Doneness test: Leather should be evenly firm, with no visible moist spots, and should still be flexible.

Tip

• Purple or blue Italian-style plums have a deeper flavor than other plums; this flavor comes through nicely when the plums are dried.

Strawberry Banana Leather

Preparation: In a food processor, purée 2 cups (500 mL) strawberries and 1 ripe banana, broken into chunks, until smooth.

Drying: Spread out to ¼-inch (0.5 cm) thickness, as evenly as possible, on a leather sheet or a drying tray lined with parchment paper, leaving it slightly thicker around the edges. Dry at 130°F (55°C).

Time: 5 to 7 hours.

Special instructions: Start checking leather after 3 hours. When top is very firm and edges are easy to lift, carefully peel leather from sheet, flip over and continue drying.

Doneness test: Leather should be evenly firm, with no visible moist spots, and should still be flexible.

Tip

• Use very ripe bananas (with brown spots) for the best flavor. Underripe bananas aren't sweet or moist enough to make a nice leather.

Tropical Fruit Leather

Preparation: In a food processor, purée 1 cup (250 mL) chopped pineapple, 1 cup (250 mL) chopped mango and 1 ripe banana, broken into chunks, until smooth.

Drying: Spread out to ¼-inch (0.5 cm) thickness, as evenly as possible, on a leather sheet or a drying tray lined with parchment paper, leaving it slightly thicker around the edges. Dry at 130°F (55°C).

Time: 8 to 10 hours.

Special instructions: Start checking leather after 5 hours. When top is very firm and edges are easy to lift, carefully peel leather from sheet, flip over and continue drying.

Doneness test: Leather should be evenly firm, with no visible moist spots, and should still be flexible.

Tips

• Use ripe but not overripe fruit for the best flavor and texture.
• Sprinkle the purée with 2 tbsp (25 mL) sweetened shredded coconut, if desired.

VEGETABLE AND SAUCE LEATHERS

Tomato Pasta Sauce Leather

Preparation: Choose a homemade or prepared tomato pasta sauce with no meat, dairy or oil (or as little oil as possible). If sauce is chunky, purée in a food processor or blender until smooth.

Drying: Spread out to ¼-inch (0.5 cm) thickness, as evenly as possible, on a leather sheet or a drying tray lined with parchment paper, leaving it slightly thicker around the edges. Dry at 130°F (55°C).

Time: 12 to 16 hours.

Special instructions: Start checking leather after 10 hours. When top is very firm and edges are easy to lift, carefully peel leather from sheet, flip over and continue drying.

Doneness test: Leather should be evenly dry, with no visible moist spots, and should still be flexible.

Tip
- Starting with a thicker sauce will speed up the drying time. If you're making homemade sauce, simmer it a little longer to save time in the dryer.

Tomato Paste Leather

Preparation: None.

Drying: Press to ¼-inch (0.5 cm) thickness, as evenly as possible, on a leather sheet or a drying tray lined with parchment paper, leaving it slightly thicker around the edges. Dry at 130°F (55°C).

Time: 6 to 8 hours.

Special instructions: Start checking leather after 4 hours. When top is very firm and edges are easy to lift, carefully peel leather from sheet, flip over and continue drying.

Doneness test: Leather should be evenly dry, with no visible moist spots, and should still be flexible.

Salsa Leather

Preparation: Choose a homemade or prepared tomato salsa with no oil. If salsa is chunky, purée in a food processor or blender until smooth.

Drying: Spread out to ¼-inch (0.5 cm) thickness, as evenly as possible, on a leather sheet or a drying tray lined with parchment paper, leaving it slightly thicker around the edges. Dry at 130°F (55°C).

Time: 8 to 10 hours.

Special instructions: Start checking leather after 6 hours. When top is very firm and edges are easy to lift, carefully peel leather from sheet, flip over and continue drying.

Doneness test: Leather should be evenly dry, with no visible moist spots, and should still be flexible.

Tip
- Keep in mind that the flavor of the salsa will get very intense once dried. If you use a hot salsa, be prepared for the leather to be fiery.

Barbecue Sauce Leather

Preparation: In a saucepan, combine 1 clove garlic, minced, ¼ cup (50 mL) packed brown sugar, 1 tsp (5 mL) chili powder, ½ tsp (2 mL) dry mustard, ¼ tsp (1 mL) each celery seed, salt and pepper, 1 cup (250 mL) tomato paste and ¼ cup (50 mL) each cider vinegar and water. Bring to a boil over medium heat, whisking constantly. Simmer, whisking, for 3 minutes to blend flavors.

Drying: Spread out to ¼-inch (0.5 cm) thickness, as evenly as possible, on a leather sheet or a drying tray lined with parchment paper, leaving it slightly thicker around the edges. Dry at 130°F (55°C).

Time: 16 to 20 hours.

Special instructions: Start checking leather after 12 hours. When top is very firm and edges are easy to lift, carefully peel leather from sheet, flip over and continue drying.

Doneness test: Leather should be evenly dry, with no visible moist spots, and should still be flexible.

Tip
- This barbecue sauce was specially created to make leather. Commercial sauces generally have too much sugar and thickeners to dry properly.

Carrot Leather

Preparation: In a saucepan, cover 4 cups (1 L) chopped carrots with water. Bring to a boil over high heat. Reduce heat and boil gently for about 7 minutes, or until carrots are very soft. Drain, reserving cooking liquid. In a food processor, purée carrots, adding as much of the reserved cooking liquid as necessary to make a smooth, thick paste. Season to taste with salt and pepper, if desired.

Drying: Press to ¼-inch (0.5 cm) thickness, as evenly as possible, on a leather sheet or a drying tray lined with parchment paper, leaving it slightly thicker around the edges. Dry at 130°F (55°C).

Time: 6 to 9 hours.

Special instructions: Start checking leather after 4 hours. When top is very firm and edges are easy to lift, carefully peel leather from sheet, flip over and continue drying.

Doneness test: Leather should be evenly dry, with no visible moist spots, and should still be flexible.

Tip
- This leather tastes terrific on its own or can be broken into pieces or finely chopped and added to soups or stews.

Sweet Potato and Red Pepper Leather

Preparation: Pierce 1 large sweet potato (about 1 lb/500 g) all over with a fork. Place on a baking sheet and bake in a 350°F (180°C) oven for about 1 hour or until fork-tender. Let cool. Peel and cut into chunks. In a food processor, purée sweet potato and 1 cup (250 mL) chopped red bell pepper until smooth. Season to taste with salt and pepper, if desired.

Drying: Press to ¼-inch (0.5 cm) thickness, as evenly as possible, on a leather sheet or a drying tray lined with parchment paper, leaving it slightly thicker around the edges. Dry at 130°F (55°C).

Time: 6 to 9 hours.

Special instructions: Start checking leather after 4 hours. When top is very firm and edges are easy to lift, carefully peel leather from sheet, flip over and continue drying.

Doneness test: Leather should be evenly dry, with no visible moist spots, and should still be flexible.

Tip

- This leather tastes terrific on its own or can be broken into pieces or finely chopped and added to soups or stews.

Green Pea Leather

Preparation: In a food processor, purée 2 cups (500 mL) cooked or thawed frozen green peas until smooth, adding a little water if necessary. Season to taste with salt and pepper, if desired.

Drying: Press to $\frac{1}{4}$-inch (0.5 cm) thickness, as evenly as possible, on a leather sheet or a drying tray lined with parchment paper, leaving it slightly thicker around the edges. Dry at 130°F (55°C).

Time: 8 to 10 hours.

Special instructions: Start checking leather after 5 hours. When top is very firm and edges are easy to lift, carefully peel leather from sheet, flip over and continue drying.

Doneness test: Leather should be evenly dry and crisp.

Tip

- Green pea leather is quite hard, so it is best used as a powder or broken into small pieces. Add to soups and stews.

Roasted Winter Squash or Pumpkin Leather

Preparation: On a baking sheet lined with parchment paper, toss 4 cups (1 L) cubed winter squash ($\frac{1}{2}$-inch/1 cm cubes) with 2 tbsp (25 mL) cider vinegar. Roast in a 350°F (180°C) oven for about 30 minutes or until browned and tender. Let cool. In a food processor, purée roasted squash until smooth. Season to taste with salt and pepper, if desired.

Drying: Press to $\frac{1}{4}$-inch (0.5 cm) thickness, as evenly as possible, on a leather sheet or a drying tray lined with parchment paper, leaving it slightly thicker around the edges. Dry at 130°F (55°C).

Time: 8 to 10 hours.

Special instructions: Start checking leather after 6 hours. When top is very firm and edges are easy to lift, carefully peel leather from sheet, flip over and continue drying.

Doneness test: Leather should be evenly dry, with no visible moist spots, and should still be flexible.

Tip

- Butternut squash is the easiest to peel and chop and has a drier texture than some other squash. Avoid soft, pulpy squash, as they can make a crumbly leather.

Mushroom Leather

Preparation: In a skillet over medium-high heat, sauté 1 lb (500 g) mushrooms, chopped, $\frac{1}{2}$ cup (125 mL) chopped onion, 3 cloves garlic, minced, and

½ tsp (2 mL) crumbled dried rosemary for about 10 minutes, or until liquid is evaporated and mushrooms start to brown. Let cool. In a food processor, purée until fairly smooth. Season to taste with salt and pepper, if desired.

Drying: Press to ¼-inch (0.5 cm) thickness, as evenly as possible, on a leather sheet or a drying tray lined with parchment paper, leaving it slightly thicker around the edges. Dry at 130°F (55°C).

Time: 8 to 10 hours.

Special instructions: Start checking leather after 5 hours. When top is very firm and edges are easy to lift, carefully peel leather from sheet, flip over and continue drying.

Doneness test: Leather should be evenly dry and slightly flexible.

Tip

- Use pieces of this leather in soups and stews — or add some when making vegetable stock to boost the flavor.

Spinach Leather

Preparation: In a food processor, purée 2 cups (500 mL) drained cooked or thawed frozen spinach (about 12 oz/375 g) until fairly smooth. Season to taste with salt and pepper, if desired.

Drying: Press to ¼-inch (0.5 cm) thickness, as evenly as possible, on a leather sheet or a drying tray lined with parchment paper, leaving it slightly thicker around the edges. Dry at 130°F (55°C).

Time: 8 to 10 hours.

Special instructions: Start checking leather after 5 hours. When top is very firm and edges are easy to lift, carefully peel leather from sheet, flip over and continue drying.

Doneness test: Leather should be evenly dry and crisp.

Tip

- Dried spinach is best used as a powder. Break cooled leather into chunks and chop in a food processor to a fine powder. Add to soups, rice, stews or eggs.

Dehydrating Beans, Tofu, Grains and Dairy

BEANS AND TOFU

Canned or Cooked Beans

Preparation: Drain and rinse canned or cooked black beans, kidney beans, white pea (navy) beans, Romano beans or chickpeas. Drain well.

Drying: Place on mesh drying trays. Dry at 130°F (55°C).

Time: 5 to 6 hours.

Doneness test: Beans should be light, crisp and dry throughout.

Tip

- Some beans burst open and crumble slightly while drying. Just scoop up all of the small bits and add to the beans when packaging. The small bits help thicken recipes that use dried cooked beans.

Basic Veggie Burger Blend

Preparation: In a food processor, combine 1 cup (250 mL) cooked long-grain brown rice, 1 cup (250 mL) drained, rinsed canned or cooked chickpeas and 1 cup (250 mL) drained, rinsed canned or cooked brown lentils. Pulse until finely chopped but not puréed.

Drying: Spread out to 1/4-inch (0.5 cm) thickness, as evenly as possible, on a fine-mesh drying tray, a leather sheet or a drying tray lined with parchment paper. Dry at 130°F (55°C).

Time: 4 to 6 hours.

Doneness test: Pieces should be very crisp and dry throughout.

Tip

- The small pieces may fall through even a fine-mesh drying tray, so the leather sheet or parchment may work better for you, though they do slow drying time. If using the fine-mesh tray, place a leather sheet on an empty rack below to catch any pieces that fall through.

Tofu

Slices

Preparation: Use extra-firm or firm tofu. Remove from package and rinse well. Cut into slices about 1/4 inch (0.5 cm) thick.

Drying: Place on mesh drying trays. Dry at 130°F (55°C).

Time: 12 to 14 hours.

Special instructions: After about 8 hours, flip the tofu pieces to speed up drying, if desired.

Doneness test: Slices should feel very dry and firm and should break easily when bent.

Tips

- For extra flavor, marinate tofu in any of the jerky marinades or rubs (pages 70 to 74) for 30 minutes; drain off excess, if necessary, before drying.
- Because tofu contains fat, it is best stored in the refrigerator, where it will keep for up to 6 months; it can be stored at room temperature for up to 2 weeks.

Crumbled

Preparation: Use extra-firm or firm tofu. Remove from package and rinse well. Break into 1/4- to 1/2-inch (0.5 to 1 cm) pieces.

Drying: Spread out as thinly and evenly as possible on fine-mesh drying trays. Dry at 130°F (55°C).

Time: 12 to 14 hours.

Special instructions: During drying, rearrange tofu on the tray to separate any clumps.

Doneness test: Pieces should feel very dry and firm.

Tips

- For even drying, make sure the tofu pieces are uniform in size.
- For extra flavor, marinate tofu in any of the jerky marinades or rubs (pages 70 to 74) for 30 minutes; drain off excess, if necessary, before drying.
- Because tofu contains fat, it is best stored in the refrigerator, where it will keep for up to 6 months; it can be stored at room temperature for up to 2 weeks.

Shredded

Preparation: Use extra-firm or firm tofu. Remove from package and rinse well. Using the coarse side of a box cheese grater, grate into shreds.

Drying: Spread out as thinly and evenly as possible on fine-mesh drying trays. Dry at 130°F (55°C).

Time: 10 to 12 hours.

Special instructions: During drying, rearrange tofu on the tray to separate any clumps.

Doneness test: Shredded tofu should feel very dry and firm.

Tips

- The color of tofu will darken considerably as it dries.
- Use fine-mesh tray liners (e.g., Clean-A-Screen) if necessary to prevent pieces from falling through trays.

- Because tofu contains fat, it is best stored in the refrigerator, where it will keep for up to 6 months; it can be stored at room temperature for up to 2 weeks.

Puréed

Preparation: Use firm tofu. Remove from package and rinse well. In a food processor, purée until smooth.

Drying: Spread out to ¼-inch (0.5 cm) thickness, as evenly as possible, on leather sheets or on drying trays lined with parchment paper, leaving it slightly thicker around the edges. Dry at 130°F (55°C).

Time: 12 to 14 hours.

Special instructions: Start checking tofu after 8 hours. When top is firm and edges are easy to lift, carefully peel from trays, flip over and continue drying.

Doneness test: Sheets should be evenly dry and crisp.

To use: Sheets can be crumbled into pieces or ground in a food processor or mini chopper, then added to recipes.

Tips

- Be sure there are no lumps in the purée, as they will not dry properly.
- Because tofu contains fat, it is best stored in the refrigerator, where it will keep for up to 6 months; it can be stored at room temperature for up to 2 weeks.

COOKED GRAINS AND PASTA

White Rice

Preparation: Cook long-grain white rice according to package directions until tender. Rinse under cold running water to cool and rinse off excess starch. Drain well.

Drying: Spread out as evenly as possible on fine-mesh drying trays. Dry at 130°F (55°C).

Time: 5 to 6 hours.

Special instructions: Stir occasionally to break up any clumps and ensure even drying.

Doneness test: Rice should be translucent, very firm and dry throughout.

Tip

- Use fine-mesh tray liners (e.g., Clean-A-Screen) if necessary to prevent rice from falling through trays.

Brown Rice

Preparation: Cook long-grain brown rice according to package directions until tender. Rinse under cold running water to cool and rinse off excess starch. Drain well.

Drying: Spread out as evenly as possible on fine-mesh drying trays. Dry at 130°F (55°C).

Time: 6 to 8 hours.

Special instructions: Stir occasionally to break up any clumps and ensure even drying.

Doneness test: Rice should be translucent, very firm and dry throughout.

Tip

- Use fine-mesh tray liners (e.g., Clean-A-Screen) if necessary to prevent rice from falling through trays.

Wild Rice

Preparation: Cook wild rice according to package directions until tender. Rinse under cold running water to cool and rinse off excess starch. Drain well.

Drying: Spread out as evenly as possible on fine-mesh drying trays. Dry at 130°F (55°C).

Time: 6 to 8 hours.

Special instructions: Stir occasionally to break up any clumps and ensure even drying.

Doneness test: Rice grains should be firm, should snap easily when bent and should be dry throughout.

Tips

- Wild rice is rather expensive. You may want to experiment with small amounts to perfect your drying technique before drying larger quantities.
- Some wild rice grains are much larger than others. Large grains will take longer to cook and to dry.

Wheat Berries

Preparation: Cook wheat berries until tender. Rinse under cold running water to cool and rinse off excess starch. Drain well.

Drying: Spread out as evenly as possible on fine-mesh drying trays. Dry at 130°F (55°C).

Time: 3 to 4 hours.

Special instructions: Stir occasionally to break up any clumps and ensure even drying.

Doneness test: Wheat berries should be very firm and dry throughout.

Tips

- Wheat berries are whole kernels of wheat. They can be found at natural food stores and bulk stores, or where other whole grains are sold.
- Use fine-mesh tray liners (e.g., Clean-A-Screen) if necessary to prevent grains from falling through trays.

Barley

Preparation: Cook whole (hulled) barley, pot barley or pearl barley until tender. Drain and rinse under cold running water. Drain well.

Drying: Spread out as evenly as possible on fine-mesh drying trays. Dry at 130°F (55°C).

Time: 3 to 4 hours.

Special instructions: Stir occasionally to break up any clumps and ensure even drying.

Doneness test: Barley should be very firm and dry throughout.

Tips

- Use fine-mesh tray liners (e.g., Clean-A-Screen) if necessary to prevent grains from falling through trays.
- Whole barley is less refined than pot or pearl barley, so it takes longer to cook, but the extra nutrition is worth it.

Whole Oats

Preparation: Cook whole (hulled) oats until tender. Drain and rinse under cold running water. Drain well.

Drying: Spread out as evenly as possible on fine-mesh drying trays. Dry at 130°F (55°C).

Time: 3 to 4 hours.

Special instructions: Stir occasionally to break up any clumps and ensure even drying.

Doneness test: Oats should be very firm and dry throughout.

Tip

- Use fine-mesh tray liners (e.g., Clean-A-Screen) if necessary to prevent oats from falling through trays.

Steel-Cut Oats

Preparation: Cook steel-cut oats according to package directions until thickened and tender.

Drying: Spread out to ¼-inch (0.5 cm) thickness, as evenly as possible, on leather sheets or on drying trays lined with parchment paper, leaving it slightly thicker around the edges. Dry at 130°F (55°C).

Time: 7 to 10 hours.

Special instructions: Start checking oats after 5 hours. When top is very firm and edges are easy to lift, carefully peel from leather sheets, flip over and continue drying.

Doneness test: Sheets should be evenly dry and crisp and should break easily when bent.

To use: Break sheets into small pieces and process in a mini chopper, food processor or blender until fairly finely chopped and about one-quarter is powdery. Rehydrate by soaking 1 part ground oats in 3 parts water for 20 minutes, then bring to a boil.

Tip

- Cooked large-flake rolled oats can also be dried in this way.

Elbow Macaroni

Preparation: Cook pasta according to package directions until tender but firm (al dente). Rinse well under cold running water to remove excess starch. Drain well.

Drying: Place on fine-mesh drying trays. Dry at 130°F (55°C).

Time: 2 to 4 hours.

Special instructions: Rearrange pasta on the tray as necessary to separate pieces.

Doneness test: Pasta should be very light, evenly firm and dry throughout.

To use: Soak dried cooked pasta in room-temperature water for about 30 minutes. Or add to boiling water and boil for 3 to 5 minutes.

Tips

- Use fine-mesh tray liners (e.g., Clean-A-Screen) if necessary to prevent pasta from falling through trays.
- Dried cooked pasta doesn't shrink much in size but does rehydrate easily with room-temperature water, making it perfect for eating away from home.

Fusilli or Rotini Pasta

Preparation: Cook pasta according to package directions until tender but firm (al dente). Rinse well under cold running water to remove excess starch. Drain well.

Drying: Place on mesh drying trays. Dry at 130°F (55°C).

Time: 2 to 4 hours.

Special instructions: Rearrange pasta on the tray as necessary to separate pieces.

Doneness test: Pasta should be very light, evenly firm and dry throughout.

To use: Soak dried cooked pasta in room-temperature water for about 30 minutes. Or add to boiling water and boil for 3 to 5 minutes.

Tip

- Open pasta shapes with a lot of surface area work best for drying and rehydrating.

Bread Crumbs

Preparation: Cut fresh bread, buns or rolls into slices about $1/2$ inch (1 cm) thick.

Drying: Place on mesh drying trays. Dry at 155°F (68°C).

Time: 1 to 3 hours.

Doneness test: Slices should be very firm and crisp throughout.

To store: Let dried bread cool completely. Transfer to a bowl and crumble to coarse crumbs, or in a food processor, process to fine crumbs. Store in an airtight container at room temperature for up to 6 months.

Tip

- Crumbs made from breads with nuts or seeds will not keep as long because of the oils. Store crumbs made from these breads in the freezer.

DAIRY

Cottage Cheese

Preparation: Use 1% (low-fat) cottage cheese. Stir to blend evenly.

Drying: Spread out to ¼-inch (0.5 cm) thickness, as evenly as possible, on leather sheets or on drying trays lined with parchment paper, leaving it slightly thicker around the edges. Dry at 130°F (55°C).

Time: 10 to 14 hours.

Special instructions: If possible, flip over after 5 to 6 hours or once the cheese is easy to lift from the leather sheets; this will speed up drying.

Doneness test: Sheets should be thoroughly dry and very hard.

To use: Break dried cottage cheese into small pieces to simmer in sauces. Use a mini chopper to grind dried cottage cheese to a powder for use in other recipes.

Tips

- For maximum shelf life, dried cottage cheese is best stored in the refrigerator, where it will keep for up to 6 months; it can be stored at room temperature for up to 1 week.
- Do not attempt to use higher-fat cottage cheese, as it may go rancid quickly when heated and stored at room temperature.

Puréed

Preparation: Use 1% (low-fat) cottage cheese. Using an immersion blender in a tall cup, or in a food processor or blender, purée cottage cheese until smooth.

Drying: Spread out to ¼-inch (0.5 cm) thickness, as evenly as possible, on leather sheets or on drying trays lined with parchment paper, leaving it slightly thicker around the edges. Dry at 130°F (55°C).

Time: 10 to 14 hours.

Special instructions: If possible, flip over after 5 to 6 hours or once the cheese is easy to lift from the leather sheets; this will speed up drying.

Doneness test: Sheets should be thoroughly dry and very hard.

To use: Break dried cottage cheese into small pieces to simmer in sauces. Use a mini chopper to grind dried cottage cheese to a powder for use in other recipes.

Tips

- For maximum shelf life, dried cottage cheese is best stored in the refrigerator, where it will keep for up to 6 months; it can be stored at room temperature for up to 1 week.
- Do not attempt to use higher-fat cottage cheese, as it may go rancid quickly when heated and stored at room temperature.

Yogurt

Plain

Preparation: Use 1% (low-fat) yogurt. Stir until smooth and blended.

Drying: Spread out to ¼-inch (0.5 cm) thickness, as evenly as possible, on leather sheets or on drying trays lined with parchment paper, leaving it slightly thicker around the edges. Dry at 130°F (55°C).

Time: 12 to 14 hours.

Special instructions: If possible, flip over after about 8 hours or once the yogurt is easy to lift from the leather sheets; this will speed up drying.

Doneness test: Sheets should be firm and should break easily.

Tips

- Avoid any yogurts with gelatin or other thickeners, as they won't dry thoroughly.
- Do not attempt to use higher-fat yogurt, as it may go rancid quickly when heated and stored at room temperature.
- For maximum shelf life, dried yogurt is best stored in the refrigerator, where it will keep for up to 6 months; it can be stored at room temperature for up to 1 week.

Fruit-Flavored

Preparation: Use 1% (low-fat) fruit-flavored yogurt. Stir until smooth and blended.

Drying: Spread out to ¼-inch (0.5 cm) thickness, as evenly as possible, on leather sheets or on drying trays lined with parchment paper, leaving it slightly thicker around the edges. Dry at 130°F (55°C).

Time: 14 to 20 hours.

Special instructions: Start checking yogurt after 10 hours. When top is very firm and edges start to lift, carefully peel from leather sheets, flip over and continue drying. Or, if desired, you can cut sheet into small pieces and transfer pieces to a mesh drying tray for a chewy snack.

Doneness test: Dried yogurt should be evenly dry and firm but still flexible.

Tips

- Avoid any yogurts with gelatin or other thickeners, as they won't dry thoroughly.
- Flavored yogurts contain varying amounts of added sugars. Those higher in sugar will take longer to dry. Avoid yogurts with artificial sweeteners.
- For maximum shelf life, dried yogurt is best stored in the refrigerator, where it will keep for up to 6 months; it can be stored at room temperature for up to 1 week.

Dehydrating Meat, Poultry and Fish

Making Jerky

Dried meat, fish and poultry have sustained people around the world for centuries. Leftover meat that wasn't eaten right away was cut into strips and left to dry, sometimes over a fire, for later use. Removing the moisture made it last longer and made it lighter to pack and carry for nomadic populations. We have learned from those historical populations to preserve meat, fish and poultry and have expanded the practice by making it taste even more delicious by adding flavorful marinades and rubs.

In this chapter, we have provided some recipes for jerky strips and ground meat jerky. You can certainly experiment with the flavors, but the method should be followed carefully to make sure the jerky you make at home gets preserved properly and is safe to eat. Use only fresh meat, poultry or fish that you are confident is of the highest quality.

Lean cuts are necessary to make jerky that lasts. Higher-fat cuts do not dry properly, and the residual fats in the meat will go rancid and spoil the jerky. Cuts with marbling of fat through the meat also tend to break apart as the meat is cooked and dried, and the fat leaches out, so you don't end up with nice strips.

All meat, poultry and fish (even the lean cuts) will have a small amount of fat that cooks out when the strips are first baked, and some may continue to rise to the surface during drying. These small amounts of fat are easy to blot off with paper towels after cooking and during drying to ensure a high-quality jerky.

Jerky recipes made with ground meats also benefit from the use of lean meat. Ground meat jerky is easiest if you have a specially designed jerky gun, but with some patience you can hand-shape strips with a piping bag or simple spoons. The advantage of making jerky with ground meats is that you can incorporate seasoning elements right into the meat for extra flavor. Jerky made with ground meat is also much more tender, which is particularly good for kids and those who don't like the toothsome texture of traditional jerky made from meat strips.

For the utmost food safety, we recommend that only fully cooked meats, poultry and fish be used to make jerky at home. Historically, raw meats have been used, but new research suggests that, to protect against food-borne illnesses, the only safe way to make jerky is to cook the meat to well done before drying it.

Storing Jerky

To store jerky, once it has cooled, place it in an airtight container lined with a paper towel. Check it periodically to see if any more fat has come out of the jerky; if so, replace the paper towel with a fresh one. When storing jerky, keep different flavors separate to be sure the flavors stay true.

Commercial jerky generally contains nitrites as a preservative, which creates a softer texture, brighter color and longer shelf life. We prefer not to use any preservatives, other than common salt; therefore, the recipes have been tested without added nitrites. For that reason, we recommend storing at room temperature for a maximum of 1 month. However, jerky can be safely refrigerated for up to 6 months or frozen for up to 1 year.

Dried products take up much less space in the fridge or freezer than fresh and are stable for packing without refrigeration for a short time, making them perfect for camping and hiking.

Suitable Cuts for Jerky Strips

Any of these cuts can be used to make jerky strips (pages 70 to 74).

Beef, Venison, Elk, Moose, Bison

- flank steak
- eye of round
- outside round
- sirloin tip

Chicken, Turkey, Farmed Duck, Wild Goose

- boneless skinless breast

Ostrich, Emu

- fan (thigh)
- inside strip
- outside strip
- top strip
- back tender

Fish

- low-fat fish fillets, such as catfish, cod, ocean perch, pickerel (northern pike), pollock, rainbow trout, striped bass, rock bass or tilapia
- salmon fillets are traditional for jerky, but their fat content makes them unsuitable for room-temperature storage; store salmon jerky in the refrigerator for up to 1 month or in the freezer for up to 6 months

Before purchasing fish, always learn what you can about sustainability and fishing practices. Good North American resources are

- www.montereybayaquarium.org/cr/SeafoodWatch/web/sfw_regional.aspx
- www.seachoice.org

Using Bottled Marinades to Prepare Jerky

Look for bottled marinades or sauces that don't contain a high amount of sugar, as sugar tends to lengthen the drying time significantly. Many bottled products also contain some amount of oil, which will decrease the shelf life of the jerky, as oils tend to go rancid over time. Choose oil-free marinades or those with as little oil as possible. Be judicious in your use of bottled marinade: excess marinade tends to congeal and clump, forming overly intense flavor in those spots.

Sea Salt and Peppercorn Jerky

Makes about 24 strips

A light seasoning makes this jerky versatile: you can use it in a wide array of recipes or simply enjoy it as is.

- Large rimmed baking sheets, lined with parchment paper

1 lb	meat, poultry or fish, trimmed	500 g
1 tsp	sea salt	5 mL
½ tsp	freshly ground black pepper	2 mL

1. For easier slicing, put the meat in the freezer for about 25 minutes or until firm but not solid. Meanwhile, preheat oven to 350°F (180°C).

2. Using a sharp knife, cut meat into strips about ¼ inch (0.5 cm) thick, cutting with the grain for chewy strips or across the grain for more brittle strips (which will be easier to chew).

3. In a bowl, toss meat strips with salt and pepper, coating evenly. Arrange on prepared baking sheets, leaving space between each strip.

4. Bake in preheated oven for 10 minutes or until meat is no longer pink inside (or fish is firm and opaque). Transfer to a baking sheet lined with paper towels, turning to blot both sides.

5. Place cooked meat strips on mesh drying trays. Dry at 155°F (68°C) for 6 to 8 hours, occasionally blotting any fat that rises to the surface with paper towels, until jerky is firm and flexes and cracks, but doesn't break, when gently bent. Transfer to a clean baking sheet lined with paper towels and let cool completely, turning once to blot thoroughly.

Cajun Jerky

Makes about 24 strips

Sweetness, spice and heat combine to make a zesty jerky.

Tips

Experiment with your favorite prepared dry rubs and spice blends. On average, use about $1/3$ cup (75 mL) per pound (500 g) meat, poultry or fish.

Fish, chicken breasts and tender ostrich and emu cuts only need to stand in the rub for 15 minutes to 1 hour. For other meats, refrigerate for 30 minutes or longer.

• Large rimmed baking sheets, lined with parchment paper

1 lb	meat, poultry or fish, trimmed	500 g
2 tbsp	sweet paprika	25 mL
4 tsp	packed brown sugar	20 mL
2 tsp	salt	10 mL
2 tsp	dry mustard	10 mL
$1/2$ tsp	ground ginger	2 mL
$1/2$ tsp	cayenne pepper	2 mL
$1/4$ tsp	ground allspice	1 mL

1. For easier slicing, put the meat in the freezer for about 25 minutes or until firm but not solid.

2. Using a sharp knife, cut meat into strips about $1/4$ inch (0.5 cm) thick, cutting with the grain for chewy strips or across the grain for more brittle strips (which will be easier to chew).

3. In a bowl, combine paprika, brown sugar, salt, mustard, ginger, cayenne and allspice. Add meat strips and toss to coat. Let stand at room temperature for 15 minutes, or cover and refrigerate for up to 8 hours (see tip, at left). Meanwhile, preheat oven to 350°F (180°C).

4. Arrange meat strips on prepared baking sheets, leaving space between each strip. Bake in preheated oven for 10 minutes or until meat is no longer pink inside (or fish is firm and opaque). Transfer to a baking sheet lined with paper towels, turning to blot both sides.

5. Place cooked meat strips on mesh drying trays. Dry at 155°F (68°C) for 6 to 8 hours, occasionally blotting any fat that rises to the surface with paper towels, until jerky is firm and flexes and cracks, but doesn't break, when gently bent. Transfer to a clean baking sheet lined with paper towels and let cool completely, turning once to blot thoroughly.

Maple and Grainy Dijon Jerky

Makes about 24 strips

This jerky marinade gives the classic honey-mustard idea a gourmet twist by combining sweet maple syrup with tangy mustard.

Tip

Fish, chicken breast and tender ostrich and emu cuts only need to marinate for 15 minutes to 1 hour. For other meats, marinate for 30 minutes or longer.

- Large rimmed baking sheets, lined with parchment paper

1 lb	meat, poultry or fish, trimmed	500 g
¼ tsp	salt	1 mL
2 tbsp	grainy Dijon mustard	25 mL
2 tbsp	pure maple syrup	25 mL

1. For easier slicing, put the meat in the freezer for about 25 minutes or until firm but not solid.

2. Using a sharp knife, cut meat into strips about ¼ inch (0.5 cm) thick, cutting with the grain for chewy strips or across the grain for more brittle strips (which will be easier to chew).

3. In a bowl, combine salt, mustard and maple syrup. Add meat strips and toss to coat. Let stand at room temperature for 15 minutes, or cover and refrigerate for up to 8 hours (see tip, at left). Meanwhile, preheat oven to 350°F (180°C).

4. Remove meat from marinade, discarding excess marinade and accumulated juices. Arrange meat strips on prepared baking sheets, leaving space between each strip. Bake in preheated oven for 10 minutes or until meat is no longer pink inside (or fish is firm and opaque). Transfer to a baking sheet lined with paper towels, turning to blot both sides.

5. Place cooked meat strips on mesh drying trays. Dry at 155°F (68°C) for 6 to 8 hours, occasionally blotting any fat that rises to the surface with paper towels, until jerky is firm and flexes and cracks, but doesn't break, when gently bent. Transfer to a clean baking sheet lined with paper towels and let cool completely, turning once to blot thoroughly.

Teriyaki Jerky

Makes about 24 strips

Teriyaki is one of the most popular seasonings for jerky, and once you taste this version you'll know why. This marinade gives a depth of flavor you just don't get from bottled sauces.

Tip

Fish, chicken breast and tender ostrich and emu cuts only need to marinate for 15 minutes to 1 hour. For other meats, marinate for 30 minutes or longer.

• Large rimmed baking sheets, lined with parchment paper

1 lb	meat, poultry or fish, trimmed	500 g
2 tbsp	packed brown sugar	25 mL
1/2 tsp	ground ginger	2 mL
1/2 tsp	freshly ground black pepper	2 mL
2 tbsp	soy sauce	25 mL
1 tsp	Asian chili sauce	5 mL
1 tsp	rice vinegar	5 mL

1. For easier slicing, put the meat in the freezer for about 25 minutes or until firm but not solid.

2. Using a sharp knife, cut meat into strips about 1/4 inch (0.5 cm) thick, cutting with the grain for chewy strips or across the grain for more brittle strips (which will be easier to chew).

3. In a bowl, combine brown sugar, ginger, pepper, soy sauce, chili sauce and vinegar. Add meat strips and toss to coat. Let stand at room temperature for 15 minutes, or cover and refrigerate for up to 8 hours (see tip, at left). Meanwhile, preheat oven to 350°F (180°C).

4. Remove meat from marinade, discarding excess marinade and accumulated juices. Arrange meat strips on prepared baking sheets, leaving space between each strip. Bake in preheated oven for 10 minutes or until meat is no longer pink inside (or fish is firm and opaque). Transfer to a baking sheet lined with paper towels, turning to blot both sides.

5. Place cooked meat strips on mesh drying trays. Dry at 155°F (68°C) for 6 to 8 hours, occasionally blotting any fat that rises to the surface with paper towels, until jerky is firm and flexes and cracks, but doesn't break, when gently bent. Transfer to a clean baking sheet lined with paper towels and let cool completely, turning once to blot thoroughly.

Jerk Jerky

Makes about 24 strips

A little taste of Jamaica spices up jerky nicely. If you like it hot, hot, hot, use the Scotch bonnet pepper.

Tip

Fish, chicken breast and tender ostrich and emu cuts only need to marinate for 15 minutes to 1 hour. For other meats, marinate for 30 minutes or longer.

- Large rimmed baking sheets, lined with parchment paper

1 lb	meat, poultry or fish, trimmed	500 g
1 tbsp	minced garlic	15 mL
1 tsp	ground allspice	5 mL
1 tsp	ground coriander	5 mL
1/2 tsp	cayenne pepper (or 1/2 Scotch bonnet pepper, minced)	2 mL
1/2 tsp	freshly ground black pepper	2 mL
1/4 tsp	ground nutmeg	1 mL
1/4 cup	freshly squeezed lime juice	50 mL

1. For easier slicing, put the meat in the freezer for about 25 minutes or until firm but not solid.

2. Using a sharp knife, cut meat into strips about 1/4 inch (0.5 cm) thick, cutting with the grain for chewy strips or across the grain for more brittle strips (which will be easier to chew).

3. In a bowl, combine garlic, allspice, coriander, cayenne, black pepper, nutmeg and lime juice. Add meat strips and toss to coat. Let stand at room temperature for 15 minutes, or cover and refrigerate for up to 8 hours (see tip, at left). Meanwhile, preheat oven to 350°F (180°C).

4. Remove meat from marinade, discarding excess marinade and accumulated juices. Arrange meat strips on prepared baking sheets, leaving space between each strip. Bake in preheated oven for 10 minutes or until meat is no longer pink inside (or fish is firm and opaque). Transfer to a baking sheet lined with paper towels, turning to blot both sides.

5. Place cooked meat strips on mesh drying trays. Dry at 155°F (68°C) for 6 to 8 hours, occasionally blotting any fat that rises to the surface with paper towels, until jerky is firm and flexes and cracks, but doesn't break, when gently bent. Transfer to a clean baking sheet lined with paper towels and let cool completely, turning once to blot thoroughly.

Herb and Garlic Ground Meat Jerky

Makes about 6 oz (175 g)

Garden-fresh herbs season the ground meat just enough to add interest, but not so much that they overwhelm the meat. You can substitute other herbs for the oregano and sage to vary the flavor.

Tips

If you don't have a jerky gun or piping bag, use a rubber spatula and a small spoon to spoon meat mixture into strips on prepared baking sheets.

To flatten strips that are piped or spooned onto baking sheets, place another sheet of parchment paper on top and press as evenly as possible. Ensure that the strips don't touch each other.

It is best to err on the side of caution and cook the beef a little longer, if necessary, to make sure it is well done.

- Preheat oven to 400°F (200°C)
- Jerky gun or piping bag fitted with a large round tip
- Large rimmed baking sheets, lined with parchment paper

1 lb	lean ground beef, venison, lamb or pork	500 g
½ cup	chopped onion	125 mL
6	cloves garlic	6
1 cup	chopped fresh parsley	250 mL
1 tbsp	chopped fresh oregano	15 mL
1 tbsp	chopped fresh sage	15 mL
1½ tsp	salt	7 mL
½ tsp	freshly ground black pepper	2 mL

1. In a food processor, combine beef, onion, garlic, parsley, oregano, sage, salt and pepper. Process until onion, garlic and herbs are finely chopped and mixture has a paste-like consistency.

2. Fill jerky gun according to manufacturer's directions, or using a piping bag, pipe strips of beef mixture onto prepared baking sheets, leaving at least ½ inch (1 cm) between strips. Flatten, if necessary, to ¼-inch (0.5 cm) thickness (see tip, at left).

3. Bake in preheated oven for about 20 minutes or until beef is well done. Transfer strips to a plate lined with paper towels and blot dry.

4. Place cooked strips on mesh drying trays. Dry at 155°F (68°C) for 5 to 6 hours, occasionally blotting any fat that rises to the surface with paper towels, until jerky is firm and flexes and cracks, but doesn't break, when gently bent. Transfer to a clean baking sheet lined with paper towels and let cool completely, turning once to blot thoroughly.

Peppercorn Ground Meat Jerky

Makes about 6 oz (175 g)

This jerky is definitely for fans of the bold peppercorn! Use high-quality peppercorns and coarsely grind just before using for the best flavor.

Tips

If you don't have a jerky gun or piping bag, use a rubber spatula and a small spoon to spoon meat mixture into strips on prepared baking sheets.

To flatten strips that are piped or spooned onto baking sheets, place another sheet of parchment paper on top and press as evenly as possible. Ensure that the strips don't touch each other.

It is best to err on the side of caution and cook the beef a little longer, if necessary, to make sure it is well done.

- Preheat oven to 400°F (200°C)
- Jerky gun or piping bag fitted with a large round tip
- Large rimmed baking sheets, lined with parchment paper

1 lb	lean ground beef, venison, lamb or pork	500 g
½ cup	chopped onion	125 mL
6	cloves garlic	6
1½ tsp	salt	7 mL
2 tsp	coarsely ground black pepper (approx.), divided	10 mL

1. In a food processor, combine beef, onion, garlic, salt and 1 tsp (5 mL) of the pepper. Process until onion and garlic are finely chopped and mixture has a paste-like consistency.

2. Fill jerky gun according to manufacturer's directions, or using a piping bag, pipe strips of beef mixture onto prepared baking sheets, leaving at least ½ inch (1 cm) between strips. Flatten, if necessary, to ¼-inch (0.5 cm) thickness (see tip, at left). Sprinkle remaining pepper liberally over meat strips.

3. Bake in preheated oven for about 20 minutes or until beef is well done. Transfer strips to a plate lined with paper towels and blot dry.

4. Place cooked strips on mesh drying trays. Dry at 155°F (68°C) for 5 to 6 hours, occasionally blotting any fat that rises to the surface with paper towels, until jerky is firm and flexes and cracks, but doesn't break, when gently bent. Transfer to a clean baking sheet lined with paper towels and let cool completely, turning once to blot thoroughly.

Maple and Whisky Ground Meat Jerky

Makes about 6 oz (175 g)

Maple and whisky add a rustic Canadian touch to jerky. You might just be able to imagine yourself trekking through the back woods when you taste this one. And if you eat it while actually trekking in the woods, it'll be all the more terrific.

Tips

If you don't have a jerky gun or piping bag, use a rubber spatula and a small spoon to spoon meat mixture into strips on prepared baking sheets.

To flatten strips that are piped or spooned onto baking sheets, place another sheet of parchment paper on top and press as evenly as possible. Ensure that the strips don't touch each other.

It is best to err on the side of caution and cook the beef a little longer, if necessary, to make sure it is well done.

- Preheat oven to 400°F (200°C)
- Jerky gun or piping bag fitted with a large round tip
- Large rimmed baking sheets, lined with parchment paper

1 lb	lean ground beef, venison, lamb or pork	500 g
½ cup	chopped onion	125 mL
1½ tsp	salt	7 mL
1 tsp	coarsely ground black pepper	5 mL
2 tbsp	pure maple syrup	25 mL
2 tbsp	Canadian whisky (rye) or bourbon	25 mL

1. In a food processor, combine beef, onion, salt, pepper, maple syrup and whisky. Process until onion is finely chopped and mixture has a paste-like consistency.

2. Fill jerky gun according to manufacturer's directions, or using a piping bag, pipe strips of beef mixture onto prepared baking sheets, leaving at least ½ inch (1 cm) between strips. Flatten, if necessary, to ¼-inch (0.5 cm) thickness (see tip, at left).

3. Bake in preheated oven for about 20 minutes or until beef is well done. Transfer strips to a plate lined with paper towels and blot dry.

4. Place cooked strips on mesh drying trays. Dry at 155°F (68°C) for 5 to 6 hours, occasionally blotting any fat that rises to the surface with paper towels, until jerky is firm and flexes and cracks, but doesn't break, when gently bent. Transfer to a clean baking sheet lined with paper towels and let cool completely, turning once to blot thoroughly.

Asian Ground Meat Jerky

Makes about 6 oz (175 g)

Sweet, sour, salty and a touch of heat — your taste buds are sure to be satisfied when you're snacking on this jerky. It also provides a great boost of flavor when used in recipes.

Tips

If you don't have a jerky gun or piping bag, use a rubber spatula and a small spoon to spoon meat mixture into strips on prepared baking sheets.

To flatten strips that are piped or spooned onto baking sheets, place another sheet of parchment paper on top and press as evenly as possible. Ensure that the strips don't touch each other.

It is best to err on the side of caution and cook the beef a little longer, if necessary, to make sure it is well done.

- Preheat oven to 400°F (200°C)
- Jerky gun or piping bag fitted with a large round tip
- Large rimmed baking sheets, lined with parchment paper

1 lb	lean ground beef, venison, lamb or pork	500 g
½ cup	chopped onion	125 mL
6	cloves garlic	6
1 tbsp	packed brown sugar	15 mL
1 tsp	ground ginger	5 mL
1 tsp	coarsely ground black pepper	5 mL
½ tsp	salt	2 mL
2 tbsp	soy sauce	25 mL
1 tbsp	rice vinegar or freshly squeezed lime juice	15 mL

1. In a food processor, combine beef, onion, garlic, brown sugar, ginger, pepper, salt, soy sauce and vinegar. Process until onion and garlic are finely chopped and mixture has a paste-like consistency.

2. Fill jerky gun according to manufacturer's directions, or using a piping bag, pipe strips of beef mixture onto prepared baking sheets, leaving at least ½ inch (1 cm) between strips. Flatten, if necessary, to ¼-inch (0.5 cm) thickness (see tip, at left).

3. Bake in preheated oven for about 20 minutes or until beef is well done. Transfer strips to a plate lined with paper towels and blot dry.

4. Place cooked strips on mesh drying trays. Dry at 155°F (68°C) for 5 to 6 hours, occasionally blotting any fat that rises to the surface with paper towels, until jerky is firm and flexes and cracks, but doesn't break, when gently bent. Transfer to a clean baking sheet lined with paper towels and let cool completely, turning once to blot thoroughly.

Southwestern Ground Meat Jerky

Makes about 6 oz (175 g)

With a touch of chili, cumin and lime, this jerky is a flavorful snack and a super starter for chili, soups and other Southwestern favorites.

Tips

If you don't have a jerky gun or piping bag, use a rubber spatula and a small spoon to spoon meat mixture into strips on prepared baking sheets.

To flatten strips that are piped or spooned onto baking sheets, place another sheet of parchment paper on top and press as evenly as possible. Ensure that the strips don't touch each other.

It is best to err on the side of caution and cook the beef a little longer, if necessary, to make sure it is well done.

- Preheat oven to 400°F (200°C)
- Jerky gun or piping bag fitted with a large round tip
- Large rimmed baking sheets, lined with parchment paper

1 lb	lean ground beef, venison, lamb or pork	500 g
½ cup	chopped onion	125 mL
6	cloves garlic	6
2 tsp	chili powder	10 mL
1½ tsp	salt	7 mL
1 tsp	coarsely ground black pepper	5 mL
1 tsp	ground cumin	5 mL
1 tbsp	freshly squeezed lime juice	15 mL

1. In a food processor, combine beef, onion, garlic, chili powder, salt, pepper, cumin and lime juice. Process until onion and garlic are finely chopped and mixture has a paste-like consistency.

2. Fill jerky gun according to manufacturer's directions, or using a piping bag, pipe strips of beef mixture onto prepared baking sheets, leaving at least ½ inch (1 cm) between strips. Flatten, if necessary, to ¼-inch (0.5 cm) thickness (see tip, at left).

3. Bake in preheated oven for about 20 minutes or until beef is well done. Transfer strips to a plate lined with paper towels and blot dry.

4. Place cooked strips on mesh drying trays. Dry at 155°F (68°C) for 4 to 6 hours, occasionally blotting any fat that rises to the surface with paper towels, until jerky is firm and flexes and cracks, but doesn't break, when gently bent. Transfer to a clean baking sheet lined with paper towels and let cool completely, turning once to blot thoroughly.

Ground Beef

Makes about 4 oz (125 g)

1 lb	extra-lean ground beef	500 g
	Salt and freshly ground black pepper	

Tips

Small pieces may fall through even a fine-mesh drying tray, so place a leather sheet on an empty rack below to catch any pieces that fall through.

1. In a large skillet, over medium heat, cook beef, breaking up with a spoon, for about 8 minutes or until no longer pink and liquid has evaporated. Transfer to a baking sheet lined with paper towels and top with more paper towels to blot any excess moisture. Season to taste with salt and pepper.

2. Place cooked meat on fine-mesh drying trays (e.g., Clean-A-Screen). Dry at 155°F (68°C) for 6 to 8 hours, rearranging occasionally as necessary to break up any clumps, until meat is very firm and dry throughout. Let cool completely.

Dried Shrimp

Makes about 3 oz (90 g)

1 lb	medium or large shrimp	500 g

1. Peel and devein shrimp. Cut in half lengthwise.

2. In a large pot of boiling salted water, cook shrimp for 2 to 3 minutes or just until firm and opaque. Using a strainer, remove from boiling water and immediately plunge into ice water; let stand until cold. Drain well and pat dry with paper towels.

3. Place on mesh drying trays. Dry at 155°F (68°C) for 4 to 5 hours or until very firm and just slightly pliable. Let cool completely.

Tips

Jumbo or extra-large shrimp tend to get tough when cooked and dried; medium or large shrimp are better suited to drying.

A non-acidic marinade can be used before drying. Avoid any marinades with citrus juice or vinegar, as these will toughen shrimp. Coat cooked shrimp with marinade, cover and refrigerate for 30 to 60 minutes. Drain well.

Part 2
Cooking on the Trail with Dehydrated Foods

Everything You Need to Know About Camp Food

About the Recipes

These recipes take advantage of convenient dried ingredients to make tasty, nutritious and quick foods with a minimum of work. Many of them require only the addition of water to be ready to serve, so they're perfect for the campsite, cottage, cabin or roadside meal.

We've taken fuel efficiency into consideration, and in many of the recipes you'll start by soaking the ingredients in cold water to get the rehydration started, then heat and cook for a minimum amount of time. If time is of the essence, you can usually heat the food right away and cook it a little longer, rather than cold-soaking. We've noted recipes where this won't work well. There are even recipes that don't require any heat at all to prepare, and those with the option for no-heat preparation. These are perfect for those times when you don't have any fuel, it's just not practical to fire up your stove or you can't make a fire.

For many recipes, we have provided amounts for one serving, and you can multiply as necessary to make the number of servings you need. Multiple amounts of dry ingredients can be mixed together in the same bags or containers; just keep in mind that you'll need a pan large enough to cook the larger amount of food.

We do use a few commercially prepared dried ingredients. Instant skim milk powder and powdered eggs are readily available, convenient and of far better quality than anything you can make at home. In combination with your own dried foods, these convenience foods make packing supplies and preparing recipes a breeze.

The most important thing is to plan ahead. Make sure you have enough food for the entire trip, enough water for rehydration and all of the equipment you'll need to prepare the food. Read the recipes before you leave home and bring the serving and cooking instructions with you. Then savor your made-from-scratch camp meals!

Equipment

In general, these recipes were designed to use small camping-style saucepans and skillets, to keep your equipment needs at a minimum.

Essential

- **Small saucepan with lid:** A 2-cup (500 mL) pan will work for the single portions of these recipes. If you don't have a lid, pack some foil to cover the pan when necessary. It can usually be wiped off and reused multiple times.

- **Small skillet with lid:** You'll need one that's about 6 inches (15 cm) in diameter to prepare single servings or a larger one if you're cooking for more. A cast-iron skillet is particularly helpful if you plan to cook over a wood fire, because it holds the heat well, but you certainly won't want one if you're toting your supplies in a backpack. A skillet can always sub in for a saucepan, but some things (like pancakes) won't work in a saucepan; if you can bring only one vessel, choose the skillet.

- **Wooden or other heatproof spoon or spatula**

- **Paring knife and/or small serrated knife**

- **Measuring cup for water:** Bring a plastic liquid measuring cup or mark measures on a water bottle with permanent marker before you leave home.

- **Camp stove:** Though a wood fire will work for most cooking, it helps to pack a small portable burner to make sure you can still heat your food if you can't make a fire. There's always the risk of bad weather, wet wood or restrictions on burning.

Optional (But Very Helpful)

- **Metal or foil baking pan:** Make sure it is fire-safe and uncoated (not a nonstick surface) and bring foil to wrap it in after it's been over a fire to protect your other gear from the soot (it's tricky to wash it all off).

- **Cast-iron griddle that goes over a campfire or camp stove:** This works well for cooking larger portions of pancakes, biscuits and pan breads.

- **Bowls or containers with tight-fitting lids:** These are handy when ingredients need to be soaked in water before cooking. By using a bowl, you won't tie up your saucepan, which you may need for other things.

- **Pancake flipper**

Things to Consider When Meal Planning

Will there be potable running water available?

No: Choose recipes that require the least amount of water to prepare. Pack enough water for each recipe you plan to cook, plus what you'll need to drink and extra in case of spillage.

Yes: You can bring foods that require larger quantities of water. Pack a jug or bottle to tote the water from the source to your site.

Do you plan to cook solely over a wood campfire?

Yes: Choose recipes that require as little cooking time as possible, and some that don't require any cooking at all, just in case a fire isn't possible or takes too long to get hot.

Is there a cooler or refrigeration available?

Yes: You can bring some fresh ingredients to combine with the dried foods.

No: Make sure all of the ingredients you pack are non-perishable at room temperature for the length of time you'll be toting them.

Do you have to tote everything in your backpack?

Yes: Choose recipes that indicate "just add water"; that provide the most amount of energy with the least bulk (e.g., grains versus potatoes and pasta); and that can be made in the same saucepan or skillet for the entire trip.

Will you be hiking, climbing or paddling all day?

Yes: Choose high-energy foods, particularly for breakfast and lunch, and pack snacks that don't require cooking to eat between mealtimes.

Packaging, Storing and Transporting

- For ease and space efficiency, sealable bags are good for short-term ingredient storage; however, bags can allow minute amounts of air and moisture transfer, so they're not recommended for longer storage. If you make a larger batch of mixed dried ingredients and want to store it for longer than 1 month, store it in a glass jar or airtight plastic container and transfer to the sealable bag or smaller container as you pack for your trip.

- You can place small sealable bags together in one larger sealable bag or an airtight container, but be sure not to pack foods with strong flavors and aromas in the same container with milder-flavored foods (e.g., keep onions in a separate container from your pancake mix).

- On a small piece of paper, jot the ingredients, the amount of water you'll need to prepare the recipe and the basic gist of the cooking instructions. Staple it to the bag (above the seal) so it's right where you need it when it's time to cook.

- Pack a separate sealable bag with seasonings and condiments such as salt and pepper, a small plastic bottle of vegetable oil (if necessary) and packets of ketchup, soy sauce, mustard, jam, honey and sugar, just in case. A few condiments can go a long way in perking up flavors.

- Plan the meals for your trip and pack food in reverse order of when you'll need it. Keep the equipment and condiments on top, since you'll need them each time.

Cooking in the Bag

Many recipes can be prepared, or at least soaked, directly in the sealable plastic bag rather than using a pot or bowl. However, a few safety issues do need to be considered. Good-quality, thicker-grade bags are much more likely to stay intact when packed, toted and then used for soaking. Lower-quality bags are more likely to split at the seams, leak at the seal or get small holes, causing problems when water is added. Before pouring water, particularly hot water, into a bag for soaking, place the bag in a heatproof bowl or pot to stabilize it from tipping and protect yourself from getting wet or scalded. If there is a leak, the water will go into the bowl, not onto you!

Don't be tempted to reuse bags for food storage or preparation unless they have been thoroughly washed, sanitized and dried first. Once rehydrated, food spoils as though it was fresh, so food safety becomes an issue if bags are contaminated with bacteria that then have a moist environment to grown in.

Using the bag the food was packed in does reduce dish washing, so it's a handy trick, especially when water is scarce. Of course, if you prefer to keep your bags clean and dry to pack out, any instruction that says to soak ingredients in the bag can be done in a bowl or other container instead.

No-Heat "Cooking"

There are times when you just can't use your camp stove (you've run out of fuel — oh no!) or an open fire is prohibited or just won't start. You still need to eat. It's best to plan ahead for these situations by packing at least a few meals that don't require heat (as noted on the recipes) to prepare. We've flagged recipes that are "No Heat Required" and those with a "No-Heat Option," including instructions to modify the preparation where necessary, so you can easily identify the recipes that work particularly well with cold water.

When you're planning to rehydrate foods without heat or hot water, for the best flavor and texture use dried ingredients that are cooked or blanched before they are dried. Some dried raw foods, such as onions and celery, tend to be tough when rehydrated with cold water. Foods such as cooked pasta, cooked rice, cooked beans, softer vegetables, fruits and leathers (all varieties) rehydrate particularly well without heat.

Tips for Group Meals

If you're camping with a large group, there are different ways to approach the task of preparing and packing meals for the trip. A group effort is likely easier than everyone packing their own food individually.

One approach is to delegate each meal to a different person or family. They can gather and pack all the dried items necessary for each dish they're responsible for preparing. Do the math in advance: if a recipe feeds four, and you have 12 people, you'll need to triple every ingredient in the recipe. It's much easier for one person to prepare a large recipe than it is for three people to prepare the recipe individually.

Another approach is to assign different people to dry larger amounts of specific items, rather than having everyone dry a little bit of each. Decide on the menu and plan well ahead, at the beginning of the harvest season. Then divide up the items for each person or family to dry. For instance, one person or family can do all of the carrots, onions and potatoes, another can do the meats and other vegetables, and someone else can do the fruits and grains. Keep seasonality in mind and make sure that one person (or part of the group) won't be overwhelmed by the need to dry everything on their list all at once. Once you've dried enough ingredients, gather everyone together and package the recipes for the trip. Working together turns a rather mundane activity into an event. (This can work even if you're not taking a trip: it can be fun to gather a group together to pack up meals to make at home.)

Menu Plans

By taking the time to prepare and plan for your camping trip, you can make sure that all of your meals are easy to find, easy to prepare, satisfying and delicious. Some trips require a very tight timeline to reach your destinations before dark or to rendezvous at a specific time and place. A well-planned menu can remove some of the time-management challenges that a day in the wilderness or on the road can present.

Don't forget, just because you're cooking in the bush or on the road, food doesn't need to be inferior to what you'd eat at home. Bring small containers of sea salt, a pepper grinder and some hot pepper flakes for seasoning. Find compromises as far as weight goes. If you're backpacking, pick one or two things you can live without, such as an alarm clock or an extra book, and trade them in for some good Parmesan cheese (it's hard, dry and travels fairly well in cool weather) or a small plastic bottle of olive oil. Bring maple sugar granules to sprinkle on your porridge, or dried bananas, raisins and coconut flakes for garnishes on curry night. If you're traveling by canoe or kayak rather than on foot, it will be easier to carry a greater variety of food, but do keep in mind any possible portages!

When packing for your trip, put the ingredients for each recipe into labeled sealable plastic bags, then put the recipe bags for each meal into larger sealable bags labeled Breakfast 1, Lunch 1, etc. Organize the bags by days, packing the last day's food at the bottom of your pack and working your way up to the first day. Keep one bag with all of your condiments handy at the top.

For the following menus, we've assumed that you will eat your first prepared meal on the first evening, but it's very easy to adjust the order to accommodate your schedule. And of course, these recipes are just suggestions. Substitute recipes you prefer, but do keep in mind flavor and texture balance and the equipment you'll have at the campsite.

Light Camping

Here are two menu plans for a variety of easily prepared meals that provide high amounts of energy for hitting the trails, tackling the river or scaling the cliffs. For light camping, we've kept equipment, preparation and stove use to a minimum, taking into consideration that you're likely cooking on a single-burner stove or over a campfire.

If you're wilderness camping, take along a strong waterproof bag that can be used to hang your food from a tree or a pole to prevent animals from raiding your pantry.

2-Day Menu

Supper 1:	Smoked Sausage Risotto (page 167)
	Citrus-Marinated Chickpea Salad (page 173)
	Raspberry Chocolate Pudding (page 230)
Breakfast 1:	Brown Rice, Maple and Berry Porridge (page 108)
	Cottage Cheese Breakfast Biscuits (page 104)
Lunch 1:	Hearty Minestrone Soup (page 115)
	Sesame Teriyaki Veggie Trail Mix (page 195)
	Tropical Fruit Compote (page 234)
Supper 2:	Cajun Shrimp and Rice (page 162)
	Warm Broccoli, Leek and Raisin Salad (page 172)
	Cheese and Herb Skillet Biscuits (page 187)
	Campfire Apple Crumble (page 222)
Breakfast 2:	Granola Pancakes (page 99)
	Warm Peaches with Ginger (page 233)
Lunch 2:	Almost-Instant Mac and Cheese (page 152)
	No-Bake Blueberry Cheesecakes (page 227)

5-Day Menu

Supper 1: Chicken and Potato Stew (page 131)
Broccoli and Cottage Cheese Gratin (page 177)
Banana Peanut Butter S'mores (page 220)

Breakfast 1: Scrambled Huevos Rancheros (page 94)

Lunch 1: Peppered Beef and Noodles (page 137)
Sesame Teriyaki Veggie Trail Mix (page 195)

Supper 2: Vegetable Bean Chili (page 126)
Chili Cornmeal Cakes (page 188)
Pear Cherry Ginger Crumble (page 223)

Breakfast 2: Blueberry Pancakes (page 100)

Lunch 2: Moroccan Couscous with Chickpeas (page 168)
Double Pumpkin Biscotti Crisps (page 207)

Supper 3: Tex-Mex Beef Fajitas (page 141)
Spanish Brown Rice (page 185)
Banana Coconut Pudding (page 231)

Breakfast 3: Wake-Up! Omelets (page 95)
Campfire Hash Browns (page 98)

Lunch 3: Wheat Berries Parmesan (page 169)
Brown Rice, Apple and Cranberry Salad (page 174)
GORP with a Twist (page 194)

Supper 4: Teriyaki Tofu Stir-Fry (page 139)
Egg Noodles with Teriyaki Veggies (page 184)
Apple Spice Rice Pudding (page 229)

Breakfast 4: Brown Rice, Maple and Berry Porridge (page 108)

Lunch 4: One-Pot Simple Spaghetti (page 155)
Jerky 'n' Veg Trail Mix (page 196)
Tropical Fruit Compote (page 234)

Supper 5: Lemon Honey Garlic Chicken (page 150)
Stovetop Scalloped Potatoes (page 180)
Moroccan Braised Beans and Lentils (page 182)
Campfire Apple Crumble (page 222)

Breakfast 5: Jerked Beef Hash with Potatoes and Peppers (page 97)

Lunch 5: Tofu, Vegetable and Fruit Curry (page 134)
Warm Peaches with Ginger (page 233)

Heavy Camping

When you're traveling by car, canoe, horse, motorcycle, RV or boat, or setting up camp once and staying put, you have a little more flexibility in your menu planning than if you're carrying all of your food and equipment on your back. It's easier to bring along an extra pot for cooking more than one dish at a time or a cooler to include fresh ingredients like meat, chicken, milk and eggs to mix in with your dried items. A good option is to do some baking ahead and freeze items like your favorite loaf, which you can use as an ice block until it has thawed and then enjoy on the second or third day of your trip.

It's also likely that you can bring along a more sophisticated camp stove with multiple burners. If you're using an RV or a boat, you may have a barbecue that you can use as an oven, if desired.

These menus include dried and fresh items in combination. Plan on consuming fresh or premade items early in your trip and save the recipes that use only dried foods for later on.

2-Day Menu

Supper 1:	Curried Chicken with Apples (page 135) *or* barbecued chicken
	Moroccan Braised Beans and Lentils (page 182)
	Pumpkin Pie Pudding (page 228)
Breakfast 1:	Strawberry Pan Bread (page 106)
	Peanut Banana Chews (page 212)
Lunch 1:	Beef and Barley Soup (page 121)
	Cheese and Herb Skillet Biscuits (page 187)
	Tropical Fruit Compote (page 234)
Supper 2:	Catch of the Day Foil-Packet Fish (page 145)
	Easy Mushroom Risotto (page 165)
	Warm Broccoli, Leek and Raisin Salad (page 172)
	Campfire Apple Crumble (page 222)
Breakfast 2:	Sweet Cornmeal Pancakes (page 101) with Berry Sauce (page 238)
Lunch 2:	Beef Stroganoff (page 136)
	Oatmeal Raisin Pan Cookies (page 221)

7-Day Menu

Supper 1:	Chicken à la King (page 148)
	Broccoli and Cottage Cheese Gratin (page 177)
	Foil-Baked Apples (page 235)
Breakfast 1:	Banana Nut Oatmeal (page 107)
Lunch 1:	Veggie Pasta (page 156)
	Skillet Carrot Pineapple Cakes (page 226)
Supper 2:	Tex-Mex Beef Fajitas (optional: use fresh steaks) (page 141)
	Cajun Rice and Black Beans (page 161)
	Fudgy Skillet Brownies (page 225)
Breakfast 2:	Cornbread Johnny Cakes (page 103)
	Tropical Fruit Compote (page 234)
Lunch 2:	Teriyaki Tofu Stir-Fry (page 139)
	Banana Peanut Butter S'mores (page 220)
Supper 3:	Venison Chili (page 129)
	Potatoes "Anna" and Onion Gratin (page 181)
	Chocolate Toffee Bread Pudding (page 232)
Breakfast 3:	Wake-Up! Omelets (page 95)
	Campfire Hash Browns (page 98)
Lunch 3:	Chicken Noodle Soup (page 120)
	GORP with a Twist (page 194)
Supper 4:	Shrimp and Herb Pasta (page 157)
	Warm Broccoli, Leek and Raisin Salad (page 172)
	Apple Spice Rice Pudding (page 229)
Breakfast 4:	Jerked Beef Hash with Potatoes and Peppers (page 97)
Lunch 4:	No-Luck Corn Chowder and Dumplings (page 124)
	Jerky 'n' Veg Trail Mix (page 196)
	No-Bake Blueberry Cheesecakes (page 227)
Supper 5:	Smoked Sausage Risotto (page 167)
	Citrus-Marinated Chickpea Salad (page 173)
	Raspberry Chocolate Pudding (page 230)
Breakfast 5:	Scrambled Huevos Rancheros (page 94)
	Oat and Grain Hard Tack (page 210)
Lunch 5:	Almost-Instant Mac and Cheese (page 152)
	Warm Peaches with Ginger (page 233)

Supper 6:	Tofu, Lentil and Peanut Stovetop "Meatloaf" (page 142)
	Jerky and Vegetable Pasta Salad (page 159)
	Campfire Apple Crumble (page 222)
Breakfast 6:	Blueberry Pancakes (page 100)
	Tropical Fruit Compote (page 234)
Lunch 6:	Hearty Minestrone Soup (page 115)
	Cottage Cheese Breakfast Biscuits (page 104)
Supper 7:	Orange and Sweet Pepper Chicken (page 149)
	Moroccan Braised Beans and Lentils (page 182)
	Mixed Fruit Cobbler (page 224)
Breakfast 7:	Cinnamon Apple Multigrain Porridge (page 109)
Lunch 7:	Chipotle Beef Chili (page 128)
	Cornbread Johnny Cakes (page 103)

Breakfast

Scrambled Huevos Rancheros

You won't believe that a few simple ingredients mixed with a little water can taste so good until you try it. Add more vegetables if you've got them on hand.

Tip

If desired, toast tortilla wedges in a dry skillet over medium heat or over a campfire before cooking the eggs.

Variation

In place of fresh eggs, use 2 tbsp (25 mL) powdered eggs and add them to the bag with the leather when you prep at home. Add 3 tbsp (45 mL) extra water when softening the leather mixture.

Prep at Home

1	2-inch (5 cm) square Salsa Leather	1
1 tbsp	dried cooked black beans	15 mL
1	small flour tortilla, cut into wedges	1

To Serve

2 tbsp	water	25 mL
2	eggs (see variation, at left)	2
	Vegetable oil	

Prep at Home

1. Tear leather into very small pieces. In a sealable plastic bag, combine leather and beans. Seal and store at room temperature for up to 1 month. Place tortilla wedges in another bag; seal and store at room temperature for up to 5 days.

To Serve

1. In a bowl, pour water over the leather mixture. Let soak for about 15 minutes or until leather starts to soften. Using a fork, whisk in eggs until blended.

2. In a skillet, heat a thin layer of oil over medium-low heat. Add egg mixture and cook, stirring, for about 2 minutes or until eggs are just set. Serve eggs with tortilla wedges.

Wake Up! Omelets

Makes 1 serving

This breakfast will give your day a terrific kick-start. Add some toast and a piece of fruit on the side, and you'll be raring to go.

Tip

Use scissors to snip tomatoes, chile peppers and onions into very small pieces.

Prep at Home

2 tbsp	powdered eggs	25 mL
1 tsp	finely chopped dried tomatoes	5 mL
1 tsp	finely chopped dried hot chile peppers	5 mL
1 tsp	finely chopped dried onions	5 mL
1 tsp	crumbled dried parsley	5 mL
Pinch	chili powder	Pinch
Pinch	ground cumin	Pinch
Pinch	salt	Pinch

To Serve

1/3 cup	water	75 mL
	Vegetable oil	

Prep at Home

1. In a sealable plastic bag, combine eggs, tomatoes, chile peppers, onions, parsley, chili powder, cumin and salt. Seal and store at room temperature for up to 1 month.

To Serve

1. In a bowl, combine egg mixture and water. Let stand for 15 minutes or until vegetables are softened. Using a fork, whisk until frothy.

2. In a skillet, heat a thin layer of oil over medium-low heat. Add egg mixture and swirl to coat pan evenly. Cook, without stirring, for about 3 minutes or until eggs are just set.

Fresh Addition

Omit the powdered eggs when prepping at home and decrease the water to 3 tbsp (45 mL). Whisk in 2 to 3 fresh eggs after rehydrating the vegetable mixture.

Beef Jerky, Scrambled Egg and Mushroom Wrap

Need a power-packed breakfast? This is sure to satisfy even the hungriest camper.

Tips

If desired, warm the tortillas in the skillet before adding the oil and eggs, or wrap in foil and warm over the campfire.

Add a spoonful of Anytime Salsa (page 199) with the egg mixture when wrapping it in the tortillas.

Prep at Home

½ oz	beef jerky (any flavor), torn into small pieces	15 g
3 tbsp	powdered eggs	45 mL
1 tbsp	dried mushroom slices, crumbled	15 mL
1 tsp	snipped dried chives	5 mL
⅛ tsp	dried thyme	0.5 mL
Pinch	salt	Pinch

To Serve

6 tbsp	water	90 mL
	Vegetable oil	
2	small flour tortillas	2

Prep at Home

1. In a sealable plastic bag, combine jerky, eggs, mushrooms, chives, thyme and salt. Seal and store at room temperature for up to 1 month.

To Serve

1. In a bowl, combine jerky mixture and water. Cover and let stand for 20 minutes or until jerky and mushrooms start to soften. Using a fork, whisk until frothy.

2. In a skillet, heat a thin layer of oil over medium-low heat. Add egg mixture and cook, stirring, for about 2 minutes or until eggs are just set.

3. Spoon half the egg mixture in the center of each tortilla. Fold up bottom and fold in both sides to enclose filling.

> **Fresh Addition**
> Omit the powdered eggs when prepping at home and decrease the water to 3 tbsp (45 mL). Whisk in 3 fresh eggs after rehydrating the jerky mixture.

Jerked Beef Hash with Potatoes and Peppers

Makes 1 serving

Just Add Water

Hearty jerky and potatoes give a terrific start to a busy day of trekking or paddling.

Tip

This can also be cooked over a campfire. Use a foil pan or a flameproof skillet covered with foil or a lid. Place covered pan on a rack over the hot fire and cook for about 20 minutes or until potatoes are tender. Uncover and cook, stirring occasionally, for 5 to 10 minutes or until liquid is evaporated and potatoes start to brown.

Prep at Home

1/2 oz	Jerk Beef Jerky, torn into small pieces	15 g
1/2 cup	dried potato cubes	125 mL
1 tbsp	dried onion pieces	15 mL
1 tbsp	dried green bell pepper pieces	15 mL
1 tbsp	dried red bell pepper pieces	15 mL
1/2 tsp	crumbled dried cilantro or oregano	2 mL
1/8 tsp	salt	0.5 mL

To Serve

1 1/4 cups	water	300 mL

Prep at Home

1. In a sealable plastic bag, combine jerky, potatoes, onions, green and red peppers, cilantro and salt. Seal and store at room temperature for up to 1 month.

To Serve

1. In a skillet, combine jerky mixture and water. Cover and let stand for 30 minutes or until potatoes start to soften.

2. Bring to a boil over medium heat. Reduce heat to low, cover and simmer for about 15 minutes or until potatoes are soft. Uncover and simmer, increasing heat as necessary, for about 5 minutes or until liquid is evaporated and potatoes start to brown.

Campfire Hash Browns

Makes 1 serving

Just Add Water

Serve these with a side of bacon or grilled sausages for a classic campfire breakfast.

Tip

Turn this into a side dish for supper by adding ½ tsp (2 mL) Cajun seasoning or ¼ tsp (1 mL) minced dried lemon zest and replace the paprika with crumbled dried dill.

• Foil pan or flameproof skillet, with foil or lid to cover

Prep at Home

½ cup	dried potato cubes	125 mL
1 tbsp	dried onion pieces	15 mL
1 tsp	crumbled dried parsley	5 mL
½ tsp	snipped dried chives	2 mL
¼ tsp	salt	1 mL
¼ tsp	pepper	1 mL
Pinch	paprika	Pinch

To Serve

1 cup	water	250 mL

Prep at Home

1. In a sealable plastic bag, combine potatoes, onions, parsley, chives, salt, pepper and paprika. Seal and store at room temperature for up to 1 month.

To Serve

1. In foil pan, combine potato mixture and water. Cover and let stand for 30 minutes or until potatoes start to soften. Meanwhile, prepare campfire.

2. Place covered pan on a rack over the hot fire and cook for about 20 minutes or until potatoes are tender. Uncover and cook, stirring occasionally, for 5 to 10 minutes or until liquid is evaporated and potatoes start to brown.

Granola Pancakes

→

**Makes about
4 pancakes**

Hearty pancakes are a
terrific start to the day.
You can customize the
flavor by adding different
fruit and spices.

Tip

To toast a small amount of
nuts, in a small dry skillet
over medium heat, toast
chopped nuts, stirring
constantly, for about
2 minutes or until fragrant.
Transfer to a bowl and let
cool.

Variation

If powdered eggs aren't
available, substitute
powdered egg replacer,
using the package
instructions to substitute
for 1 egg. Alternatively,
omit the powdered eggs
when prepping at home
and decrease the water to
6 tbsp (90 mL). Whisk in
1 fresh egg with the oil.

Prep at Home

2 tbsp	dried cooked grains (barley, wheat berries, whole oats, wild rice)	25 mL
2 tbsp	dried cranberries or raisins	25 mL
1/2 cup	all-purpose flour	125 mL
1 tbsp	powdered eggs	15 mL
1 tbsp	packed brown sugar	15 mL
1 tbsp	toasted finely chopped almonds or pecans	15 mL
1/2 tsp	baking powder	2 mL
1/4 tsp	ground cinnamon or nutmeg	1 mL
Pinch	salt	Pinch

To Serve

1/2 cup	water	125 mL
	Vegetable oil	

Prep at Home

1. In a mini chopper or small food processor, process grains until finely chopped and about one-quarter is powdery. Transfer to a sealable plastic bag and add cranberries. In another bag, combine flour, eggs, brown sugar, almonds, baking powder, cinnamon and salt. Seal both bags and store at room temperature for up to 1 month.

To Serve

1. In a bowl, combine grain mixture and water. Cover and let stand for 30 minutes or until grains start to soften. Stir in 1 tsp (5 mL) oil. Shake flour mixture in bag to mix and pour into grain mixture. Stir just until evenly moistened.

2. Heat a skillet over medium heat until warmed. Add a thin layer of oil. Pour in about 1/4 cup (50 mL) batter per pancake. Cook for 2 to 3 minutes or until bubbles break on the surface but don't fill in and bottom is golden. Turn and cook for about 2 minutes or until golden brown. Repeat with remaining batter, adding oil to the pan and adjusting heat as necessary.

Blueberry Pancakes

There's nothing like classic pancakes studded with your own dried blueberries to make a good camping trip even better.

Variation

If powdered eggs aren't available, substitute powdered egg replacer, using the package instructions to substitute for 1 egg. Alternatively, omit the powdered eggs when prepping at home and decrease the water to 6 tbsp (90 mL). Whisk in 1 fresh egg with the oil.

Prep at Home

½ cup	all-purpose flour	125 mL
1 tbsp	powdered eggs	15 mL
1 tbsp	instant skim milk powder	15 mL
2 tsp	granulated sugar	10 mL
½ tsp	baking powder	2 mL
Pinch	salt	Pinch
2 tbsp	dried blueberries, chopped	25 mL

To Serve

½ cup	water	125 mL
	Vegetable oil	

Prep at Home

1. In a sealable plastic bag, combine flour, eggs, milk powder, sugar, baking powder and salt. Place blueberries in another bag. Seal both bags and store at room temperature for up to 1 month.

To Serve

1. In a bowl, combine blueberries and water. Let stand for 15 minutes or until blueberries are softened. Stir in 1 tsp (5 mL) oil. Shake flour mixture in bag to mix and pour into blueberry mixture. Stir just until evenly moistened.

2. Heat a skillet over medium heat until warmed. Add a thin layer of oil. Pour in about ¼ cup (50 mL) batter per pancake. Cook for 2 to 3 minutes or until bubbles break on the surface but don't fill in and bottom is golden. Turn and cook for about 2 minutes or until golden brown. Repeat with remaining batter, adding oil to the pan and adjusting heat as necessary.

Sweet Cornmeal Pancakes

Makes about 4 pancakes

With a slather of jam, a drizzle of syrup or simply on their own, these delightful pancakes are sure to start your day off right.

Variations

If powdered eggs aren't available, substitute powdered egg replacer, using the package instructions to substitute for 1 egg. Alternatively, omit the powdered eggs when prepping at home and decrease the water to 6 tbsp (90 mL). Whisk in 1 fresh egg with the oil.

Add 2 tbsp (25 mL) chopped dried fruit or berries with the corn.

Prep at Home

2 tbsp	dried corn kernels	25 mL
1/2 cup	all-purpose flour	125 mL
2 tbsp	cornmeal	25 mL
1 tbsp	granulated sugar	15 mL
1 tbsp	powdered eggs	15 mL
1 tbsp	instant skim milk powder	15 mL
1/2 tsp	baking powder	2 mL
Pinch	salt	Pinch

To Serve

1/2 cup	water	125 mL
	Vegetable oil	

Prep at Home

1. In a mini chopper or small food processor, process corn until finely chopped. Transfer to a sealable plastic bag. In another bag, combine flour, cornmeal, sugar, eggs, milk powder, baking powder and salt. Seal both bags and store at room temperature for up to 1 month.

To Serve

1. In a bowl, combine corn and water. Cover and let stand for 20 minutes or until corn is tender. Stir in 1 tsp (5 mL) oil. Shake flour mixture in bag to mix and pour into corn mixture. Stir just until evenly moistened.

2. Heat a skillet over medium heat until warmed. Add a thin layer of oil. Pour in about 1/4 cup (50 mL) batter per pancake. Cook for 2 to 3 minutes or until bubbles break on the surface but don't fill in and bottom is golden. Turn and cook for about 2 minutes or until golden brown. Repeat with remaining batter, adding oil to the pan and adjusting heat as necessary.

Fresh Addition

Fry an egg and sandwich it between two pancakes for a heartier breakfast. Drizzle the egg with a little ketchup, if desired.

Vanilla Cinnamon French Toast

Makes 1 serving

Vanilla sugar adds a boost of flavor to this incredibly easy breakfast. Sprinkle a little more on the hot toast for extra tastiness — you won't even need syrup.

Tip

Serve topped with Tropical Fruit Compote (page 234) or Berry Sauce (page 238).

Variation

In place of powdered eggs, substitute 1 fresh egg and omit the water. Whisk with vanilla sugar until frothy and proceed with step 3.

Prep at Home

2 tbsp	powdered eggs	25 mL
1½ tsp	vanilla sugar (see tip, page 234)	7 mL

To Serve

¼ cup	water	50 mL
2	slices bread	2
	Butter or vegetable oil	

Prep at Home

1. In a sealable plastic bag, combine eggs and vanilla sugar. Seal and store at room temperature for up to 1 month.

To Serve

1. In a shallow container, whisk egg mixture with water.

2. Heat a skillet over medium heat until hot.

3. Dip one slice of bread into egg mixture, flipping to coat both sides and letting egg mixture soak into bread slightly. Add butter to skillet and swirl to coat. Add soaked bread and cook, turning once, for about 3 minutes per side or until golden brown. Repeat with remaining slice of bread and egg mixture.

Cornbread Johnny Cakes

Makes
1 or 2 servings

This traditional simple cake was introduced to early settlers by Native North Americans. There are many theories about the origin of the name, but it is most commonly said to be a derivation of "journey cakes" or "Shawnee cakes." We've added fruit and spice to liven up the flavor.

Tip

Serve topped with Berry Sauce (page 238) or Tropical Fruit Compote (page 234), or simply with a drizzle of honey or maple syrup.

Variation

Substitute chopped dried apples or blueberries for the cherries.

● 6- to 8-inch (15 to 20 cm) nonstick or cast-iron skillet

Prep at Home

1 cup	cornmeal	250 mL
1 tbsp	packed brown sugar	15 mL
1 tsp	baking powder	5 mL
¼ tsp	salt	1 mL
¼ tsp	ground ginger	1 mL
¼ cup	dried corn kernels	50 mL
1 tbsp	dried sweet cherries, chopped	15 mL

To Serve

1 cup	water	250 mL
	Vegetable oil	

Prep at Home

1. In a sealable plastic bag, combine cornmeal, brown sugar, baking powder, salt and ginger. Place corn and cherries in another bag. Seal both bags and store at room temperature for up to 1 month.

To Serve

1. In a saucepan, bring water to a boil over high heat. Remove from heat and add corn mixture. Cover and let stand for about 10 minutes or until corn is softened. Shake cornmeal mixture in bag to mix and pour into corn mixture. Using a fork, stir just until evenly moistened. Let stand for 10 minutes.

2. Meanwhile, heat skillet over medium-low heat until warm. Add a thin layer of oil. Spread the batter in skillet. Reduce heat to low, cover and cook for about 5 minutes or until bottom is golden brown. Flip cake and cook, uncovered, for about 2 minutes or until browned. Cut into quarters and serve hot.

Cottage Cheese Breakfast Biscuits

Sweet biscuits studded with fruit are a nice change from cereal in the morning. Any extras can be packed along and eaten with a slice of cheese or a smear of nut butter for a snack.

Tip

These can be cooked over a campfire. Just heat the pan on a rack over the hottest part of the fire, then move it to the cooler edge to cook the biscuits. The timing will depend on the fire, so keep an eye on them.

- 6- to 8-inch (15 to 20 cm) skillet, preferably cast-iron, with lid or foil to cover

Prep at Home

³⁄₄ cup	all-purpose flour	175 mL
2 tbsp	powdered dried cottage cheese	25 mL
2 tbsp	granulated sugar	25 mL
1 tsp	baking powder	5 mL
¹⁄₂ tsp	ground cinnamon or ginger	2 mL
¹⁄₄ tsp	salt	1 mL
¹⁄₄ cup	chopped dried fruit (apples, pears, peaches, cherries, berries)	50 mL

To Serve

²⁄₃ cup	water	150 mL
	Vegetable oil or butter	

Prep at Home

1. In a sealable plastic bag, combine flour, cottage cheese, sugar, baking powder, cinnamon and salt. Seal and store at room temperature for up to 1 week or in the refrigerator for up to 6 months. Place fruit in another bag; seal and store at room temperature for up to 6 months.

To Serve

1. In a bowl, combine fruit and water. Cover and let stand for 15 minutes or until fruit is softened.

2. Meanwhile, heat skillet over medium heat until warmed.

3. Shake flour mixture in bag to mix and pour into fruit mixture. Using a fork, stir just until evenly moistened.

4. Add a thin layer of oil to skillet. Spoon dough into 4 mounds in skillet. Reduce heat to low, cover and cook for 3 minutes. Uncover and cook for about 1 minute or until bottoms are golden brown and edges are no longer shiny. Flip over and cook for about 2 minutes or until biscuits are puffed and firm. Serve hot.

Jerky, Cheese and Dried Tomato Biscuits

Makes 4 biscuits

Savory biscuits add new life to breakfast. They're satisfying on their own and also make a nice change from toast, served with scrambled eggs or an omelet.

Tip

Let extra biscuits cool and seal in a plastic bag for a snack later in the day. Wrap in foil and heat over a campfire to refresh them.

• 6- to 8-inch (15 to 20 cm) skillet, preferably cast-iron, with lid or foil to cover

Prep at Home

½ oz	beef or other meat jerky (any flavor), broken into very small pieces	15 g
1 tbsp	finely chopped dried tomatoes	15 mL
1 tsp	crumbled dried parsley	5 mL
1 tsp	crumbled dried basil or oregano	5 mL
¾ cup	whole wheat flour	175 mL
2 tbsp	powdered dried cottage cheese	25 mL
2 tsp	granulated sugar	10 mL
1 tsp	baking powder	5 mL
¼ tsp	salt	1 mL

To Serve

½ cup	water	125 mL
	Vegetable oil or butter	

Prep at Home

1. In a sealable plastic bag, combine jerky, tomatoes, parsley and basil. In a separate bag, combine flour, cottage cheese, sugar, baking powder and salt. Seal both bags and store at room temperature for up to 1 week or in the refrigerator for up to 6 months.

To Serve

1. In a saucepan, bring water to a boil over high heat. Remove from heat and add jerky mixture. Cover and let stand for about 30 minutes or until jerky is soft and water is cooled to room temperature.

2. Meanwhile, heat skillet over medium heat until warmed.

3. Shake flour mixture in bag to mix and pour into jerky mixture. Using a fork, stir just until evenly moistened.

4. Add a thin layer of oil to skillet. Spoon dough into 4 mounds in skillet. Reduce heat to low, cover and cook for 3 minutes. Uncover and cook for about 1 minute or until bottoms are golden brown and edges are no longer shiny. Flip over and cook for about 2 minutes or until biscuits are puffed and firm. Serve hot.

Strawberry Pan Bread

Heartier than a pancake but just as easy, this strawberry-studded bread makes a nice breakfast served with yogurt and fresh fruit.

Tip

This can be cooked over a campfire. Just heat the pan on a rack over the hottest part of the fire, then move it to the cooler edge to cook the bread. The timing will depend on the fire, so peek under the lid frequently (but don't lift it off).

- 6- to 8-inch (15 to 20 cm) skillet, preferably cast-iron, with lid or foil to cover

Prep at Home

¼ cup	all-purpose flour	50 mL
¼ cup	whole wheat flour	50 mL
1 tbsp	instant skim milk powder or buttermilk powder	15 mL
1 tbsp	packed brown sugar	15 mL
½ tsp	baking powder	2 mL
⅛ tsp	salt	0.5 mL
2 tbsp	chopped dried strawberries	25 mL
¼ tsp	finely chopped dried orange or lemon zest	1 mL

To Serve

⅓ cup	water or orange juice	75 mL
	Vegetable oil or butter	

Prep at Home

1. In a sealable plastic bag, combine all-purpose and whole wheat flours, milk powder, brown sugar, baking powder and salt. Seal and store at room temperature for up to 2 weeks or in the refrigerator for up to 6 months. Place strawberries and orange zest in another bag; seal and store at room temperature for up to 6 months.

To Serve

1. In a bowl, combine strawberry mixture and water. Cover and let stand for 10 minutes or until fruit is softened.

2. Meanwhile, heat skillet over medium heat until warmed.

3. Shake flour mixture in bag to mix and pour into berry mixture. Using a fork, stir just until evenly moistened.

4. Add a thin layer of oil to skillet. Spread dough in skillet. Reduce heat to low, cover and cook for about 8 minutes or until bottom is brown and top is no longer shiny. Uncover, flip over and cook for about 1 minute or until bottom is dry. Cut into quarters and serve hot.

Banana Nut Oatmeal

Makes 1 serving

Just Add Water

Whole oats are hearty and tasty and have a more toothsome texture than rolled oats. Try them with dried bananas and pecans and you'll never go back to the instant kind.

Tip

Place the oat mixture in a covered bowl and measure the water before you go to sleep. When you wake up, mix them together, then get the stove ready and wash up. The soaking time will be finished before you know it, and a hot breakfast will be just minutes away.

Variation

Substitute quick-cooking rolled oats for the dried cooked whole oats. Reduce the soaking time to 15 minutes and reduce the cooking time to 2 to 3 minutes.

Prep at Home

1/3 cup	dried cooked whole oats	75 mL
1 tbsp	dried banana slices	15 mL
1 tbsp	toasted chopped pecans (see tip, page 99)	15 mL
1 tbsp	instant skim milk powder	15 mL
1 tsp	packed brown sugar (or to taste)	5 mL
Pinch	ground nutmeg (optional)	Pinch
Pinch	salt	Pinch

To Serve

1 cup	water (approx.)	250 mL

Prep at Home

1. In a mini chopper or small food processor, process oats until finely chopped and about one-quarter is powdery. Transfer to a sealable plastic bag and add bananas, pecans, milk powder, brown sugar, nutmeg (if using) and salt. Seal and store at room temperature for up to 1 month.

To Serve

1. In a saucepan, combine oat mixture and water. Cover and let stand for 30 minutes or until oats start to soften.

2. Uncover and bring to a boil over medium heat, stirring often. Reduce heat and simmer, stirring often, for about 5 minutes or until oats are tender and porridge is thickened. Thin with more water, if desired.

Brown Rice, Maple and Berry Porridge

Makes 1 serving

Just Add Water

This hearty, nutritious hot cereal makes a nice change from regular oatmeal. Grinding the dried cooked rice slightly gives the cereal a creamy texture — perfect for a chilly morning.

Tip

You can find maple sugar granules at farmers' markets and specialty food stores. If you can't find them, use 1 tsp (5 mL) packed brown sugar or granulated sugar, or omit them for an unsweetened version.

Variation

Replace the berries with your favorite dried fruit. Try chopped figs, apples, pears, peaches or raisins.

Prep at Home

½ cup	dried cooked long-grain brown rice	125 mL
2 tbsp	dried berries, chopped if large	25 mL
2 tbsp	instant skim milk powder (optional)	25 mL
2 tsp	maple sugar granules	10 mL
Pinch	salt	Pinch

To Serve

1 cup	water	250 mL

Prep at Home

1. In a mini chopper or small food processor, process rice until finely chopped and about one-quarter is powdery. Transfer to a sealable plastic bag and add berries, milk powder (if using), maple sugar and salt. Seal and store at room temperature for up to 1 month.

To Serve

1. In a saucepan, combine rice mixture and water. Cover and let stand for 20 minutes or until rice starts to soften.

2. Uncover and bring to a boil over medium heat, stirring often. Reduce heat and simmer, stirring often, for about 5 minutes or until rice is tender and porridge is thickened.

Cinnamon Apple Multigrain Porridge

Makes 1 serving

Just Add Water

Hot cooked multigrain porridge usually takes 30 minutes or more to cook — not practical for a camp stove! Now you can get all the benefits of whole grains in a fraction of the cooking time with dried cooked whole grains.

Variations

Use 6 tbsp (90 mL) of any combination of dried cooked whole grains.

In place of the whole oats, substitute dried cooked steel-cut or large-flake rolled oats. Break the sheet into small pieces and grind until very finely chopped, with some powder. Measure, then add the other grains and grind again.

Add 1 tbsp (15 mL) dried cranberries or blueberries and 1 tbsp (15 mL) toasted chopped almonds with the apples.

Prep at Home

2 tbsp	dried cooked whole oats	25 mL
2 tbsp	dried cooked long-grain brown rice	25 mL
1 tbsp	dried cooked wheat berries	15 mL
1 tbsp	dried cooked whole or pot barley	15 mL
1 tsp	flax seeds (whole or ground)	5 mL
2 tbsp	chopped dried apples	25 mL
1 tbsp	instant skim milk powder	15 mL
1 tsp	packed brown sugar (or to taste)	5 mL
$\frac{1}{8}$ tsp	ground cinnamon	0.5 mL
Pinch	salt	Pinch

To Serve

1 cup	water (approx.)	250 mL

Prep at Home

1. In a mini chopper or small food processor, process oats, rice, wheat berries, barley and flax seeds until finely chopped and about one-quarter is powdery. Transfer to a sealable plastic bag and add apples, milk powder, brown sugar, cinnamon and salt. Seal and store at room temperature for up to 1 month.

To Serve

1. In a saucepan, combine oat mixture and water. Cover and let stand for 30 minutes or until grains start to soften.

2. Uncover and bring to a boil over medium heat, stirring often. Reduce heat and simmer, stirring often, for about 5 minutes or until grains are tender and porridge is thickened. Thin with more water, if desired.

Crispy, Crunchy Granola Cereal

By making your own granola, you control the flavor, and you know exactly what's in it.

Tip

Granola stays crunchier when stored in a cookie tin or a glass jar. A plastic container tends to make it soft. A sealable bag or plastic container is fine for short-term storage when you're packing granola for the trail.

Variation

Replace some or all of the rolled oats with barley flakes or spelt flakes.

- Preheat oven to 350°F (180°C)
- Rimmed baking sheet, lined with parchment paper

3 cups	large-flake (old-fashioned) rolled oats	750 mL
1/2 cup	wheat germ or natural bran	125 mL
1/2 cup	chopped nuts	125 mL
1/2 cup	green pumpkin seeds	125 mL
1/2 cup	sunflower seeds	125 mL
3/4 cup	unsweetened apple juice or other fruit juice	175 mL
1/4 cup	liquid honey	50 mL
1 tsp	vanilla extract	5 mL
1 cup	chopped dried fruit	250 mL

1. In a bowl, combine oats, wheat germ, nuts, pumpkin seeds and sunflower seeds.

2. In a measuring cup or bowl, whisk together apple juice, honey and vanilla. Pour over dry ingredients and toss to coat.

3. Spread out on prepared baking sheet. Bake in preheated oven, stirring two or three times, for about 30 minutes or until golden brown, dry and fragrant. Let cool completely on pan on a wire rack, stirring occasionally.

4. Transfer to a cookie tin or a glass jar and add dried fruit; shake to combine. Store in a cool, dry place for up to 1 month.

No-Cook Grains and Fruit

Makes 1 serving

Just Add Water

No Heat Required

A hearty whole-grain cereal that's cold-soaked is sure to satisfy you on those mornings when there's no time or fuel to cook. The flax seeds not only provide nutrition, but also help thicken the cereal and give it a nice texture.

Tip

Softer dried fruits, such as raisins, strawberries and peaches, work best for this no-cook cereal.

Variation

For added flavor and energy, use fruit juice instead of water to rehydrate your cereal.

Prep at Home

¼ cup	dried cooked whole oats, wheat berries and/or barley	50 mL
¼ cup	whole wheat couscous	50 mL
2 tsp	flax seeds (whole or ground)	10 mL
2 tbsp	finely chopped dried fruit	25 mL
1 tbsp	instant skim milk powder	15 mL
1½ tsp	vanilla sugar (see tip, page 234) or packed brown sugar (or to taste)	7 mL
Pinch	salt	Pinch

To Serve

¾ cup	water (approx.)	175 mL

Prep at Home

1. In a blender or mini chopper, process oats, couscous and flax seeds until most are powdery. Transfer to a sealable plastic bag and add dried fruit, milk powder, vanilla sugar and salt. Seal and store at room temperature for up to 1 month.

To Serve

1. In a sealable bag, or in a container or bowl, combine cereal mixture and water. Cover and let stand for at least 30 minutes, until grains are softened, or overnight. Thin with more water, if necessary.

Pack-In Breakfast Bars

Makes 16 bars

These sturdy bars, which keep and travel well, make a filling, nutritious start to the day, wherever you find yourself.

Tips

Use the coarse side of a cheese grater to shred the apples. Or, for a faster method, use a food processor fitted with the metal blade and pulse coarsely chopped apples until in small pieces but not puréed.

Bars can be wrapped individually in plastic wrap, then frozen in an airtight container or freezer bag for up to 2 months.

Variation

Stir 1 cup (250 mL) chopped toasted pecans, walnuts or peanuts into cereal mixture before adding egg.

- Preheat oven to 375°F (190°C)
- 13- by 9-inch (33 by 23 cm) metal baking pan, lined with greased foil with a 2-inch (5 cm) overhang

2 cups	shredded or finely chopped apples (about 4)	500 mL
2 cups	bran cereal, such as All-Bran or 100% Bran	500 mL
3/4 cup	plain yogurt (not fat-free)	175 mL
1 1/2 cups	whole wheat flour	375 mL
2 tsp	baking powder	10 mL
1 1/2 tsp	ground cinnamon	10 mL
1/2 tsp	baking soda	2 mL
1/2 tsp	salt	2 mL
1	egg, beaten	1
2/3 cup	liquid honey	150 mL
2 tsp	vanilla extract	10 mL

1. In a bowl, combine apples, cereal and yogurt. Let stand for 10 minutes or until cereal is moistened.

2. In a large bowl, combine whole wheat flour, baking powder, cinnamon, baking soda and salt.

3. Stir egg, honey and vanilla into cereal mixture. Pour over dry ingredients and stir just until moistened.

4. Spread into prepared pan, smoothing top. Bake for about 40 minutes or until a tester inserted in the center comes out clean. Let cool completely in pan on a wire rack. Using the foil overhang as handles, remove from pan and transfer to a cutting board. Cut into bars.

Main Courses

continued...

Hearty Minestrone Soup

Makes 1 serving

Just Add Water

This classic soup can be made with ease with your own dried ingredients. The tomato sauce leather adds a boost of flavor with little work.

Tip

Use a spice grinder or mini chopper to grind dried garlic slices into powder.

Prep at Home

1	1-inch (2.5 cm) square Tomato Pasta Sauce Leather	1
½ cup	dried cooked fusilli	125 mL
¼ cup	dried cooked red kidney beans or Romano beans	50 mL
2 tbsp	crumbled beef jerky (optional, any flavor)	25 mL
1 tbsp	dried carrot pieces	15 mL
1 tbsp	dried celery slices	15 mL
¼ tsp	crumbled dried basil	1 mL
Pinch	powdered dried garlic	Pinch

To Serve

1½ cups	water	375 mL

Prep at Home

1. Tear leather into small pieces. In a sealable plastic bag, combine leather, fusilli, beans, jerky (if using), carrots, celery, basil and garlic. Seal and store at room temperature for up to 1 month (or up to 6 months if jerky is not used).

To Serve

1. In a saucepan, combine vegetable mixture and water. Let stand for 15 minutes or until vegetables start to soften.

2. Bring to a boil over medium heat, stirring often. Reduce heat and boil gently, stirring often, for about 10 minutes or until vegetables are softened.

Fresh Addition

Top hot soup with 1 tbsp (15 mL) shredded cheese.

Squash and Lentil Soup

Makes 1 serving

Just Add Water

Winter squash adds substance to this tasty soup, and the lentils and rice add texture and complete the protein.

Prep at Home

¼ cup	dried cooked lentils	50 mL
2 tbsp	dried grated winter squash	25 mL
2 tbsp	dried cooked brown rice	25 mL
1 tbsp	dried onion pieces	15 mL
½ tsp	crumbled dried parsley	2 mL
¼ tsp	finely chopped dried garlic	1 mL
⅛ tsp	ground cumin or curry powder	0.5 mL
¼ tsp	salt	1 mL
	Freshly ground black pepper	

To Serve

2 cups	water	500 mL

Prep at Home

1. In a sealable plastic bag, combine lentils, squash, rice, onions, parsley, garlic, cumin, salt and pepper to taste. Seal and store at room temperature for up to 1 month.

To Serve

1. In a saucepan, combine vegetable mixture and water. Let stand for 15 minutes or until squash starts to soften.

2. Bring to a boil over medium heat, stirring often. Reduce heat and boil gently, stirring often and mashing lentils slightly to thicken soup, for about 10 minutes or until vegetables are softened.

Sweet Potato and Red Pepper Soup

Makes 1 serving

Just Add Water

Sweet potatoes and red bell peppers are a terrific flavor and color combination, and both are highlighted in this warming soup.

Prep at Home

¼ cup	crumbled dried sweet potato slices	50 mL
2 tbsp	dried red bell pepper pieces	25 mL
2 tbsp	dried cooked brown or white rice	25 mL
1 tbsp	dried celery slices	15 mL
¼ tsp	crumbled dried basil	1 mL
¼ tsp	salt	1 mL
Pinch	powdered dried garlic	Pinch
	Freshly ground black pepper	

To Serve

2 cups	water	500 mL

Prep at Home

1. In a sealable plastic bag, combine sweet potatoes, red peppers, rice, celery, basil, salt, garlic and pepper to taste. Seal and store at room temperature for up to 1 month.

To Serve

1. In a saucepan, combine vegetable mixture and water. Let stand for 20 minutes or until sweet potato starts to soften.

2. Bring to a boil over medium heat, stirring often. Reduce heat and boil gently, stirring often, for about 10 minutes or until vegetables are softened.

Three Sisters Soup

Makes 1 serving

Just Add Water

In Native North American culture, the three sisters are represented by corn, beans and squash, which are traditionally grown together to complement the nutrients they each draw from and add to the earth. The flavors complement each other beautifully in this soup, too.

Variation

For a thicker soup, whisk 2 tsp (10 mL) all-purpose flour with 2 tbsp (25 mL) water and whisk into the soup after 10 minutes of simmering in step 2; stir often after adding flour.

Prep at Home

2 tbsp	dried corn kernels	25 mL
2 tbsp	dried green bean pieces	25 mL
2 tbsp	dried winter squash pieces	25 mL
1 tbsp	crumbled dried potato slices	15 mL
2 tsp	dried onion pieces	10 mL
2 tsp	dried celery slices	10 mL
1/2 tsp	crumbled dried parsley	2 mL
1/4 tsp	minced dried garlic	1 mL
1/4 tsp	crumbled dried thyme	1 mL
1/4 tsp	salt	1 mL
	Freshly ground black pepper	

To Serve

2 cups	water	500 mL

Prep at Home

1. In a sealable plastic bag, combine corn, green beans, squash, potatoes, onions, celery, parsley, garlic, thyme, salt and pepper to taste. Seal and store at room temperature for up to 1 month.

To Serve

1. In a saucepan, combine vegetable mixture and water. Let stand for 20 minutes or until corn starts to soften.

2. Bring to a boil over medium heat, stirring often. Reduce heat and boil gently, stirring often, for about 10 minutes or until vegetables are softened.

Pumping Iron Pea Soup

Makes 1 serving

Just Add Water

Easy, fast, nutritious and great-tasting — you can't ask for a better way to get more greens in your diet.

Prep at Home

1	3-inch (7.5 cm) square Spinach Leather	1
2 tbsp	dried green peas	25 mL
2 tbsp	dried cooked lentils or white beans	25 mL
1 tbsp	dried onion pieces	15 mL
1 tbsp	instant skim milk powder	15 mL
¼ tsp	crumbled dried basil	1 mL
¼ tsp	salt	1 mL
⅛ tsp	finely chopped dried lemon or orange zest	0.5 mL
	Freshly ground black pepper	

To Serve

2 cups	water	500 mL

Prep at Home

1. In a mini chopper or blender, process leather, peas, lentils, onions, milk powder, basil, salt, lemon zest and pepper to taste until vegetables are finely chopped and fairly powdery. Transfer to a sealable plastic bag, seal and store at room temperature for up to 1 month.

To Serve

1. In a saucepan, combine vegetable mixture and water. Let stand for 15 minutes or until vegetables start to soften.

2. Bring to a boil over medium heat, stirring often. Reduce heat and boil gently, stirring often, for about 5 minutes or until vegetables are softened.

Chicken Noodle Soup

Makes 1 serving

Just Add Water

Even on the best camping trip, a little comfort food might be in order. Here's the chicken noodle soup that you won't believe came out of your pack.

Tip

Dried chicken tends to keep a toothsome texture even when rehydrated. Chopping it into very small pieces does help to soften it.

Prep at Home

1 oz	Sea Salt and Peppercorn Chicken Jerky or Cajun Chicken Jerky, finely chopped	30 g
1 tbsp	dried carrot pieces, finely chopped	15 mL
1 tbsp	dried celery slices, finely chopped	15 mL
1 tbsp	dried onion pieces, finely chopped	15 mL
1 tbsp	crumbled dried parsley	15 mL
¼ tsp	salt	1 mL
⅛ tsp	freshly ground black pepper	0.5 mL
¼ cup	broken spaghettini	50 mL

To Serve

2 cups	water	500 mL

Prep at Home

1. In a sealable plastic bag, combine chicken, carrots, celery, onions, parsley, salt and pepper. Place spaghettini in another bag. Seal both bags and store at room temperature for up to 1 month.

To Serve

1. In a saucepan, bring water to a boil. Add chicken mixture, remove from heat, cover and let stand for 20 minutes or until chicken starts to soften.

2. Uncover and bring to a boil over medium heat, stirring often. Add spaghettini. Reduce heat and boil gently, stirring often, for about 10 minutes or until pasta is tender.

Beef and Barley Soup

Just Add Water

Start with a flavored jerky, add a few dried vegetables and you've got a scrumptious soup to enjoy.

Tip

Heating the water before adding the beef mixture speeds up the soaking time and gives a better texture to the barley. If you don't want to fire up the stove twice, you can soak the mixture in cold water for about 1 hour or until the barley is softened.

Prep at Home

1/2 oz	Maple and Whisky Ground Beef Jerky or Southwestern Ground Beef Jerky, broken into small pieces	15 g
2 tbsp	dried cooked barley	25 mL
1 tbsp	dried carrot pieces, finely chopped	15 mL
1 tbsp	dried celery slices, finely chopped	15 mL
2 tsp	dried onion pieces or leek slices, finely chopped	10 mL
1/4 tsp	crumbled dried thyme	1 mL
1/4 tsp	salt	1 mL
1/8 tsp	freshly ground black pepper	0.5 mL

To Serve

2 cups	water	500 mL

Prep at Home

1. In a sealable plastic bag, combine beef, barley, carrots, celery, onions, thyme, salt and pepper. Seal and store at room temperature for up to 1 month.

To Serve

1. In a saucepan, bring water to a boil. Add beef mixture, remove from heat, cover and let stand for 20 minutes or until beef starts to soften.

2. Uncover and bring to a boil over medium heat, stirring often. Reduce heat and boil gently, stirring often, for about 10 minutes or until beef and barley are tender.

> **Fresh Addition**
> Add a dash of hot pepper sauce, Worcestershire sauce or steak sauce for an extra kick of flavor.

Hamburger Soup

Just Add Water

The secret ingredient (instant coffee) in this one comes from Jennifer's mom, Patricia, who always added a touch to enrich the broth when she made hamburger soup. You'll be surprised at the fabulous flavor for a just-add-water soup.

Variation

Flavored ground meat jerky can be used in place of the ground beef. Try Herb and Garlic Ground Meat Jerky, Maple and Whisky Ground Meat Jerky, or Southwestern Ground Meat Jerky, broken into very small pieces.

Prep at Home

2 tbsp	dried cooked ground beef	25 mL
1 tbsp	finely chopped dried tomatoes	15 mL
1 tbsp	dried carrot pieces, finely chopped	15 mL
1 tbsp	dried celery slices, finely chopped	15 mL
1 tbsp	dried mushroom slices, crumbled	15 mL
1 tsp	dried onion pieces, finely chopped	5 mL
1/2 tsp	instant coffee granules	2 mL
1/4 tsp	paprika	1 mL
1/4 tsp	crumbled dried rosemary	1 mL
1/4 tsp	salt	1 mL
	Freshly ground black pepper	

To Serve

2 cups	water	500 mL

Prep at Home

1. In a sealable plastic bag, combine beef, tomatoes, carrots, celery, mushrooms, onions, coffee granules, paprika, rosemary, salt and pepper to taste. Seal and store at room temperature for up to 1 month.

To Serve

1. In a saucepan, combine beef mixture and water. Cover and let stand for 15 minutes or until vegetables start to soften.

2. Uncover and bring to a boil over medium heat, stirring often. Reduce heat and boil gently, stirring often, for about 10 minutes or until beef and vegetables are tender.

Fisherman's Chowder

Makes 1 serving

This tasty fish chowder will make you proud of your catch and your cooking skills. Serve with biscuits for a hearty meal after a hard day's work.

Tip

Crumbled dried potato slices cook quickly and add body to the chowder. You can break them into small pieces by hand or pulse them in a mini chopper.

Variation

Pack ½ oz (15 g) dried cooked shrimp, finely chopped, to add with the potato mixture just in case you don't catch a keeper.

Prep at Home

¼ cup	crumbled dried potato slices	50 mL
1 tbsp	dried celery slices, finely chopped	15 mL
1 tbsp	dried carrot pieces, finely chopped	15 mL
1 tbsp	instant skim milk powder	15 mL
1 tbsp	all-purpose flour	15 mL
1 tsp	dried leek slices or onion pieces, finely chopped	5 mL
¼ tsp	crumbled dried thyme or rosemary	1 mL
¼ tsp	salt	1 mL
Pinch	cayenne pepper	Pinch

To Serve

2 cups	water	500 mL
1	fresh fish, filleted, skinned and cut into bite-size pieces	1

Prep at Home

1. In a sealable plastic bag, combine potatoes, celery, carrots, milk powder, flour, leeks, thyme, salt and cayenne. Seal and store at room temperature for up to 1 month.

To Serve

1. In a saucepan, combine potato mixture and water. Let stand for 15 minutes or until vegetables start to soften.

2. Bring to a boil over medium heat, stirring often. Reduce heat and boil gently, stirring often, for about 10 minutes or until vegetables are almost tender. Stir in fish, reduce heat and simmer for about 5 minutes or until fish flakes easily with a fork and vegetables are tender.

No-Luck Corn Chowder and Dumplings

Just Add Water

If the big one got away and you had your heart set on chowder, a steaming bowl of this corn version, complete with dumplings, makes a fine consolation prize.

Prep at Home

¼ cup	crumbled Sweet Potato and Red Pepper Leather	50 mL
¼ cup	dried corn kernels	50 mL
2 tbsp	crumbled dried potato slices	25 mL
2 tbsp	instant skim milk powder	25 mL
1 tbsp	dried celery slices	15 mL
¼ tsp	crumbled dried thyme	1 mL
¼ tsp	paprika	1 mL
¼ tsp	salt	1 mL
	Freshly ground black pepper	

Dumplings

⅓ cup	all-purpose flour	75 mL
1 tbsp	instant skim milk powder	15 mL
1 tsp	crumbled dried parsley	5 mL
½ tsp	baking powder	2 mL
Pinch	salt	Pinch
Pinch	freshly ground black pepper	Pinch

To Serve

2⅓ cups	water, divided	575 mL

Prep at Home

1. In a sealable plastic bag, combine leather, corn, potatoes, milk powder, celery, thyme, paprika, salt and pepper to taste. Seal and store at room temperature for up to 1 month.

2. *For the dumplings:* In another bag, combine flour, milk powder, parsley, baking powder, salt and pepper. Seal and store at room temperature for up to 1 month.

To Serve

1. In a saucepan, combine corn mixture and 2 cups (500 mL) of the water. Let stand for 20 minutes or until corn starts to soften.

Tip

Don't be tempted to lift the lid when cooking dumplings. You need to keep the heat and steam in the pan for proper cooking.

Variation

Substitute $\frac{1}{4}$ cup (50 mL) dried sweet potato cubes and 1 tbsp (15 mL) dried red bell pepper pieces for the Sweet Potato and Red Pepper Leather.

2. Bring to a boil over medium heat, stirring often. Reduce heat to low, cover and simmer, stirring occasionally, for about 15 minutes or until vegetables are almost tender.

3. Meanwhile, in a bowl, stir dumpling mixture to blend. Add the remaining water and, using a fork, stir just until moistened. Drop by spoonfuls on top of simmering chowder. Cover and simmer for about 10 minutes or until dumplings are puffed and a tester inserted in a dumpling comes out clean.

Vegetable Bean Chili

Makes 1 serving

Just Add Water

A spicy mixture of beans and vegetables, this satisfying chili is even better served over rice or with toast.

Tip

Chipotle pepper powder is available at well-stocked spice or bulk food stores and some supermarkets. If you can't find it, you can grind a dry chipotle pepper in a spice grinder.

Prep at Home

¼ cup	dried cooked black beans or chickpeas	50 mL
¼ cup	dried cooked kidney beans	50 mL
2 tbsp	finely chopped dried tomatoes	25 mL
1 tbsp	dried red or green bell pepper pieces	15 mL
1 tbsp	dried mushroom slices, crumbled	15 mL
1 tbsp	dried onion pieces	15 mL
¾ tsp	chili powder	3 mL
½ tsp	crumbled dried oregano	2 mL
Pinch	chipotle pepper powder	Pinch
Pinch	salt	Pinch

To Serve

1⅓ cups	water	325 mL

Prep at Home

1. In a sealable plastic bag, combine black beans, kidney beans, tomatoes, red peppers, mushrooms, onions, chili powder, oregano, chipotle powder and salt. Seal and store at room temperature for up to 1 month.

To Serve

1. In a saucepan, combine bean mixture and water. Let stand for 20 minutes or until vegetables start to soften.

2. Bring to a boil over medium heat, stirring often. Reduce heat and boil gently, stirring often, for about 10 minutes or until vegetables are soft and chili is thickened.

> **Fresh Addition**
> Serve on top of torn fresh lettuce, sprinkle with diced avocado and serve with tortilla chips for a taco salad.

Tofu Chili

Makes 1 serving

Just Add Water

You can't beat a rich-flavored chili that's warm, hearty and filling after a day of extreme trekking.

Tip

Barbecue sauce leather adds a deep, rich flavor to the chili. If you don't have it, increase the chili powder to 1 tsp (5 mL) and stir in some liquid barbecue sauce before serving.

Prep at Home

1	1-inch (2.5 cm) square Barbecue Sauce Leather	1
¼ cup	dried crumbled tofu	50 mL
¼ cup	dried cooked kidney or black beans	50 mL
2 tbsp	finely chopped dried tomatoes	25 mL
1 tbsp	dried grated carrots	15 mL
1 tbsp	dried onion pieces	15 mL
1 tbsp	dried celery slices	15 mL
1 tsp	crumbled dried parsley	5 mL
½ tsp	chili powder	2 mL
¼ tsp	finely chopped dried garlic	1 mL
¼ tsp	ground cumin	1 mL
¼ tsp	salt	1 mL

To Serve

1¼ cups	water	300 mL

Prep at Home

1. Tear leather into small pieces. In a sealable plastic bag, combine leather, tofu, beans, tomatoes, carrots, onions, celery, parsley, chili powder, garlic, cumin and salt. Seal and store at room temperature for up to 1 month.

To Serve

1. In a saucepan, bring water to a boil. Add leather mixture, remove from heat, cover and let stand for 15 minutes or until tofu is softened.

2. Uncover and bring to a boil over medium heat, stirring often. Boil, stirring often, for about 10 minutes or until vegetables are soft and chili is thickened.

Chipotle Beef Chili

Makes 1 serving

Just Add Water

A super-satisfying hot bowl of chili is made even better with a touch of smoky heat from the chipotles and your own dried vegetables and jerky.

Tip

Chipotle pepper powder is available at well-stocked spice or bulk food stores and some supermarkets. If you can't find it, you can grind a dry chipotle pepper in a spice grinder.

Prep at Home

½ oz	Cajun Beef Jerky or Southwestern Ground Beef Jerky, broken into small pieces	15 g
¼ cup	dried cooked kidney or black beans	50 mL
2 tbsp	finely chopped dried tomatoes	25 mL
1 tbsp	dried red or green bell pepper pieces	15 mL
2 tsp	dried onion pieces	10 mL
½ tsp	crumbled dried oregano	2 mL
½ tsp	chili powder	2 mL
Pinch	chipotle pepper powder	Pinch
Pinch	salt	Pinch

To Serve

1¼ cups	water	300 mL

Prep at Home

1. In a sealable plastic bag, combine beef, beans, tomatoes, red peppers, onions, oregano, chili powder, chipotle powder and salt. Seal and store at room temperature for up to 1 month.

To Serve

1. In a saucepan, combine beef mixture and water. Cover and let stand for 30 minutes or until vegetables start to soften.

2. Uncover and bring to a boil over medium heat, stirring often. Reduce heat and boil gently, stirring often, for about 15 minutes or until vegetables are soft.

> ### Fresh Additions
> Replace ¼ cup (50 mL) of the water with beer.
>
> Sprinkle with shredded Cheddar cheese or dollop with sour cream to serve.

Blueberry Pancakes (page 100)

Three Sisters Soup (page 118)

Chipotle Beef Chili (page 128)

Pan-Seared Chicken
with a Side of Stuffing (page 151)

Thai Noodles (page 158)

Curried Squash and
Chickpeas (page 178)

GORP with a Twist
(page 194)

Pear Cherry Ginger Crumble (page 223)

Venison Chili

Makes 1 serving

Just Add Water

This chili has a little kick from the spices and rich venison flavor. Serve with corn cakes or tortilla chips, and this meal will make the top five list of camping memories.

Variation
If you don't have tomato paste leather, use 2 tbsp (25 mL) finely chopped dried tomatoes.

Prep at Home

1	2-inch (5 cm) piece Tomato Paste Leather	1
1/2 oz	Southwestern Ground Venison Jerky or Cajun Venison Jerky, broken into small pieces	15 g
1/4 cup	dried cooked chickpeas, kidney beans or black beans	50 mL
1 tbsp	dried grated carrots	15 mL
1 tbsp	dried mushroom slices, crumbled	15 mL
2 tsp	dried onion pieces	10 mL
1/2 tsp	crumbled dried oregano	2 mL
3/4 tsp	chili powder	3 mL
1/4 tsp	salt	1 mL
Pinch	hot pepper flakes	Pinch

To Serve

1 1/4 cups	water	300 mL

Prep at Home
1. Tear leather into very small pieces. In a sealable plastic bag, combine leather, venison, chickpeas, carrots, mushrooms, onions, oregano, chili powder, salt and hot pepper flakes. Seal and store at room temperature for up to 1 month.

To Serve
1. In a saucepan, combine venison mixture and water. Cover and let stand for 30 minutes, mashing leather occasionally, until vegetables start to soften.

2. Uncover and bring to a boil over medium heat, stirring often. Reduce heat and boil gently, stirring often, for about 15 minutes or until vegetables and venison are tender and chili is slightly thickened.

> **Fresh Addition**
> Top with a dollop of sour cream and some diced avocado.

No-Cook "Baked" Beans

Makes 1 serving

Just Add Water

No Heat Required

We'll be the first to admit this isn't quite gourmet fare; however, if you have no fuel and want a satisfying meal, this recipe certainly fits the bill.

Tip

For the best flavor in this recipe, use a flavorful barbecue sauce or tomato sauce to make the leather. Taste the leather before using it, and if it isn't very rich-tasting, tear up a 1-inch (2.5 cm) square of tomato paste leather and add it to the bean mixture.

Variation

This can be served hot, too. Just add ¼ cup (50 mL) extra water, reduce the soaking time to 15 minutes and simmer in a saucepan, stirring often, for about 5 minutes or until thickened and beans are soft.

Prep at Home

1	2-inch (5 cm) square Barbecue Sauce Leather or Tomato Sauce Leather	1
⅔ cup	dried cooked kidney beans or black beans	150 mL
¼ tsp	packed brown sugar	1 mL
¼ tsp	salt	1 mL

To Serve

¾ cup	water	175 mL

Prep at Home

1. Tear leather into very small pieces. In a sealable plastic bag, combine leather, beans, sugar and salt. Seal and store at room temperature for up to 1 month.

To Serve

1. In a bowl, combine bean mixture and water. Cover and let stand for 30 minutes, mashing leather occasionally, until beans are softened.

Chicken and Potato Stew

Makes 1 serving

Just Add Water

A stick to your ribs stew is just what you need when there's a chill in the air and you've had an active day. This is an all-in-one meal, but a biscuit or bread on the side might be in order to sop up the sauce.

Variation

Substitute your favorite dried vegetables in place of the squash, carrots and celery. Just be sure to use a total of about ¼ cup (50 mL).

Prep at Home

1 oz	Maple and Grainy Dijon Chicken Jerky or Sea Salt and Peppercorn Chicken Jerky, finely chopped	30 g
¼ cup	dried potato cubes	50 mL
2 tbsp	dried winter squash cubes	25 mL
1 tbsp	dried carrot pieces	15 mL
1 tbsp	dried celery slices	15 mL
1 tbsp	all-purpose flour	15 mL
1 tsp	crumbled dried parsley	5 mL
¼ tsp	crumbled dried tarragon or thyme	1 mL
¼ tsp	salt	1 mL
	Freshly ground black pepper	

To Serve

1½ cups	water	375 mL

Prep at Home

1. In a sealable plastic bag, combine chicken, potatoes, squash, carrots, celery, flour, parsley, tarragon, salt and pepper to taste. Seal and store at room temperature for up to 1 month.

To Serve

1. In a saucepan, combine chicken mixture and water. Cover and let stand for 30 minutes or until jerky starts to soften.

2. Uncover and bring to a boil over medium heat, stirring often. Reduce heat and boil gently, stirring often, for about 15 minutes or until potatoes and chicken are tender and liquid is slightly thickened.

Viking Stew

← •

Makes 1 serving

Just Add Water

The name of this stew comes from Jay's childhood. It's what his mom called a stew when she used all of the leftover bits of vegetables from the fridge to make it. The kids thought it was fantastic and even dressed in costume to eat it. It wasn't until years later that they realized it had nothing to do with Norsemen or ships, but rather that their fridge was a Viking brand! You can clean out your dried goods pantry for this version.

Variation

Replace ¼ cup (50 mL) of the water with beer.

Prep at Home

1	1-inch (2.5 cm) square Tomato Pasta Sauce Leather or Barbecue Sauce Leather	1
1 oz	meat jerky (any type), broken into small pieces	30 g
¼ cup	dried potato cubes or crumbled dried potato slices	50 mL
¼ cup	dried vegetables (any type)	50 mL
1 tbsp	all-purpose flour	15 mL
1 tsp	crumbled dried herbs	5 mL
½ tsp	finely chopped dried garlic	2 mL
¼ tsp	salt	1 mL
¼ tsp	freshly ground black pepper	1 mL

To Serve

1½ cups	water	375 mL

Prep at Home

1. Tear leather into very small pieces. In a sealable plastic bag, combine leather, jerky, potatoes, vegetables, flour, herbs, garlic, salt and pepper. Seal and store at room temperature for up to 1 month.

To Serve

1. In a saucepan, combine leather mixture and water. Cover and let stand for 30 minutes, mashing leather occasionally, until vegetables start to soften.

2. Uncover and bring to a boil over medium heat, stirring often. Reduce heat and boil gently, stirring often, for about 15 minutes or until potatoes and meat are tender and liquid is slightly thickened.

> ### Fresh Addition
> Spice the stew up with a little hot pepper sauce before serving.

Venison, Potato and Apple Stew

Makes 1 serving

Just Add Water

When you need something warm and hearty on a crisp night, this is the stew that will satisfy you.

Variations

You can use any type of meat or poultry jerky in this stew in place of the venison.

Barbecue sauce leather adds a good depth of flavor to this stew. If you don't have it, add a splash of liquid barbecue sauce or steak sauce before serving.

Prep at Home

1	1-inch (2.5 cm) square Barbecue Sauce Leather	1
½ oz	Sea Salt and Peppercorn Venison Jerky or Maple and Grainy Dijon Venison Jerky, broken into small pieces	15 g
¼ cup	dried potato slices, broken into pieces	50 mL
2 tbsp	dried apple slices	25 mL
1 tbsp	dried carrot pieces	15 mL
1 tbsp	dried celery slices	15 mL
¼ tsp	crumbled dried rosemary or thyme	1 mL
¼ tsp	salt	1 mL
Pinch	dry mustard	Pinch
	Freshly ground black pepper	

To Serve

1½ cups	water	375 mL

Prep at Home

1. Tear leather into very small pieces. In a sealable plastic bag, combine leather, venison, potatoes, apples, carrots, celery, rosemary, salt, mustard and pepper to taste. Seal and store at room temperature for up to 1 month.

To Serve

1. In a saucepan, combine leather mixture and water. Cover and let stand for 30 minutes, mashing leather occasionally, until vegetables start to soften.

2. Uncover and bring to a boil over medium heat, stirring often. Reduce heat and boil gently, stirring often, for about 15 minutes or until potatoes and venison are tender and liquid is slightly thickened.

Tofu, Vegetable and Fruit Curry

Just Add Water

There's dazzling color and flavor and a variety of textures in this satisfying vegetarian curry.

Tips

For the lime flesh, dry whole lime slices, then cut off the rind. Chop the flesh into small pieces.

Heating the water to soak the tofu gives it a much better texture than cold-soaking.

Prep at Home

1/4 cup	dried crumbled tofu	50 mL
2 tbsp	dried cooked lentils	25 mL
2 tbsp	dried mushroom slices, crumbled	25 mL
2 tbsp	dried red bell pepper pieces	25 mL
1 tbsp	finely chopped dried peaches or apricots	15 mL
1 tbsp	raisins	15 mL
1 tbsp	sweetened shredded coconut or finely chopped dried coconut	15 mL
1 tbsp	chopped dried lime flesh (optional)	15 mL
2 tsp	dried onion pieces	10 mL
1/2 tsp	curry powder	2 mL
1/4 tsp	finely chopped dried gingerroot	1 mL
1/4 tsp	salt	1 mL

To Serve

1 1/4 cups	water	300 mL

Prep at Home

1. In a sealable plastic bag, combine tofu, lentils, mushrooms, red peppers, peaches, raisins, coconut, lime (if using), onions, curry powder, ginger and salt. Seal and store at room temperature for up to 1 month.

To Serve

1. In a saucepan or skillet, bring water to a boil. Add tofu mixture, remove from heat, cover and let stand for 15 minutes or until tofu is softened.

2. Uncover and bring to a boil over medium heat, stirring often. Boil, stirring often, for about 5 minutes or until mixture is hot and liquid is absorbed.

> **Fresh Addition**
> Serve with lime wedges to squeeze over top and add a dollop of plain yogurt.

Curried Chicken with Apples

Just Add Water

Fragrant spices and sweet apples warm up a simple chicken dish. Serve it over rice or with lentils.

Variation

If you like a fiery hot curry, use a hot curry powder or add ⅛ tsp (0.5 mL) cayenne pepper.

Prep at Home

1 oz	Sea Salt and Peppercorn Chicken Jerky, finely chopped	30 g
¼ cup	dried sweet potato cubes	50 mL
2 tbsp	dried apple slices	25 mL
2 tbsp	dried red bell pepper pieces	25 mL
1 tbsp	dried onion pieces	15 mL
1 tsp	crumbled dried cilantro or parsley	5 mL
½ tsp	curry powder	2 mL
¼ tsp	ground cumin	1 mL
¼ tsp	finely chopped dried gingerroot	1 mL
¼ tsp	salt	1 mL

To Serve

1½ cups	water	375 mL

Prep at Home

1. In a sealable plastic bag, combine chicken, sweet potatoes, apples, red peppers, onions, cilantro, curry powder, cumin, ginger and salt. Seal and store at room temperature for up to 1 month.

To Serve

1. In a saucepan, combine chicken mixture and water. Cover and let stand for 30 minutes or until chicken starts to soften.

2. Uncover and bring to a boil over medium heat, stirring often. Reduce heat and boil gently, stirring often, for about 15 minutes or until potatoes are tender and liquid is slightly thickened.

Beef Stroganoff

Just Add Water

This simplified version of the classic noodle, beef and mushroom dish will surprise you because it's so easy and tasty.

Variation

Other flavors of beef jerky can be used. Try Cajun Beef Jerky, Herb and Garlic Ground Beef Jerky or Maple and Whisky Ground Beef Jerky.

Prep at Home

1/2 oz	Sea Salt and Peppercorn Beef Jerky, broken into small pieces	15 g
2 tbsp	dried mushroom slices	25 mL
2 tsp	crumbled dried parsley	10 mL
1/4 tsp	paprika	1 mL
1 cup	broad egg noodles (about 2 oz/60 g)	250 mL
2 tbsp	instant skim milk powder	25 mL
1 tbsp	crumbled dried cottage cheese	15 mL

To Serve

1 1/4 cups	water	300 mL
	Salt and pepper	

Prep at Home

1. In a sealable plastic bag, combine beef, mushrooms, parsley and paprika. In another bag, combine noodles, milk powder and cottage cheese. Seal both bags and store at room temperature for up to 1 month.

To Serve

1. In a saucepan, combine beef mixture and water. Cover and let stand for 15 minutes or until beef starts to soften.

2. Uncover and bring to a boil over high heat. Stir in noodle mixture, reduce heat and boil gently, stirring often, for about 5 minutes or until noodles are tender. Season to taste with salt and pepper.

> ### Fresh Addition
> Omit the cottage cheese when prepping at home and stir in 2 tbsp (25 mL) sour cream after removing from heat.

Peppered Beef and Noodles

Just Add Water

Plenty of flavor and the four major food groups in one pot make this a winner. The other campers will surely be curious about the fantastic aromas emanating from your site.

Prep at Home

¹/₂ oz	Peppercorn Ground Beef Jerky Strips, broken into small pieces	15 g
1 cup	broad egg noodles (about 2 oz/60 g)	250 mL
¹/₄ cup	instant skim milk powder	50 mL
2 tbsp	halved dried red bell pepper slices	25 mL
¹/₂ tsp	crumbled dried basil	2 mL
¹/₄ tsp	salt	1 mL
	Freshly ground black pepper	

To Serve

1¹/₄ cups	water	300 mL

Prep at Home

1. In a sealable plastic bag, combine beef, noodles, milk powder, red peppers, basil, salt and pepper to taste. Seal and store at room temperature for up to 1 month.

To Serve

1. In a saucepan, combine beef mixture and water. Cover and let stand for 15 minutes or until beef starts to soften.

2. Uncover and bring to a boil over high heat. Reduce heat and boil gently, stirring often, for about 5 minutes or until noodles and peppers are tender.

> **Fresh Addition**
> At the end, stir in 1 cup (250 mL) baby spinach until wilted.

Sloppy Joes

Makes 1 serving

Just Add Water

Serve this savory, saucy beef mixture over toast or biscuits, or with tortilla chips.

Tip

For extra flavor, add 1 tbsp (15 mL) chili powder per pound (500 g) of ground beef when cooking it and before drying and use the seasoned dried beef in this recipe.

Variation

Vegetarian Sloppy Joes: In place of ground beef, substitute $\frac{1}{2}$ cup (125 mL) dried Basic Veggie Burger Blend or $\frac{1}{4}$ cup (50 mL) each dried Basic Veggie Burger Blend and dried shredded tofu.

Prep at Home

1	2-inch (5 cm) square Barbecue Sauce Leather or Tomato Sauce Leather	1
$\frac{1}{2}$ cup	dried cooked ground beef	125 mL
1 tbsp	dried bell pepper pieces (any color)	15 mL
$\frac{1}{4}$ tsp	crumbled dried oregano	1 mL
$\frac{1}{8}$ tsp	salt	0.5 mL
Pinch	hot pepper flakes or chipotle powder	Pinch

To Serve

$1\frac{1}{4}$ cups	water	300 mL
	Salt and pepper (optional)	

Prep at Home

1. Tear leather into small pieces. In a sealable plastic bag, combine leather, beef, bell peppers, oregano, salt and hot pepper flakes. Seal and store at room temperature for up to 1 month.

To Serve

1. In a saucepan, combine beef mixture and water. Cover and let stand for 15 minutes or until beef starts to soften.

2. Uncover and bring to a boil over high heat. Reduce heat and boil gently, stirring often, for about 10 minutes or until peppers are tender and sauce is reduced. Season with salt and pepper to taste, if desired.

Teriyaki Tofu Stir-Fry

Makes 1 serving

Just Add Water

The idea for this super-easy, satisfying recipe was given to Jennifer and Jay by their friend Christopher Campbell, a professional photographer, avid camper and fervent foodie.

Tip

To make dried crumbled teriyaki tofu, marinate crumbled tofu in Teriyaki Jerky marinade (page 73) and dry according to the instructions on page 60.

Variation

Substitute $1/2$ oz (15 g) chopped Asian Ground Meat Jerky for the tofu.

Prep at Home

$1/3$ cup	dried cooked long-grain brown rice	75 mL
$1/4$ cup	dried crumbled teriyaki tofu (see tip, at left)	50 mL
1 tbsp	dried grated carrots	15 mL
1 tbsp	dried zucchini or red bell pepper slices	15 mL
1 tbsp	dried cauliflower florets, broken into small pieces	15 mL
$1/4$ tsp	finely chopped dried gingerroot	1 mL

To Serve

$1 1/4$ cups	water	300 mL

Prep at Home

1. In a sealable plastic bag, combine rice, tofu, carrots, zucchini, cauliflower and ginger. Seal and store at room temperature for up to 2 weeks or refrigerate for up to 1 month.

To Serve

1. In a saucepan or skillet, bring water to a boil. Add rice mixture, remove from heat, cover and let stand for 15 minutes or until tofu is softened.

2. Uncover and bring to a boil over medium heat, stirring often. Boil, stirring often, for about 5 minutes or until mixture is hot and liquid is absorbed.

Bean Fajitas

Makes 1 serving

Make your own fried beans right over the camp stove. You'll love the terrific "fresh" flavor.

Tip

If desired, warm the tortillas in a skillet or wrap in foil and warm over the campfire.

No-Heat Option

To make this filling without heating it, decrease the water to $2/3$ cup (150 mL), soak in sealable bag or bowl for 30 minutes and skip step 2.

Prep at Home

1	2-inch (5 cm) square Salsa Leather	1
$1/2$ cup	dried cooked black beans	125 mL
1 tbsp	dried onion slices	15 mL
1 tbsp	dried red or green bell pepper pieces	15 mL
Pinch	salt	Pinch

To Serve

1 cup	water	250 mL
2	flour tortillas	2

Prep at Home

1. Tear leather into very small pieces. In a sealable plastic bag, combine leather, beans, onions, red peppers and salt. Seal and store at room temperature for up to 1 month.

To Serve

1. In a saucepan or skillet, combine bean mixture and water. Let stand for 20 minutes, mashing leather occasionally, until vegetables start to soften.

2. Bring to a boil over medium heat, stirring often. Reduce heat and boil gently, stirring often and mashing beans, for about 5 minutes or until mixture is thick and hot.

3. Spoon half the bean mixture into the center of each tortilla. Fold up bottom and fold in both sides to enclose filling.

> **Fresh Addition**
> Spoon 1 tbsp (15 mL) shredded Monterey Jack, pepper Jack or Cheddar cheese and 1 tbsp (15 mL) sour cream over the bean mixture before folding the tortilla.

Tex-Mex Beef Fajitas

Hearty fajitas, a campfire — just add a cold beer, and you've got a fiesta under the stars.

Tip
If desired, warm the tortillas in a skillet or wrap in foil and warm over the campfire.

No-Heat Option

To make this filling without heating it, decrease the water to ⅔ cup (150 mL), soak in sealable bag or bowl for 30 to 45 minutes and skip step 2.

Prep at Home

1	2-inch (5 cm) square Salsa Leather	1
1 oz	Cajun Beef Jerky or Southwestern Ground Beef Jerky, broken into small pieces	30 g
¼ cup	dried red and/or green bell pepper slices	50 mL
1 tbsp	dried cooked black or kidney beans	15 mL
1 tbsp	dried onion slices	15 mL
¼ tsp	finely chopped dried hot chile peppers (optional)	1 mL
Pinch	salt	Pinch

To Serve

1 cup	water	250 mL
2	flour tortillas	2

Prep at Home

1. Tear leather into very small pieces. In a sealable plastic bag, combine leather, beef, red peppers, beans, onions, chile peppers (if using) and salt. Seal and store at room temperature for up to 1 month.

To Serve

1. In a saucepan or skillet, combine beef mixture and water. Let stand for 20 minutes, mashing leather occasionally, until vegetables start to soften.

2. Bring to a boil over medium heat, stirring often. Reduce heat and boil gently, stirring often and mashing beans, for about 10 minutes or until mixture is thick and hot.

3. Spoon half the beef mixture into the center of each tortilla. Fold up bottom and fold in both sides to enclose filling.

Fresh Additions
Omit the jerky when prepping at home and add 4 oz (125 g) fresh boneless beef grilling steak, cut into thin strips. Sauté it separately in a skillet, then stir into the cooked bean mixture. Alternatively, grill a whole piece of steak, slice it thinly, then stir into bean mixture for the last minute.

Sprinkle with a little shredded Monterey Jack or pepper Jack cheese before folding the tortillas.

Tofu, Lentil and Peanut Stovetop "Meatloaf"

Moisture, lots of texture and great flavor — you won't miss the meat in this loaf, which can be made on a stove or over a campfire.

Tip

This can be cooked over a campfire. Place the wrapped loaf in a flameproof metal or foil pan and cook over the moderately hot part of the fire. It may take a little longer to heat through, but you should hear it sizzling once it's hot.

- 9-inch (23 cm) square piece of foil
- Skillet with a lid

Prep at Home

1/4 cup	dried Basic Veggie Burger Blend	50 mL
1/4 cup	dried crumbled tofu	50 mL
1/4 cup	chopped peanuts	50 mL
1/4 cup	chopped dried tomatoes	50 mL
1 tsp	dried roasted onions	5 mL
1 tsp	crumbled dried parsley	5 mL
1/4 tsp	salt	1 mL
1/4 tsp	freshly ground black pepper	1 mL

To Serve

2/3 cup	water	150 mL
	Vegetable oil	

Prep at Home

1. In a sealable plastic bag, combine veggie burger blend, tofu, peanuts, tomatoes, onions, parsley, salt and pepper. Seal and store at room temperature for up to 1 month.

To Serve

1. In a saucepan, bring water to a boil. Add tofu mixture, remove from heat, cover and let stand for 15 minutes or until tofu is softened and liquid is absorbed.

2. Oil the center of the foil square. Form tofu mixture into a loaf about 4 by 2 by 1 inch (10 by 5 by 2.5 cm) in size and place on the oiled foil. Wrap tightly.

3. Place the foil package in a skillet over low heat. Cover and cook for 10 minutes, then flip foil package and heat for about 8 minutes or until loaf is heated through.

Veggie Burger on a Stick

Start with your own dried grain and lentil blend, add in dried veggies and peanut butter, and voila! You've got a fantastic veggie burger to cook over the campfire.

Variation

To make burger patties instead, shape mixture into two 1/2-inch (1 cm) thick patties. Heat a thin layer of oil in a skillet over medium heat and cook patties, turning once, for about 5 minutes or until both sides are golden brown and inside is hot.

- Two 1/2-inch (1 cm) thick sticks, at least 2 feet (60 cm) long
- Two 8-inch (20 cm) pieces of foil

Prep at Home

1/4 cup	dried Basic Veggie Burger Blend	50 mL
3 tbsp	quick-cooking rolled oats	45 mL
2 tsp	dried grated carrots	10 mL
1/2 tsp	finely chopped dried onions	2 mL
1/2 tsp	crumbled dried parsley	2 mL
1/4 tsp	salt	1 mL
Pinch	ground cumin	Pinch
Pinch	ground coriander	Pinch
	Freshly ground black pepper	

To Serve

1/4 cup	water	50 mL
2 tsp	natural peanut butter or almond butter	10 mL
1/2 tsp	freshly squeezed lime juice (optional)	2 mL

Prep at Home

1. In a sealable plastic bag, combine veggie burger blend, oats, carrots, onions, parsley, salt, cumin, coriander and pepper to taste. Seal and store at room temperature for up to 1 month.

To Serve

1. Prepare campfire.

2. In a bowl, combine burger mixture and water. Let stand for 15 minutes or until grains are softened and liquid is absorbed. Stir in peanut butter and lime juice (if using).

3. Wrap a square of foil around one end of each stick, covering at least 4 inches (10 cm). Divide mixture in half and squeeze one piece around the foil-wrapped section of each stick, making sure it is about 1/2 inch (1 cm) thick on all sides of the stick.

4. Cook burgers on sticks over the fire, holding them over a medium-hot area if possible and turning often, until golden brown and firm.

Tomato and Herb Tofu

Just Add Water

Pack more protein into your meal by replacing pasta with tofu seasoned with zesty Italian flair.

Variation

Substitute 1 tsp (5 mL) plain dried onions for the roasted onions.

Prep at Home

½ cup	dried shredded tofu	125 mL
2 tbsp	finely chopped dried tomatoes	25 mL
1 tbsp	dried roasted onions	15 mL
1 tsp	crumbled dried basil	5 mL
1 tsp	crumbled dried parsley	5 mL
½ tsp	crumbled dried oregano	2 mL
¼ tsp	crumbled dried roasted garlic or finely chopped dried garlic	1 mL
¼ tsp	salt	1 mL
Pinch	hot pepper flakes	Pinch

To Serve

1 cup	water	250 mL

Prep at Home

1. In a sealable plastic bag, combine tofu, tomatoes, onions, basil, parsley, oregano, garlic, salt and hot pepper flakes. Seal and store at room temperature for up to 1 month.

To Serve

1. In a saucepan, bring water to a boil. Add tofu mixture, remove from heat, cover and let stand for 15 minutes or until tofu is softened.

2. Uncover and bring to a boil over medium heat, stirring often. Boil, stirring often, for about 8 minutes or until tomatoes are soft and liquid is absorbed.

> **Fresh Addition**
> Top with shredded mozzarella or Parmesan cheese.

Catch of the Day Foil-Packet Fish

Makes 1 serving

If you happen to be lucky enough to make a good catch, here's a simple recipe to dress up that prize fish. (If you go into town and find a good fish market, you never have to divulge the truth.)

Variation

If you want to use dried lemon slices, pack them separately from the leek mixture and soak them in boiling water for about 15 minutes or until softened, then drain before stuffing the fish. Omit the extras for serving on top.

- 12-inch (30 cm) square piece of foil
- Grill rack (for campfire cooking)

Prep at Home

1 tbsp	dried leek slices or onion pieces	15 mL
1 tsp	dried garlic slices	5 mL
1/4 tsp	crumbled dried thyme	1 mL
1/4 tsp	salt	1 mL
1/4 tsp	freshly ground black pepper	1 mL

To Serve

1 tbsp	butter, softened, divided	15 mL
1/2	lemon, sliced	1/2
1	whole fresh fish, dressed and scaled (1 to 2 lbs/500 g to 1 kg)	1

Prep at Home

1. In a sealable plastic bag, combine leeks, garlic, thyme, salt and pepper. Seal and store at room temperature for up to 1 month.

To Serve

1. Prepare campfire (if using) and position grill rack over fire.

2. Spread half the butter across the center of the foil. Stuff the leek mixture, 2 of the lemon slices and the remaining butter in the cavity of the fish. Place on the buttered foil and wrap tightly.

3. Place on grill rack over hot coals or in a skillet over medium heat on a stove and cook for about 10 minutes per inch (2.5 cm) of thickness, turning once, until fish flakes easily with a fork. Serve with the remaining lemon slices to squeeze over top.

Fire-Grilled Fish Stuffed with Red Peppers, Lime and Oregano

Makes 1 serving

A hint of wood smoke makes fresh-caught fish all the better. The lime and savory seasonings add moisture and zest.

Variations

If you want to use dried lime slices, pack them separately from the vegetable mixture and soak them in boiling water for about 15 minutes or until softened, then drain before stuffing the fish.

To cook in a skillet on a stove, heat oil over medium-high heat. Add fish, reduce heat to medium-low and cook as directed in step 4.

- Grill rack

Prep at Home

1 tbsp	dried red bell pepper pieces	15 mL
1 tbsp	dried onion pieces	15 mL
1 tsp	finely chopped dried garlic	5 mL
1/2 tsp	crumbled dried oregano	2 mL
1/4 tsp	salt	1 mL
1/4 tsp	freshly ground black pepper	1 mL

To Serve

2 tbsp	water	25 mL
1	lime, sliced	1
1	whole fresh fish, dressed and scaled (1 to 2 lbs/500 g to 1 kg)	1
1 tbsp	olive or vegetable oil	15 mL

Prep at Home

1. In a sealable plastic bag, combine peppers, onions, garlic, oregano, salt and pepper. Seal and store at room temperature for up to 1 month.

To Serve

1. Prepare campfire and position grill rack over fire.

2. In a bowl, combine vegetable mixture and water. Let stand for about 15 minutes or until softened. Carefully drain off any excess water, trying not to lose the herbs.

3. Stuff the cavity of the fish with lime slices and vegetable mixture. Secure with toothpicks or skewers, or tie with soaked string. Brush the outside of the fish with olive oil.

4. Place on grill rack and cook over medium coals for about 10 minutes per inch (2.5 cm) of thickness, turning once, until the skin is crisp and golden brown and fish flakes easily with a fork.

Cajun Blackened Seasoning Mix

**Makes about
1/3 cup (75 mL)**

This seasoning mix is terrific to have on hand in case you make that big catch and have some fish fillets to fry up, or you take a trip into town and pick up some fresh chicken, steaks or pork chops.

Prep at Home

1/4 cup	paprika	50 mL
1 tbsp	crumbled dried oregano	15 mL
1 tbsp	crumbled dried thyme	15 mL
1 1/2 tsp	salt	7 mL
1 tsp	finely chopped dried garlic	5 mL
1 tsp	finely chopped dried lemon zest	5 mL
1 tsp	cayenne pepper	5 mL
1 tsp	freshly ground black pepper	5 mL

Prep at Home

1. In a sealable plastic bag, combine paprika, oregano, thyme, salt, garlic, lemon zest, cayenne and black pepper. Seal and store at room temperature for up to 1 month.

To Serve

1. Spread about 1 tsp (5 mL) seasoning mix over each portion of fish fillets, chicken, steaks or pork chops and grill or fry as desired.

Chicken à la King

Just Add Water

This classic dish never goes out of style. You might have to forgo the puff pastry shell at the campfire, but biscuits would be just as nice alongside.

Tip
Dried chicken tends to keep a toothsome texture even when rehydrated. Chopping it into very small pieces does help to soften it.

Prep at Home

1 oz	Maple and Grainy Dijon Chicken Jerky or Sea Salt and Peppercorn Chicken Jerky, finely chopped	30 g
1 tbsp	dried onion pieces	15 mL
1 tbsp	dried mushroom slices, crumbled	15 mL
1 tbsp	dried carrot pieces	15 mL
1 tbsp	dried green peas	15 mL
1 tbsp	instant skim milk powder	15 mL
1 tbsp	all-purpose flour	15 mL
1/4 tsp	crumbled dried thyme	1 mL
1/4 tsp	dry mustard	1 mL
1/4 tsp	salt	1 mL
	Freshly ground black pepper	

To Serve

1 1/2 cups	water	375 mL

Prep at Home

1. In a sealable plastic bag, combine chicken, onions, mushrooms, carrots, peas, milk powder, flour, thyme, mustard, salt and pepper to taste. Seal and store at room temperature for up to 1 month.

To Serve

1. In a saucepan, combine chicken mixture and water. Cover and let stand for 30 minutes or until chicken starts to soften.

2. Uncover and bring to a boil over medium heat, stirring constantly. Reduce heat and simmer, stirring often, for about 15 minutes or until chicken and vegetables are tender and liquid is slightly thickened.

Orange and Sweet Pepper Chicken

Makes 1 serving

Just Add Water

Oranges and red bell peppers are such a fresh-tasting combination, you won't believe you made this dish from dried ingredients. Serve it over rice or pasta.

Tip

This is a thin sauce that soaks nicely into rice or pasta. If you prefer a thickened sauce, whisk ½ tsp (2 mL) cornstarch into 1 tbsp (15 mL) cold water and stir into the sauce for the last 2 minutes of cooking.

Prep at Home

1 oz	Sea Salt and Peppercorn Chicken Jerky or Teriyaki Chicken Jerky, finely chopped	30 g
2 tbsp	dried red bell pepper slices	25 mL
1 tbsp	dried onion slices	15 mL
1 tbsp	dried carrot slices	15 mL
½ tsp	finely chopped dried orange zest	2 mL
¼ tsp	salt	1 mL
¼ tsp	paprika	1 mL
	Freshly ground black pepper	

To Serve

1¼ cups	water	300 mL

Prep at Home

1. In a sealable plastic bag, combine chicken, red peppers, onions, carrots, orange zest, salt, paprika and pepper to taste. Seal and store at room temperature for up to 1 month.

To Serve

1. In a saucepan, combine chicken mixture and water. Cover and let stand for 30 minutes or until chicken starts to soften.

2. Uncover and bring to a boil over medium heat, stirring constantly. Reduce heat and simmer, stirring often, for about 15 minutes or until chicken and vegetables are tender and liquid is slightly thickened.

Fresh Addition

Omit the dried chicken when prepping at home and add 4 oz (125 g) fresh chicken, thinly sliced, to the saucepan after it comes to a simmer; simmer until chicken is no longer pink inside.

Lemon Honey Garlic Chicken

Even if you're hundreds of miles away from the nearest Chinese takeout, you can have a fast dinner with that classic flavor you love. It's worth toting a few fresh ingredients for the best lemon and honey taste. Serve over rice or noodles.

Tip

This is a thin sauce that nicely soaks into rice or coats noodles. If you prefer a thickened sauce, whisk ½ tsp (2 mL) cornstarch into 1 tbsp (15 mL) cold water and stir into the sauce for the last 2 minutes of cooking.

Prep at Home

1 oz	Teriyaki Chicken Jerky, finely chopped	30 g
1 tbsp	dried green bean pieces	15 mL
1 tbsp	dried onion pieces	15 mL
1 tsp	crumbled dried parsley	5 mL
½ tsp	finely chopped dried garlic	2 mL
½ tsp	finely chopped dried lemon zest	2 mL
Pinch	salt	Pinch
Pinch	hot pepper flakes	Pinch

To Serve

1 cup	water	250 mL
2 tbsp	freshly squeezed lemon juice	25 mL
1 tsp	liquid honey	5 mL

Prep at Home

1. In a sealable plastic bag, combine chicken, green beans, onions, parsley, garlic, lemon zest, salt and hot pepper flakes. Seal and store at room temperature for up to 1 month.

To Serve

1. In a saucepan, combine chicken mixture and water. Cover and let stand for 30 minutes or until chicken starts to soften.

2. Uncover and bring to a boil over medium heat, stirring constantly. Reduce heat and simmer, stirring often, for about 15 minutes or until chicken and vegetables are tender and liquid is slightly thickened. Stir in lemon juice and honey.

Pan-Seared Chicken with a Side of Stuffing

Makes 1 serving

When you bring fresh chicken along with you to camp, pair it with this delicious "stuffing" mix that you make with your own dried ingredients and you'll think it's a special occasion. You might just find yourself making it even when you're not heading out on the trail.

Tips

Use a chicken breast that is no thicker than about ½ inch (1 cm) to make sure it cooks quickly in the skillet. If your chicken is thicker, cut it in half horizontally to butterfly it, or cut it into strips.

Prep at Home

1 tbsp	dried celery slices	15 mL
1 tbsp	chopped dried apple slices or cranberries	15 mL
1 tbsp	dried red bell pepper pieces	15 mL
2 tsp	dried onion pieces, preferably roasted onion	10 mL
1 tsp	crumbled dried sage, basil, oregano and/or thyme	5 mL
½ tsp	finely chopped dried garlic	2 mL
⅛ tsp	salt	0.5 mL
	Freshly ground black pepper	
½ cup	coarse dried bread crumbs	125 mL

To Serve

1 tsp	butter or vegetable oil	5 mL
1	boneless skinless chicken breast (see tip, at left)	1
	Salt and pepper	
¾ cup	water	175 mL

Prep at Home

1. In a sealable plastic bag, combine celery, apples, red peppers, onions, sage, garlic, salt and pepper to taste. Place bread crumbs in another bag. Seal both bags and store at room temperature for up to 1 month.

To Serve

1. In a small saucepan or the sealable plastic bag, combine vegetable mixture and water. Cover or seal and let stand for 15 minutes or until vegetables start to soften.

2. Meanwhile, season chicken with salt and pepper. Heat a skillet over medium-high heat until hot. Reduce heat to medium, add oil and swirl to coat pan. Add chicken and cook, turning once and adjusting heat as necessary to prevent burning, for about 10 minutes or until both sides are well browned and chicken is no longer pink inside. Set aside and keep warm, if necessary.

3. Uncover saucepan or pour vegetable mixture into skillet and bring to a boil over medium heat, stirring constantly. Reduce heat and simmer, stirring often, for about 5 minutes or until vegetables are tender. Gently stir in bread crumbs. Remove from heat, cover and let stand for 5 minutes or until liquid is absorbed.

Almost-Instant Mac and Cheese

Makes 1 serving

Just Add Water

Made from scratch, this macaroni and cheese, which needs just a couple of minutes on the stove to heat up, might just become your new favorite.

No-Heat Option

Decrease the water to ¾ cup (175 mL), increase the soaking time to 30 to 45 minutes and stir the macaroni mixture occasionally while it's soaking. For best results, grind the dried cottage cheese to a powder in a mini chopper or blender instead of crumbling.

Prep at Home

1 cup	dried cooked macaroni	250 mL
2 tbsp	crumbled dried cottage cheese	25 mL
2 tbsp	skim milk powder	25 mL
¼ tsp	dry mustard	1 mL
¼ tsp	crumbled dried basil (optional)	1 mL
	Salt and pepper	

To Serve

1 cup	water	250 mL

Prep at Home

1. In a sealable plastic bag, combine macaroni, cottage cheese, milk powder, mustard, basil (if using) and salt and pepper to taste. Seal and store at room temperature for up to 2 weeks or refrigerate for up to 3 months.

To Serve

1. In a saucepan, combine macaroni mixture and water. Let stand for 15 minutes or until pasta is softened.

2. Bring to a boil over medium heat, stirring constantly. Reduce heat and boil gently, stirring often, for about 1 minute or until sauce is reduced and thickened.

Fresh Additions

Add drained canned tuna or fresh grilled fish.

Add chopped fresh tomatoes or the traditional squeeze of ketchup.

Chili Mac and Cheese

Just Add Water

Give macaroni and cheese a zesty kick with some spices and a crunchy topping.

No-Heat Option

Decrease the water to ¾ cup (175 mL), increase the soaking time to 30 to 45 minutes and stir the macaroni mixture occasionally while it's soaking. For best results, grind the dried cottage cheese to a powder in a mini chopper or blender instead of crumbling.

Prep at Home

1 cup	dried cooked macaroni	250 mL
2 tbsp	crumbled dried cottage cheese	25 mL
1 tbsp	finely chopped dried tomatoes	15 mL
1 tbsp	instant skim milk powder	15 mL
¼ tsp	crumbled dried oregano	1 mL
¼ tsp	chili powder	1 mL
⅛ tsp	ground cumin	0.5 mL
	Salt and freshly ground black pepper	
¼ cup	crumbled tortilla chips	50 mL

To Serve

1 cup	water	250 mL

Prep at Home

1. In a sealable plastic bag, combine macaroni, cottage cheese, tomatoes, milk powder, oregano, chili powder, cumin and salt and pepper to taste. Place tortilla chips in another bag. Seal both bags and store at room temperature for up to 2 weeks (or refrigerate macaroni mixture for up to 3 months).

To Serve

1. In a saucepan, combine macaroni mixture and water. Let stand for 15 minutes or until pasta is softened.

2. Bring to a boil over medium heat, stirring constantly. Reduce heat and boil gently, stirring often, for about 1 minute or until sauce is reduced and thickened. Sprinkle tortilla chips over top.

Fresh Additions

Brown some ground beef in a skillet and stir into macaroni before topping with tortilla chips.

Squeeze a little lime juice on top or add a dollop of salsa.

No-Cook Pasta and Sauce

Just Add Water

No Heat Required

Pack this as a "just in case" meal for the time when you run out of camp stove fuel or the fire just won't start. Dried cooked pasta rehydrates wonderfully in room-temperature water. You'll never eat that stuff out of a can again.

Tip

This can be served hot. Just combine in a saucepan instead of a bowl, let stand as directed, then uncover and heat over medium heat until bubbling.

Prep at Home

1	4-inch (10 cm) square Tomato Pasta Sauce Leather	1
1 cup	dried cooked fusilli	250 mL
1 tbsp	grated Parmesan cheese	15 mL
½ tsp	crumbled dried basil or oregano	2 mL
Pinch	freshly ground black pepper	Pinch

To Serve

1 cup	water	250 mL

Prep at Home

1. Tear leather into small pieces. In a sealable plastic bag, combine leather, fusilli, Parmesan, basil and pepper. Seal and store at room temperature for up to 2 weeks or refrigerate for up to 3 months.

To Serve

1. In a bowl, combine leather mixture and water. Cover and let stand for 30 minutes, mashing leather occasionally, until pasta is tender.

One-Pot Simple Spaghetti

Just Add Water

The tomato sauce leather and jerky pack such a punch of flavor, you won't believe how fast and easy this one-pot meal is.

Tip

The smaller the leather pieces are, the better the texture of the sauce once it's rehydrated.

Prep at Home

1	2-inch (5 cm) square Tomato Pasta Sauce Leather	1
2 tbsp	crumbled Herb and Garlic Ground Beef Jerky	25 mL
1 tbsp	dried mushroom slices	15 mL
1 tbsp	finely chopped dried tomatoes	15 mL
1/4 tsp	salt	1 mL
Pinch	hot pepper flakes	Pinch
1/2 cup	broken spaghettini	125 mL

To Serve

1 1/2 cups	water	375 mL

Prep at Home

1. Tear leather into small pieces. In a sealable plastic bag, combine leather, beef, mushrooms, tomatoes, salt and hot pepper flakes. Place spaghettini in another bag. Seal both bags and store at room temperature for up to 1 month.

To Serve

1. In a saucepan, combine leather mixture and water. Let stand for 30 minutes or until mushrooms are softened.

2. Bring to a boil over medium heat, stirring often. Stir in spaghettini. Reduce heat and boil gently, stirring occasionally, for about 8 minutes or until pasta is tender and sauce is reduced and thickened.

> **Fresh Addition**
> Top with freshly grated Parmesan cheese or another shredded cheese.

Veggie Pasta

Makes 1 serving

Just Add Water

Color and flavor abound in this just-add-water pasta dish. Serve it on its own or as a side to grilled steak, sausage or fish.

Variation

Substitute other dried vegetables in your pantry for the mushrooms, zucchini or peppers. Try roasted onions, asparagus, hot chile peppers or green peas.

Prep at Home

1 cup	dried cooked fusilli	250 mL
2 tbsp	finely chopped dried tomatoes	25 mL
1 tbsp	dried mushroom slices, crumbled	15 mL
1 tbsp	dried zucchini slices	15 mL
1 tbsp	dried bell pepper pieces	15 mL
1 tbsp	grated Parmesan cheese	15 mL
1/2 tsp	crumbled dried basil	2 mL
1/4 tsp	crumbled dried oregano	1 mL
1/4 tsp	finely chopped dried garlic	1 mL
1/4 tsp	salt	1 mL
	Freshly ground black pepper	

To Serve

1 1/4 cups	water	300 mL

Prep at Home

1. In a sealable plastic bag, combine fusilli, tomatoes, mushrooms, zucchini, bell peppers, Parmesan, basil, oregano, garlic, salt and pepper to taste. Seal and store at room temperature for up to 2 weeks or refrigerate for up to 3 months.

To Serve

1. In a saucepan, combine fusilli mixture and water. Let stand for 20 minutes or until vegetables start to soften.

2. Bring to a boil over medium heat, stirring constantly. Reduce heat and boil gently, stirring often, for about 3 minutes or until pasta and vegetables are tender and liquid is reduced.

Shrimp and Herb Pasta

Just Add Water

A primavera-style pasta makes a nice meal on a steamy summer night. If you've packed some white wine, chill it in the lake and uncork it (or unscrew it!) to enjoy with this dinner.

Variations

Substitute chopped dried asparagus or green beans for the peas.

Use whatever herbs you like. Tarragon, sage or rosemary would also be nice.

Prep at Home

1/2 oz	dried shrimp, chopped into very small pieces	15 g
2 tbsp	finely chopped dried tomatoes	25 mL
1 tbsp	dried onion pieces or leek slices, finely chopped	15 mL
1 tbsp	dried green peas	15 mL
1 tbsp	instant skim milk powder	15 mL
1/2 tsp	crumbled dried roasted garlic	2 mL
1/2 tsp	crumbled dried basil	2 mL
1/4 tsp	crumbled dried oregano	1 mL
Pinch	crumbled dried thyme	Pinch
1/4 tsp	salt	1 mL
	Freshly ground black pepper	
1 cup	dried cooked fusilli	250 mL

To Serve

1 1/4 cups	water	300 mL

Prep at Home

1. In a sealable plastic bag, combine shrimp, tomatoes, onions, peas, milk powder, garlic, basil, oregano, thyme, salt and pepper to taste. Place fusilli in another bag. Seal both bags and store at room temperature for up to 2 weeks or refrigerate for up to 3 months.

To Serve

1. In a saucepan or skillet, bring water to a boil. Add shrimp mixture, remove from heat, cover and let stand for 20 minutes or until shrimp are softened.

2. Stir in fusilli and bring to a boil over medium heat, stirring often. Boil, stirring often, for about 5 minutes or until pasta and vegetables are tender.

Thai Noodles

Makes 1 serving

Just Add Water

The peanuts add body, as well as protein, to the sauce. Add in the vegetables, ginger and a kick of heat, and this noodle dish is sure to satisfy you on an active day.

Variation

Add ¼ cup (50 mL) crumbled dried tofu or ½ oz (15 g) dried shrimp, chopped into very small pieces, with the vegetable mixture; increase the water to 1½ cups (375 mL) and increase the soaking time in step 1 to 30 minutes.

Prep at Home

2 tbsp	finely ground roasted peanuts	25 mL
2 tbsp	dried grated carrots	25 mL
1 tbsp	dried red bell pepper slices	15 mL
1 tbsp	dried leek or shallot slices	15 mL
½ tsp	finely chopped dried lime zest	2 mL
½ tsp	finely chopped dried gingerroot	2 mL
½ tsp	crumbled dried mint or cilantro	2 mL
¼ tsp	salt	1 mL
⅛ tsp	hot pepper flakes (or to taste)	0.5 mL
1 cup	broken rice vermicelli noodles	250 mL

To Serve

1⅓ cups	water	325 mL

Prep at Home

1. In a sealable plastic bag, combine peanuts, carrots, red peppers, leeks, lime zest, ginger, mint, salt and hot pepper flakes. Place noodles in another bag. Seal both bags and store at room temperature for up to 1 month.

To Serve

1. In a saucepan, combine vegetable mixture and water. Let stand for 15 minutes or until vegetables are softened.

2. Stir in noodles and bring to a boil over medium heat, stirring often. Boil, stirring often, for about 5 minutes or until noodles and vegetables are tender.

Jerky and Vegetable Pasta Salad

Makes 1 serving

All you need to do is boil water to make this delicious pasta salad. Get it started, then set up camp. By the time the tent is up, your dinner will be soaked and ready to eat.

Variation

Omit the dried herbs when prepping at home and replace the vinegar and oil with 1 tbsp (15 mL) prepared basil pesto or other pesto.

No-Heat Option

Decrease the water to ¾ cup (175 mL) and increase the soaking time to 30 to 45 minutes. Omit the vinegar and oil, if desired.

Prep at Home

½ oz	Maple and Grainy Dijon Jerky or Cajun Jerky	15 g
2 tbsp	finely chopped dried tomatoes	25 mL
1 tbsp	dried zucchini slices	15 mL
1 tbsp	dried asparagus or green bean pieces	15 mL
½ tsp	crumbled dried basil	2 mL
¼ tsp	crumbled dried rosemary	1 mL
¼ tsp	finely chopped dried garlic	1 mL
1 cup	dried cooked fusilli	250 mL
1 tbsp	grated Parmesan cheese	15 mL
¼ tsp	salt	1 mL
	Freshly ground black pepper	

To Serve

1 cup	water	250 mL
1 tbsp	vinegar (any flavor)	15 mL
1 tsp	olive or vegetable oil	5 mL

Prep at Home

1. In a sealable plastic bag, combine jerky, tomatoes, zucchini, asparagus, basil, rosemary and garlic. In another bag, combine fusilli, Parmesan, salt and pepper to taste. Seal both bags and store at room temperature for up to 2 weeks or refrigerate for up to 3 months.

To Serve

1. In a saucepan, bring water to a boil. Add jerky mixture, remove from heat, cover and let stand for 10 minutes or until jerky and vegetables start to soften.

2. Stir in fusilli mixture, cover and let stand for about 20 minutes or until pasta is tender and cooled to room temperature. Stir in vinegar and oil.

Caribbean Spiced Rice and Beans

Makes 1 serving

Just Add Water

Spiced-up rice is very nice. This classic dish gives a tropical twist to your meal.

Tip
Heating the water before adding the rice mixture speeds up the soaking time and gives a better texture to the rice. If you don't want to fire up the stove twice, you can soak the mixture in cold water for about 1 hour or until the rice is softened.

Prep at Home

1/3 cup	dried cooked long-grain brown or white rice	75 mL
1/4 cup	dried cooked kidney or black beans	50 mL
1 tbsp	dried grated carrots	15 mL
1 tbsp	finely chopped dried pineapple	15 mL
1 tsp	finely chopped dried onions	5 mL
1/2 tsp	curry powder	2 mL
1/4 tsp	salt	1 mL
Pinch	ground allspice or ginger	Pinch
Pinch	hot pepper flakes (optional)	Pinch

To Serve

1 1/4 cups	water	300 mL

Prep at Home

1. In a sealable plastic bag, combine rice, beans, carrots, pineapple, onions, curry powder, salt, allspice and hot pepper flakes (if using). Seal and store at room temperature for up to 2 weeks or refrigerate for up to 1 month.

To Serve

1. In a saucepan or skillet, bring water to a boil. Add rice mixture, remove from heat, cover and let stand for 15 minutes or until rice is softened.

2. Uncover and bring to a boil over medium heat, stirring often. Boil, stirring often, for about 5 minutes or until mixture is hot and liquid is absorbed.

Fresh Addition
Serve with fresh lime or lemon wedges to squeeze over top.

Cajun Rice and Black Beans

Just Add Water

Jumping with flavor and color, this rice and bean dish is sure to spice up your meal.

Tips

Heating the water before adding the rice mixture speeds up the soaking time and gives a better texture to the rice. If you don't want to fire up the stove twice, you can soak the mixture in cold water for about 1 hour or until the rice is softened.

If you like it fiery, use a generous pinch or $^1/_8$ tsp (0.5 mL) cayenne pepper.

Prep at Home

$^1/_3$ cup	dried cooked long-grain brown rice	75 mL
$^1/_4$ cup	dried cooked black beans	50 mL
2 tbsp	finely chopped dried tomatoes	25 mL
1 tbsp	dried onion pieces	15 mL
1 tbsp	dried celery slices	15 mL
1 tbsp	dried green bell pepper pieces	15 mL
$^1/_4$ tsp	salt	1 mL
$^1/_4$ tsp	crumbled dried thyme	1 mL
$^1/_4$ tsp	paprika	1 mL
Pinch	cayenne pepper	Pinch

To Serve

1$^1/_3$ cups	water	325 mL

Prep at Home

1. In a sealable plastic bag, combine rice, beans, tomatoes, onions, celery, green peppers, salt, thyme, paprika and cayenne. Seal and store at room temperature for up to 1 month.

To Serve

1. In a saucepan or skillet, bring water to a boil. Add rice mixture, remove from heat, cover and let stand for 15 minutes or until rice is softened.

2. Uncover and bring to a boil over medium heat, stirring often. Boil, stirring often, for about 5 minutes or until mixture is hot and liquid is absorbed.

Cajun Shrimp and Rice

Makes 1 serving

Just Add Water

A quick version of jambalaya will elevate your camp cuisine to new heights.

Tips

Heating the water before adding the rice mixture speeds up the soaking time and gives a better texture to the rice. If you don't want to fire up the stove twice, you can soak the mixture in cold water for about 1 hour or until the rice is softened.

Dried shrimp tends to keep a firm texture even when rehydrated. Chopping it into very small pieces does help to soften it.

Variations

Add 1 tbsp (15 mL) finely chopped smoked pepperette sausage or Cajun Chicken Jerky to the shrimp mixture.

Use a 2-inch (5 cm) square of Tomato Pasta Sauce Leather, torn into very small pieces, in place of the dried tomatoes.

Prep at Home

½ oz	dried cooked shrimp, chopped into very small pieces	15 g
⅓ cup	dried cooked long-grain brown or white rice	75 mL
2 tbsp	finely chopped dried tomatoes	25 mL
1 tbsp	dried onion pieces	15 mL
1 tbsp	dried red bell pepper pieces	15 mL
½ tsp	crumbled dried parsley	2 mL
¼ tsp	crumbled dried thyme	1 mL
¼ tsp	salt	1 mL
⅛ tsp	cayenne pepper	0.5 mL

To Serve

1¼ cups	water	300 mL

Prep at Home

1. In a sealable plastic bag, combine shrimp, rice, tomatoes, onions, red peppers, parsley, thyme, salt and cayenne. Seal and store at room temperature for up to 1 month.

To Serve

1. In a saucepan or skillet, bring water to a boil. Add shrimp mixture, remove from heat, cover and let stand for 15 minutes or until rice is softened.

2. Uncover and bring to a boil over medium heat, stirring often. Boil, stirring often, for about 5 minutes or until mixture is hot and liquid is absorbed.

Beef and Veggie Fried Rice

Makes 1 serving

This one-dish meal has lots of color and texture to delight the eye and the palate. Save up those packets of soy sauce when you get takeout and pack them to add that extra burst of flavor.

Tip

Heating the water before adding the rice mixture speeds up the soaking time and gives a better texture to the rice. If you don't want to fire up the stove twice, you can soak the mixture in cold water for about 1 hour or until the rice is softened.

Prep at Home

½ oz	Teriyaki Beef Jerky or Asian Ground Meat Jerky, broken into small pieces	15 g
⅓ cup	dried cooked long-grain brown or white rice	75 mL
1 tbsp	dried onion pieces	15 mL
1 tbsp	dried carrot slices	15 mL
1 tbsp	dried green or red bell pepper pieces	15 mL
1 tbsp	dried broccoli florets, broken into small pieces	15 mL
¼ tsp	finely chopped dried garlic	1 mL
¼ tsp	finely chopped dried gingerroot	1 mL
Pinch	hot pepper flakes	Pinch

To Serve

1⅓ cups	water	325 mL
1 tbsp	soy sauce (or to taste)	15 mL

Prep at Home

1. In a sealable plastic bag, combine beef, rice, onions, carrots, green peppers, broccoli, garlic, ginger and hot pepper flakes. Seal and store at room temperature for up to 1 month.

To Serve

1. In a saucepan or skillet, bring water to a boil. Add beef mixture, remove from heat, cover and let stand for 15 minutes or until rice is softened.

2. Uncover and bring to a boil over medium heat, stirring often. Boil, stirring often, for about 5 minutes or until mixture is hot and liquid is absorbed. Stir in soy sauce.

Chicken Fried Rice

Just Add Water

This classic fried rice dish can be made with ease at camp. When you use your homemade seasoned jerky and dried vegetables, you know you're eating only the most wholesome ingredients.

Tip

Heating the water before adding the chicken mixture speeds up the soaking time and gives a better texture to the rice. If you don't want to fire up the stove twice, you can soak the mixture in cold water for about 1 hour or until the rice is softened.

Prep at Home

½ oz	Asian Ground Chicken Jerky, broken into small pieces	15 g
⅓ cup	dried cooked long-grain brown or white rice	75 mL
1 tbsp	dried onion pieces	15 mL
1 tbsp	dried celery slices	15 mL
1 tbsp	dried mushroom slices	15 mL
1 tbsp	dried green peas	15 mL
¼ tsp	finely chopped dried gingerroot	1 mL
¼ tsp	salt	1 mL

To Serve

1⅓ cups	water	325 mL

Prep at Home

1. In a sealable plastic bag, combine chicken, rice, onions, celery, mushrooms, peas, ginger and salt. Seal and store at room temperature for up to 1 month.

To Serve

1. In a saucepan or skillet, bring water to a boil. Add chicken mixture, remove from heat, cover and let stand for 15 minutes or until rice is softened.

2. Uncover and bring to a boil over medium heat, stirring often. Boil, stirring often, for about 5 minutes or until mixture is hot and liquid is absorbed.

> **Fresh Addition**
> Cook a scrambled egg and add it to the fried rice for extra protein and flavor.

Easy Mushroom Risotto

Just Add Water

Although risotto is usually made with short-grain rice, this version uses slightly chopped long-grain rice, with added creaminess from the cottage cheese. It's sure to earn you a reputation as a campsite gourmet.

Variation

Substitute 1 tsp (5 mL) crumbled roasted garlic for the plain dried garlic.

Prep at Home

½ cup	dried cooked long-grain white or brown rice	125 mL
2 tbsp	dried mushroom slices, crumbled	25 mL
1 tbsp	finely chopped dried leeks or onions	15 mL
1 tbsp	powdered dried cottage cheese	15 mL
½ tsp	finely chopped dried garlic	2 mL
½ tsp	crumbled dried tarragon	2 mL
¼ tsp	salt	1 mL
	Freshly ground black pepper	

To Serve

1 cup	water	250 mL

Prep at Home

1. In a mini chopper, pulse rice until chopped and about one-quarter is powdery. Transfer to a sealable plastic bag and add mushrooms, leeks, cottage cheese, garlic, tarragon, salt and pepper to taste. Seal and store at room temperature for up to 1 month.

To Serve

1. In a saucepan, combine rice mixture and water. Cover and let stand for 30 minutes or until mushrooms are softened.

2. Uncover and bring to a boil over medium heat, stirring often. Reduce heat to low, cover and simmer, stirring twice, for about 10 minutes or until rice is tender. Uncover and simmer, stirring, until liquid is absorbed and rice is creamy.

Chicken and Tomato Risotto

Makes 1 serving

Just Add Water

Dried tomatoes and a blend of herbs add lots of flavor to this hearty risotto.

Tip
Dried chicken tends to keep a toothsome texture even when rehydrated. Chopping it into very small pieces does help to soften it.

Prep at Home

½ cup	dried cooked long-grain white rice	125 mL
1 oz	Sea Salt and Peppercorn Chicken Jerky, finely chopped	30 g
2 tbsp	chopped dried tomatoes	25 mL
1 tbsp	powdered dried cottage cheese	15 mL
½ tsp	crumbled dried basil	2 mL
¼ tsp	crumbled dried oregano	1 mL
¼ tsp	finely chopped dried garlic	1 mL
Pinch	crumbled dried rosemary	Pinch
¼ tsp	salt	1 mL
	Freshly ground black pepper	

To Serve

1¼ cups	water	300 mL

Prep at Home
1. In a mini chopper, pulse rice until chopped and about one-quarter is powdery. Transfer to a sealable plastic bag and add chicken, tomatoes, cottage cheese, basil, oregano, garlic, rosemary, salt and pepper to taste. Seal and store at room temperature for up to 2 weeks or refrigerate for up to 3 months.

To Serve
1. In a saucepan, combine rice mixture and water. Cover and let stand for 30 minutes or until chicken starts to soften.

2. Uncover and bring to a boil over medium heat, stirring often. Reduce heat to low, cover and simmer, stirring twice, for about 10 minutes or until rice is tender. Uncover and simmer, stirring, until liquid is absorbed and rice is creamy.

Smoked Sausage Risotto

Makes 1 serving

Just Add Water

With its fabulous flavor and satisfying texture, this quick risotto will have you singing "O Sole Mio" around the campfire.

Tips

It is best to buy prepared dried sausage, as it is difficult to get a safe product when drying sausage at home.

Short-grain rice is traditionally used for risotto, but it doesn't dry and rehydrate as well as long-grain. Pulsing the rice in the mini chopper first adds some creaminess to the texture.

Variation

In place of sausage, substitute crumbled Herb and Garlic Ground Meat Jerky or Southwestern Ground Meat Jerky.

Prep at Home

½ cup	dried cooked long-grain white rice	125 mL
1	2-inch (5 cm) square Tomato Pasta Sauce Leather	1
¼ cup	thinly sliced dried smoked pepperette sausage (see tip, at left)	50 mL
1 tbsp	dried onion pieces	15 mL
1 tbsp	grated Parmesan cheese	15 mL
½ tsp	crumbled dried basil	2 mL
Pinch	salt	Pinch
	Freshly ground black pepper	

To Serve

1¼ cups	water	300 mL

Prep at Home

1. In a mini chopper, pulse rice until chopped and about one-quarter is powdery. Tear leather into small pieces. In a sealable plastic bag, combine rice, leather, sausage, onions, Parmesan, basil, salt and pepper to taste. Seal and store at room temperature for up to 2 weeks or refrigerate for up to 3 months.

To Serve

1. In a saucepan, combine rice mixture and water. Cover and let stand for 30 minutes, mashing leather occasionally, until leather is soft.

2. Uncover and bring to a boil over medium heat, stirring often. Reduce heat to low, cover and simmer, stirring twice, for about 10 minutes or until rice is tender. Uncover and simmer, stirring, until liquid is absorbed and rice is creamy.

Moroccan Couscous with Chickpeas

Makes 1 serving

Just Add Water

When spiked with spices, dried fruit and the added protein of chickpeas, couscous makes a quick meal that gives a touch of the exotic to your campsite.

Tip

To toast a small amount of nuts, in a small dry skillet over medium heat, toast chopped nuts, stirring constantly, for about 2 minutes or until fragrant. Transfer to a bowl and let cool.

No-Heat Option

When prepping at home, pulse couscous in a mini chopper or blender until finely ground and fairly powdery. Decrease the water to ½ cup (125 mL), increase the soaking time to 45 minutes and stir the couscous mixture occasionally while it's soaking.

Prep at Home

2 tbsp	dried cooked chickpeas	25 mL
1 tbsp	dried grated carrots	15 mL
1 tbsp	chopped dried apricots	15 mL
1 tbsp	raisins	15 mL
¼ tsp	ground cumin	1 mL
¼ tsp	ground coriander	1 mL
⅛ tsp	salt	0.5 mL
Pinch	finely chopped dried orange or lemon zest	Pinch
Pinch	ground cinnamon	Pinch
Pinch	cayenne pepper or black pepper	Pinch
¼ cup	couscous (preferably whole wheat)	50 mL
1 tbsp	toasted sliced almonds	15 mL

To Serve

⅔ cup	water	150 mL

Prep at Home

1. In a sealable plastic bag, combine chickpeas, carrots, apricots, raisins, cumin, coriander, salt, orange zest, cinnamon and cayenne. In another bag, combine couscous and almonds. Seal both bags and store at room temperature for up to 1 month.

To Serve

1. In a saucepan, combine chickpea mixture and water. Let stand for 30 minutes or until chickpeas are softened.

2. Bring to a boil over high heat, stirring often. Remove from heat and stir in couscous mixture. Cover and let stand for 5 minutes or until liquid is absorbed. Fluff with a fork.

> **Fresh Addition**
>
> Sprinkle 1 tbsp (15 mL) freshly squeezed orange or lemon juice over top, or serve with orange wedges.

Wheat Berries Parmesan

Just Add Water

Wheat berries have a toothsome texture and make a nice change from rice or pasta. This recipe is hearty enough for a main course and is also nice as a side dish.

Variation

Replace the leather with 1 tbsp (15 mL) finely chopped dried tomatoes and add $\frac{1}{4}$ tsp (1 mL) crumbled dried roasted garlic or minced dried garlic and an extra $\frac{1}{4}$ tsp (1 mL) dried basil.

Prep at Home

1	2-inch (5 cm) square Tomato Pasta Sauce Leather	1
$\frac{1}{2}$ cup	dried cooked wheat berries	125 mL
1 tbsp	grated Parmesan cheese	15 mL
$\frac{1}{4}$ tsp	crumbled dried basil	1 mL
	Freshly ground black pepper	

To Serve

1 cup	water	250 mL

Prep at Home

1. Tear leather into small pieces. In a sealable plastic bag, combine leather, wheat berries, Parmesan, basil and pepper to taste. Seal and store at room temperature for up to 2 weeks or refrigerate for up to 1 month.

To Serve

1. In a saucepan, combine leather mixture and water. Let stand for 30 minutes, mashing leather occasionally, until wheat berries start to soften.

2. Bring to a boil over medium heat, stirring often. Reduce heat and boil gently, stirring often, for about 10 minutes or until wheat berries are tender and liquid is absorbed.

Campfire Pizza

Pizza is always a welcome dinner, and at camp it's even more of a treat. Whether you cook over a campfire or have a camp oven (or eat it cold), the rich tomato sauce and vegetable topping is sure to satisfy your craving for 'za!

Variation

Change the vegetables to suit your tastes. Try dried broccoli, tomatoes, hot peppers, roasted onions and/or eggplant.

No-Heat Option

Soak the vegetables in cold water for about 30 minutes or until softened, then drain. Add the Parmesan with the tomato sauce and spread over pita, then top with vegetables and skip the baking step.

- Grill rack or flat rocks to place close to fire

Prep at Home

1	4-inch (10 cm) square Tomato Sauce Leather	1
1/2 tsp	crumbled dried oregano	2 mL
1 tbsp	crumbled dried mushroom slices	15 mL
1 tbsp	dried red or green bell pepper pieces	15 mL
1 tbsp	dried zucchini slices	15 mL
2 tbsp	grated Parmesan cheese	25 mL

To Serve

1/3 cup	water, divided	75 mL
1	6-inch (15 cm) whole wheat pita or English muffin, split	1

Prep at Home

1. Tear leather into very small pieces. In a sealable plastic bag, combine leather and oregano. In another bag, combine mushrooms, bell peppers and zucchini. Place Parmesan in another bag. Seal bags and store at room temperature for up to 2 weeks or refrigerate for up to 3 months.

To Serve

1. Preheat camp oven or prepare a campfire and place grill rack, if using, just off to the side, over the fire.

2. In the sealable plastic bag or a bowl, combine leather mixture and 2 tbsp (25 mL) of the water. Seal or cover and let stand for 15 minutes, mashing leather occasionally, until saucy.

3. Meanwhile, in a saucepan, bring remaining water to a boil. Add vegetables, cover and remove from heat. Let stand for about 10 minutes or until softened. Drain well.

4. Spread tomato sauce over pita. Sprinkle with vegetables and Parmesan cheese. Bake in camp oven or place on grill rack and cook, rotating occasionally, until pizza is hot.

Fresh Addition

Top the pizza with chopped ham, pepperoni or cooked bacon before adding the cheese.

Add shredded mozzarella cheese along with or instead of the Parmesan.

Side Dishes and Accompaniments

Warm Broccoli, Leek and Raisin Salad

Start this salad before your other dishes to give it time to soak and cool down. It makes a refreshing, tender-crisp side to fish or stew.

Prep at Home

¼ cup	dried broccoli florets	50 mL
1 tbsp	dried leek slices, finely chopped	15 mL
1 tbsp	raisins	15 mL
½ tsp	crumbled dried oregano	2 mL
¼ tsp	finely chopped lemon or orange zest	1 mL
¼ tsp	finely chopped dried garlic	1 mL
Pinch	salt	Pinch

To Serve

⅓ cup	water	75 mL
1 tbsp	olive oil	15 mL
2 tsp	lemon juice, orange juice or vinegar	10 mL

Prep at Home

1. In a sealable plastic bag, combine broccoli, leeks, raisins, oregano, lemon zest, garlic and salt. Seal and store at room temperature for up to 1 month.

To Serve

1. In a saucepan, bring water to a boil. Add broccoli mixture, remove from heat, cover and let stand for 30 minutes, stirring occasionally, until broccoli is tender and cooled to room temperature and most of the liquid is absorbed. Stir in oil and lemon juice.

Fresh Addition

Add a fresh orange, peeled and cut into segments, with the oil and juice.

Citrus-Marinated Chickpea Salad

No Heat Required

A simple salad is sometimes just what you need. Whether it's alongside grilled fresh-caught fish, a burger or a rice dish, it's sure to perk up the meal.

Tip

Instead of the lemon juice, you can use a pinch of citric acid powder (available at pharmacies and health food stores) to add tang. Add it with the dry ingredients.

Prep at Home

¹/₃ cup	dried cooked chickpeas	75 mL
2 tbsp	dried red bell pepper pieces	25 mL
1 tsp	dried red onion pieces	5 mL
¹/₂ tsp	crumbled dried tarragon	2 mL
¹/₄ tsp	finely chopped dried lemon or orange zest	1 mL
¹/₈ tsp	salt	0.5 mL
	Freshly ground black pepper	

To Serve

¹/₂ cup	water	125 mL
1 tbsp	lemon juice or orange juice	15 mL
1 tsp	olive oil	5 mL

Prep at Home

1. In a sealable plastic bag, combine chickpeas, red peppers, red onions, tarragon, lemon zest, salt and pepper to taste. Seal and store at room temperature for up to 1 month.

To Serve

1. In a bowl, combine chickpea mixture and water. Let stand for 30 minutes, stirring occasionally, until chickpeas and vegetables are softened. Stir in lemon juice and oil.

> **Fresh Addition**
> Add a fresh orange, peeled and cut into segments, with the juice.

Brown Rice, Apple and Cranberry Salad

This salad is terrific served with a biscuit as a light lunch. It also makes a satisfying side dish for grilled fish or chicken.

Tip

You can leave out the vinegar — it just adds a little fresh zing.

Prep at Home

¼ cup	dried cooked long-grain brown rice	50 mL
2 tbsp	finely chopped dried apples	25 mL
1 tbsp	dried cranberries	15 mL
1 tsp	dried leek slices or onion pieces, finely chopped (optional)	5 mL
1 tsp	crumbled dried parsley	5 mL
⅛ tsp	salt	0.5 mL
	Freshly ground black pepper	

To Serve

½ cup	water	125 mL
1 tbsp	cider vinegar or unsweetened apple juice	15 mL

Prep at Home

1. In a sealable plastic bag, combine rice, apples, cranberries, leeks (if using), parsley, salt and pepper to taste. Seal and store at room temperature for up to 1 month.

To Serve

1. In a saucepan, bring water to a boil. Add rice mixture, remove from heat, cover and let stand for 20 minutes or until rice is tender and cooled to room temperature and most of the liquid is absorbed. Stir in vinegar.

Mediterranean Vegetable Couscous

Makes 1 serving

Just Add Water

Couscous is practically instant and makes a terrific hot or cold side dish when combined with colorful Mediterranean vegetables.

Prep at Home

1 tbsp	chopped dried eggplant slices	15 mL
1 tbsp	dried red bell pepper pieces	15 mL
1 tbsp	chopped dried tomatoes	15 mL
1 tbsp	dried grated zucchini	15 mL
½ tsp	finely chopped dried garlic, preferably roasted garlic	2 mL
½ tsp	crumbled dried basil	2 mL
¼ tsp	crumbled dried oregano	1 mL
⅛ tsp	salt	0.5 mL
	Freshly ground black pepper	
⅓ cup	whole wheat couscous	75 mL

To Serve

¾ cup	water	175 mL

Prep at Home

1. In a sealable plastic bag, combine eggplant, red peppers, tomatoes, zucchini, garlic, basil, oregano, salt and pepper to taste. Place couscous in a separate bag. Seal both bags and store at room temperature for up to 1 month.

To Serve

1. In a saucepan, combine vegetable mixture and water. Let stand for 20 minutes or until vegetables start to soften.

2. Bring to a boil over high heat; reduce heat and boil gently for 2 minutes or until vegetables are almost soft. Stir in couscous. Remove from heat, cover and let stand for 5 minutes. Fluff with a fork and serve warm or let cool completely.

> **Fresh Additions**
>
> Add 1 tbsp (15 mL) red or white wine vinegar, or red or white wine, with the couscous.
>
> Top with crumbled feta cheese or goat cheese before serving.

Tabbouleh Salad

Just Add Water

No Heat Required

Cracked wheat kernels, known as bulgur, add heartiness to this fresh-tasting salad of Lebanese origin. It's delicious on its own, stuffed in a pita or as a side for grilled fish or poultry.

Tips

Fine bulgur soaks more quickly than medium or coarse grinds. If you don't have fine, you can pulse coarser bulgur in a blender or mini chopper before combining it with the vegetables.

To speed up the preparation of this dish, soak the vegetable mixture in water in a saucepan for 10 minutes, then bring to a boil over medium heat. Remove from heat and let stand for 5 minutes. Enjoy warm or let cool.

Prep at Home

3 tbsp	fine bulgur	45 mL
2 tbsp	chopped dried tomatoes	25 mL
1 tbsp	crumbled dried parsley	15 mL
1 tsp	finely chopped dried chives	5 mL
$\frac{1}{2}$ tsp	finely chopped dried garlic	2 mL
$\frac{1}{2}$ tsp	finely chopped dried lemon zest	2 mL
$\frac{1}{2}$ tsp	crumbled dried mint	2 mL
$\frac{1}{8}$ tsp	ground cumin	0.5 mL
$\frac{1}{8}$ tsp	salt	0.5 mL
	Freshly ground black pepper	

To Serve

$\frac{1}{2}$ cup	water	125 mL

Prep at Home

1. In a sealable plastic bag, combine bulgur, tomatoes, parsley, chives, garlic, lemon zest, mint, cumin, salt and pepper to taste. Seal and store at room temperature for up to 1 month.

To Serve

1. In sealable bag or a bowl, combine vegetable mixture and water. Let stand for 30 to 45 minutes or until water is absorbed and bulgur and vegetables are softened. Fluff with a fork.

> **Fresh Additions**
>
> Add 1 tbsp (15 mL) lemon juice before serving.
>
> Add drained canned tuna to this salad.

Broccoli and Cottage Cheese Gratin

Makes 1 serving

Just Add Water

Turn a classic side dish into a camp cuisine wonder. Serve alongside a meat or rice dish.

Variation
Replace half or all of the broccoli with dried cauliflower florets.

Prep at Home

¼ cup	dried broccoli florets	50 mL
1 tbsp	crumbled dried cottage cheese	15 mL
1 tsp	dried onion pieces, finely chopped	5 mL
½ tsp	powdered dried roasted garlic (optional)	2 mL
	Freshly ground black pepper	
2 tbsp	coarse dried bread crumbs	25 mL
1 tbsp	grated Parmesan cheese	15 mL

To Serve

½ cup	water	125 mL

Prep at Home

1. In a sealable plastic bag, combine broccoli, cottage cheese, onions, garlic (if using) and pepper to taste. In another bag, combine bread crumbs and Parmesan. Seal both bags and store at room temperature for up to 2 weeks or refrigerate for up to 3 months.

To Serve

1. In a saucepan, combine broccoli mixture and water. Cover and let stand for 20 minutes or until broccoli starts to soften.

2. Uncover and bring to a boil over medium heat. Reduce heat and simmer, stirring occasionally, for about 5 minutes or until broccoli is tender and most of the liquid is absorbed. Remove from heat, sprinkle with bread crumb mixture and let stand for 5 minutes.

Curried Squash and Chickpeas

Just Add Water

Pair this spiced side dish with a rice dish or grilled meat or fish.

Prep at Home

¼ cup	dried butternut squash cubes	50 mL
2 tbsp	dried cooked chickpeas	25 mL
1 tbsp	chopped dried mangos, apricots or raisins	15 mL
1 tsp	dried onion pieces	5 mL
1 tsp	crumbled dried cilantro	5 mL
¼ tsp	finely chopped dried garlic	1 mL
¼ tsp	curry powder	1 mL
¼ tsp	salt	1 mL
⅛ tsp	ground cumin	0.5 mL
⅛ tsp	ground coriander	0.5 mL
Pinch	cayenne pepper	Pinch

To Serve

½ cup	water	125 mL

Prep at Home

1. In a sealable plastic bag, combine squash, chickpeas, mangos, onions, cilantro, garlic, curry powder, salt, cumin, coriander and cayenne. Seal and store at room temperature for up to 1 month.

To Serve

1. In a saucepan, combine squash mixture and water. Cover and let stand for 20 minutes or until starting to soften.

2. Uncover and bring to a boil over medium heat, stirring often. Reduce heat and simmer, stirring occasionally, for about 10 minutes or until squash is tender and most of the liquid is absorbed.

> **Fresh Addition**
> Add a squeeze of fresh lime or lemon juice before serving.

Ratatouille

Just Add Water

This French-inspired side dish is also terrific on top of pasta, mixed with beans, with meat or fish or on top of bread. The options are endless; the results are delicious!

Tip

The leather adds body to the sauce, but if you don't have it, substitute another vegetable leather or an additional 1 tbsp (15 mL) chopped dried tomatoes.

Prep at Home

1	1-inch (2.5 cm) square Tomato Paste Leather or Tomato Sauce Leather	1
2 tbsp	chopped dried eggplant slices	25 mL
1 tbsp	chopped dried tomatoes	15 mL
1 tbsp	chopped dried zucchini slices	15 mL
1 tbsp	dried red bell pepper pieces	15 mL
1 tsp	dried red onion pieces, finely chopped	5 mL
1/2 tsp	minced dried garlic	2 mL
1/2 tsp	crumbled dried basil	2 mL
1/4 tsp	salt	1 mL
1/8 tsp	crumbled dried thyme	0.5 mL
	Freshly ground black pepper	

To Serve

1/2 cup	water	125 mL

Prep at Home

1. Tear leather into very small pieces. In a sealable plastic bag, combine leather, eggplant, tomatoes, zucchini, red peppers, onions, garlic, basil, salt, thyme and pepper to taste. Seal and store at room temperature for up to 1 month.

To Serve

1. In a saucepan, combine vegetable mixture and water. Cover and let stand for 20 minutes or until vegetables start to soften.

2. Uncover and bring to a boil over medium heat. Reduce heat and simmer, stirring occasionally and mashing leather pieces, for about 10 minutes or until vegetables are soft and most of the liquid is absorbed.

Stovetop Scalloped Potatoes

Just Add Water

You don't need an oven and an hour to bake these creamy, herb-scented potatoes. They make a nice change from rice or pasta as a side to grilled pork, steak or sausages, or even just with some flavorful jerky.

Variation

Replace ¼ cup (50 mL) of the potatoes with dried sweet potato slices.

Prep at Home

½ cup	dried potato slices	125 mL
2 tbsp	instant skim milk powder	25 mL
1 tbsp	dried onion pieces or slices	15 mL
¼ tsp	salt	1 mL
Pinch	freshly ground black pepper	Pinch
Pinch	crumbled dried rosemary (or any other herb)	Pinch

To Serve

½ cup	water	125 mL

Prep at Home

1. In a sealable plastic bag, combine potatoes, milk powder, onions, salt, pepper and rosemary. Seal and store at room temperature for up to 1 month.

To Serve

1. In a saucepan, combine potato mixture and water. Cover and let stand for 30 minutes.

2. Uncover and bring to a boil over medium heat, stirring often. Reduce heat and simmer, gently stirring occasionally, for about 10 minutes or until potatoes are tender and sauce is thickened. Remove from heat and let stand for 5 minutes.

Potatoes "Anna" and Onion Gratin

Makes 1 serving

Just Add Water

The traditional dish Pommes Anna was named for a French courtesan. We're not sure Anna did much camping, but if she did, she surely would have been very impressed with this just-add-water version.

Tip

We generally try to avoid using stock or bouillon powder because of the high salt content and added fillers, but this dish really does benefit from the extra flavor stock powder provides. Look for one that is lower in sodium and has the most natural ingredients possible.

Prep at Home

¹/₂ cup	dried potato slices	125 mL
2 tbsp	dried onion slices	25 mL
¹/₂ tsp	vegetable or chicken stock powder (see tip, at left)	2 mL
¹/₄ tsp	salt	1 mL
Pinch	freshly ground black pepper	Pinch
2 tbsp	coarse dried bread crumbs	25 mL
1 tbsp	grated Parmesan cheese	15 mL

To Serve

¹/₂ cup	water	125 mL

Prep at Home

1. In a sealable plastic bag, combine potatoes, onions, stock powder, salt and pepper. In another bag, combine bread crumbs and Parmesan. Seal both bags and store at room temperature for up to 2 weeks.

To Serve

1. In a saucepan, combine potato mixture and water. Cover and let stand for 30 minutes.

2. Uncover and bring to a boil over medium heat, stirring often. Reduce heat and simmer, gently stirring occasionally, for about 10 minutes or until potatoes are tender and liquid is almost absorbed. Remove from heat, sprinkle with bread crumb mixture and let stand for 5 minutes.

Moroccan Braised Beans and Lentils

Just Add Water

Fragrant spices and a variety of textures might make this side dish take over as the main feature of your meal.

Variation

In place of the squash, you can use a 2-inch (5 cm) square of Roasted Winter Squash Leather or Sweet Potato and Red Pepper Leather, torn into very small pieces.

Prep at Home

¼ cup	dried cooked lentils	50 mL
¼ cup	dried cooked red kidney or black beans	50 mL
1 tbsp	finely chopped dried tomatoes	15 mL
1 tbsp	finely chopped dried winter squash	15 mL
½ tsp	crumbled dried mint	2 mL
¼ tsp	finely chopped dried lemon zest	1 mL
¼ tsp	salt	1 mL
⅛ tsp	ground cinnamon	0.5 mL
⅛ tsp	ground cumin	0.5 mL
⅛ tsp	paprika	0.5 mL

To Serve

1 cup	water	250 mL

Prep at Home

1. In a sealable plastic bag, combine lentils, beans, tomatoes, squash, mint, lemon zest, salt, cinnamon, cumin and paprika. Seal and store at room temperature for up to 1 month.

To Serve

1. In a saucepan or skillet, combine lentil mixture and water. Let stand for 15 minutes or until vegetables start to soften.

2. Bring to a boil over medium heat, stirring often. Reduce heat and boil gently, stirring often, for about 5 minutes or until vegetables are tender and liquid is absorbed.

Ramen-Style Noodles with Beans, Carrots and Onions

Toss out the seasoning packet in a ramen noodle soup (it's full of stuff you wouldn't want to eat) and add your own nutritious dried vegetables instead. The noodles themselves are fast and convenient.

Variation

Add 1 tbsp (15 mL) powdered Spinach Leather with the vegetables for an extra nutrition boost.

Prep at Home

1 tbsp	dried green bean pieces	15 mL
1 tbsp	dried carrot slices	15 mL
1 tbsp	dried onion pieces	15 mL
1 tbsp	dried celery slices	15 mL
1 tsp	crumbled dried parsley	5 mL
1/2 tsp	finely chopped dried garlic	2 mL
1/4 tsp	finely chopped dried gingerroot	1 mL
1	package (about 2 1/2 oz/80 g) instant ramen noodles, broken	1

To Serve

1 cup	water	250 mL
1 tbsp	lime juice	15 mL
2 tsp	soy sauce	10 mL

Prep at Home

1. In a sealable plastic bag, combine green beans, carrots, onions, celery, parsley, garlic and ginger. Place noodles in another bag. Seal both bags and store at room temperature for up to 1 month.

To Serve

1. In a saucepan, combine vegetable mixture and water. Let stand for 30 minutes or until vegetables are softened.

2. Bring to a boil over medium heat, stirring often. Reduce heat and simmer for about 5 minutes or until vegetables are tender. Stir in noodles, lime juice and soy sauce; heat until noodles are tender.

Egg Noodles
with Teriyaki Veggies

Makes 1 serving

Colorful vegetables and tender noodles in a lightly seasoned teriyaki sauce make a terrific side dish for plain grilled chicken or fish.

Variation
Add 1 tbsp (15 mL) finely chopped dried pineapple or mango to the vegetable mixture.

Prep at Home

2 tbsp	dried green or red bell pepper slices	25 mL
1 tbsp	dried onion slices	15 mL
1 tbsp	dried carrot slices	15 mL
1 tbsp	dried green peas	15 mL
1 tsp	packed brown sugar	5 mL
1/4 tsp	finely chopped dried gingerroot	1 mL
1/2 cup	fine egg noodles	125 mL

To Serve

2/3 cup	water	150 mL
1 tbsp	thin teriyaki sauce	15 mL

Prep at Home
1. In a sealable plastic bag, combine green peppers, onions, carrots, peas, brown sugar and ginger. Place noodles in another bag. Seal both bags and store at room temperature for up to 1 month.

To Serve
1. In a saucepan, combine vegetable mixture and water. Let stand for 15 minutes or until vegetables are softened.

2. Bring to a boil over medium heat, stirring often. Stir in noodles and teriyaki sauce. Reduce heat and boil gently, stirring often, for about 5 minutes or until vegetables and noodles are tender.

Spanish Brown Rice

Makes 1 serving

Just Add Water

Seriously, a recipe with three ingredients that tastes great? You have to try it to believe it.

Variation

If you don't have salsa leather, use 2 tsp (10 mL) finely chopped dried tomatoes, 1 tsp (5 mL) finely chopped dried red bell peppers and a pinch of cayenne pepper.

No-Heat Option

Reduce water to $\frac{1}{4}$ cup (50 mL) and soak vegetable mixture in sealable bag or a covered bowl for at least 1 hour or for up to 24 hours. Add a little more water to moisten, if necessary.

Prep at Home

1	2-inch (5 cm) square Salsa Leather	1
$\frac{1}{3}$ cup	dried cooked long-grain brown rice	75 mL
$\frac{1}{4}$ tsp	crumbled dried thyme	1 mL

To Serve

$\frac{1}{2}$ cup	water	125 mL

Prep at Home

1. Tear leather into small pieces. In a sealable plastic bag, combine leather, rice and thyme. Seal and store at room temperature for up to 1 month.

To Serve

1. In a saucepan or skillet, bring water to a boil. Add leather mixture, remove from heat, cover and let stand for 15 minutes, mashing leather occasionally, until rice is softened.

2. Uncover and bring to a boil over medium heat, stirring often. Boil, stirring often, for about 5 minutes or until mixture is hot and liquid is absorbed.

Potato and Veggie Pancakes

Pancakes don't have to
be just for breakfast. This
vegetable-studded savory
version makes a nice
replacement for bread
or crackers as a lunch or
dinner side dish.

Tip

If powdered eggs aren't
available, substitute
powdered egg replacer,
using the package
instructions to substitute
for 1 egg. Alternatively,
omit the powdered eggs
when prepping at home
and decrease the water to
6 tbsp (90 mL). Whisk in
1 fresh egg with the oil.

Prep at Home

2 tbsp	dried grated potatoes	25 mL
1 tbsp	dried grated carrots	15 mL
1 tbsp	dried grated zucchini	15 mL
1 tsp	crumbled dried herbs (basil, oregano, savory)	5 mL
1/2 cup	all-purpose flour	125 mL
1 tbsp	powdered eggs	15 mL
1 tbsp	instant skim milk powder	15 mL
2 tsp	granulated sugar	10 mL
1/2 tsp	baking powder	2 mL
Pinch	salt	Pinch

To Serve

1/2 cup	water	125 mL
	Vegetable oil	

Prep at Home

1. In a sealable plastic bag, combine potatoes, carrots, zucchini and herbs. In another bag, combine flour, eggs, milk powder, sugar, baking powder and salt. Seal both bags and store at room temperature for up to 1 month.

To Serve

1. In a bowl, combine vegetable mixture and water. Cover and let stand for 30 minutes or until vegetables are soft. Stir in 1 tsp (5 mL) oil. Shake flour mixture in bag to mix and pour into vegetable mixture. Stir just until evenly moistened.

2. Heat a skillet over medium heat until warmed. Add a thin layer of oil. Pour in about 1/4 cup (50 mL) batter per pancake. Cook for 2 to 3 minutes or until bubbles break on the surface but don't fill in and bottom is golden. Turn and cook for about 2 minutes or until golden brown. Repeat with remaining batter, adding oil to the pan and adjusting heat as necessary.

Fresh Addition
Top pancakes with sour cream, applesauce or salsa.

Cheese and Herb Skillet Biscuits

Makes 4 biscuits

The dried cottage cheese adds a fabulous gooeyness to these herb biscuits. Serve them with eggs for breakfast or with soup or stew for lunch or dinner.

Tip

These can be cooked over a campfire. Just heat the pan on a rack over the hottest part of the fire, then move it to the cooler edge to cook the biscuits. The timing will depend on the fire, so keep an eye on them.

- 6- to 8-inch (15 to 20 cm) skillet, preferably cast-iron, with lid or foil to cover

Prep at Home

³⁄₄ cup	all-purpose flour	175 mL
2 tbsp	powdered dried cottage cheese	25 mL
2 tsp	granulated sugar	10 mL
2 tsp	crumbled dried parsley	10 mL
1¹⁄₂ tsp	crumbled dried herbs (basil, oregano, thyme, chives)	7 mL
1 tsp	baking powder	5 mL
¹⁄₄ tsp	salt	1 mL
Pinch	freshly ground black pepper	Pinch

To Serve

¹⁄₂ cup	water or beer	125 mL
	Vegetable oil or butter	

Prep at Home

1. In a sealable plastic bag, combine flour, cottage cheese, sugar, parsley, herbs, baking powder, salt and pepper. Seal and store at room temperature for up to 1 week or refrigerate for up to 6 months.

To Serve

1. Heat skillet over medium heat until warmed.

2. In a bowl, combine flour mixture and water. Using a fork, stir just until evenly moistened.

3. Add a thin layer of oil to skillet. Spoon dough into 4 mounds in skillet. Reduce heat to low, cover and cook for 3 minutes. Uncover and cook for about 1 minute or until bottoms are golden brown and edges are no longer shiny. Flip over and cook for about 2 minutes or until biscuits are puffed and firm. Serve hot.

> **Fresh Addition**
>
> Add ¹⁄₄ cup (50 mL) diced ham or other deli meat or 2 tbsp (25 mL) minced smoked salmon when mixing the dough.

Chili Cornmeal Cakes

Serve these flavorful biscuits with soup or stew to round out a hearty meal perfectly.

● 6- to 8-inch (15 to 20 cm) skillet, preferably cast-iron, with lid or foil to cover

Prep at Home

1 tbsp	dried corn kernels	15 mL
1 tsp	crumbled dried parsley	5 mL
1/2 tsp	finely chopped dried hot chile peppers	2 mL
1/2 tsp	chili powder	2 mL
1/2 cup	all-purpose flour	125 mL
1/4 cup	cornmeal	50 mL
2 tbsp	instant skim milk powder	25 mL
1 tsp	granulated sugar	5 mL
1 tsp	baking powder	5 mL
1/4 tsp	salt	1 mL

To Serve

1/2 cup	water or beer	125 mL
	Vegetable oil or butter	

Prep at Home

1. In a sealable plastic bag, combine corn, parsley, chile peppers and chili powder. In another bag, combine flour, cornmeal, milk powder, sugar, baking powder and salt. Seal both bags and store at room temperature for up to 1 month.

To Serve

1. In a bowl, combine corn mixture, water and 2 tsp (10 mL) oil. Let stand for 15 minutes or until corn starts to soften.

2. Shake flour mixture in bag to mix and pour into corn mixture. Using a fork, stir just until evenly moistened. Let stand for 5 minutes.

Tip

If you don't have dried chile peppers, substitute $\frac{1}{8}$ tsp (0.5 mL) cayenne pepper.

3. Meanwhile, heat skillet over medium heat until warmed. Add a thin layer of oil. Spoon dough into 4 mounds in skillet. Reduce heat to low, cover and cook for 3 minutes. Uncover and cook for about 1 minute or until bottoms are golden brown and edges are no longer shiny. Flip over and cook for about 2 minutes or until biscuits are puffed and firm. Serve hot.

Fresh Addition

Add 1 tbsp (15 mL) shredded Cheddar or Monterey Jack cheese with the flour mixture.

Multigrain Pan Bread

This versatile bread goes well with soups, stews and chili.

Tip

This can be cooked over a campfire. Just heat the skillet on a rack over the hottest part of the fire, then move it to the cooler edge to cook the bread. The timing will depend on the fire, so peek under the lid frequently (but don't lift it off).

- 6- to 8-inch (15 to 20 cm) skillet, preferably cast iron, with lid or foil to cover

Prep at Home

¼ cup	large-flake (old-fashioned) rolled oats	50 mL
2 tbsp	barley flakes	25 mL
¼ cup	whole wheat flour	50 mL
1 tbsp	instant skim milk powder or buttermilk powder	15 mL
1 tsp	granulated sugar or packed brown sugar	5 mL
½ tsp	baking powder	2 mL
¼ tsp	salt	1 mL

To Serve

⅓ cup	water	75 mL
	Vegetable oil or melted butter	

Prep at Home

1. In a mini chopper or blender, process oats and barley flakes until fairly powdery. In a sealable plastic bag, combine oat mixture, whole wheat flour, milk powder, sugar, baking powder and salt. Seal and store at room temperature for up to 2 weeks or in the refrigerator for up to 6 months.

To Serve

1. Heat skillet over medium heat until warmed.

2. In a bowl, stir flour mixture to combine. Pour in water and 1 tbsp (15 mL) butter. Using a fork, stir just until evenly moistened.

3. Add a thin layer of oil to skillet. Spread dough in skillet. Reduce heat to low, cover and cook for about 8 minutes or until bottom is brown and top is no longer shiny. Uncover, flip over and cook for about 1 minute or until bottom is dry. Cut into quarters and serve hot.

Whole Wheat Bannock on a Stick

Makes 4 bannock

Speedy bannock is a campfire essential. Serve it with chili or soup for a hearty, warming meal.

Tips

If you don't have refrigeration, shortening is best for room-temperature storage. Use trans fat–free shortening, if available. If you do have refrigeration available to store the flour mixture until serving, use the butter — it tastes great!

If you have a camp oven, these can be formed into bread sticks and baked on a pan or a piece of greased foil instead of on sticks.

- Four ½-inch (1 cm) thick sticks, at least 2 feet (60 cm) long
- Four 8-inch (20 cm) pieces of foil

Prep at Home

½ cup	whole wheat flour	125 mL
1 tbsp	instant skim milk powder	15 mL
1 tsp	granulated sugar	5 mL
½ tsp	baking powder	2 mL
⅛ tsp	salt	0.5 mL
Pinch	freshly ground black pepper (optional)	Pinch
1 tbsp	cold shortening or butter	15 mL

To Serve

¼ cup	water	50 mL

Prep at Home

1. In a bowl, combine flour, milk powder, sugar, baking powder, salt and pepper (if using). Using a pastry blender or two knives, cut in shortening until fine crumbs form. Transfer to a sealable plastic bag. Seal and store at room temperature for up to 1 month (store in the refrigerator if butter was used).

To Serve

1. Prepare campfire.

2. In a bowl, stir flour mixture to combine. Pour in water and, using a fork, stir just until a soft dough forms. Gather with your hands and lightly knead in the bowl just until dough holds together.

3. Wrap a square of foil around one end of each stick, covering at least 4 inches (10 cm). Divide dough into quarters and squeeze one piece around the foil-wrapped section of each stick, making sure dough is about ½ inch (1 cm) thick on all sides of the stick.

4. Cook bannock on sticks over the fire, holding them over a medium-hot area if possible and turning often, until golden brown and firm.

Roasted Garlic and Parmesan Bread Stick Spirals

Pretend you're at a rustic Italian restaurant when you enjoy these bread sticks, packed with authentic flavor.

Tips

If you have a camp oven, these can be formed into bread sticks and baked on a pan or a piece of greased foil instead of on sticks.

The oil adds tenderness and flavor to the dough, but you can use an extra tablespoon (15 mL) of water instead.

- Four $1/2$-inch (1 cm) thick sticks, at least 2 feet (60 cm) long
- Four 12-inch (30 cm) pieces of foil

Prep at Home

$1/2$ cup	all-purpose flour	125 mL
2 tbsp	grated Parmesan cheese	25 mL
1 tsp	finely chopped dried roasted garlic	5 mL
$1/2$ tsp	crumbled dried basil	2 mL
$1/2$ tsp	granulated sugar	2 mL
$1/4$ tsp	baking powder	1 mL
$1/8$ tsp	freshly ground black pepper (optional)	0.5 mL

To Serve

$1/4$ cup	water	50 mL
1 tbsp	olive or vegetable oil	15 mL

Prep at Home

1. In a sealable plastic bag, combine flour, Parmesan, garlic, basil, sugar, baking powder and pepper (if using). Seal and store at room temperature for up to 2 weeks or in the refrigerator for up to 2 months.

To Serve

1. Prepare campfire.

2. In a bowl, stir flour mixture to combine. Pour in water and oil. Using a fork, stir just until a soft dough forms. Gather with your hands and lightly knead in the bowl just until dough holds together.

3. Wrap a square of foil around one end of each stick, covering at least 6 inches (15 cm). Divide dough into quarters and squeeze one piece into a long rope about $1/2$ inch (1 cm) thick. Wrap around the foil-wrapped section of each stick in a spiral, making sure dough is spaced about 1 inch (2.5 cm) apart along the stick.

4. Cook bread sticks over the fire, holding them over a medium-hot area if possible and turning often, until golden brown and firm.

Snacks

GORP with a Twist

"Good Old Raisins and Peanuts" has come a long way since we were kids. Combine as many dried fruits and nuts as you like to get your favorite combination, and pack several bags to satisfy munchies on the go.

Tip

Be sure to drink plenty of water when snacking on dried fruits. You need to replace the liquid you'd normally get from fresh fruit.

½ cup	dried cranberries	125 mL
½ cup	raisins	125 mL
½ cup	chopped dried apricots	125 mL
½ cup	chopped dried pineapple	125 mL
½ cup	salted peanuts	125 mL
½ cup	salted cashews or almonds	125 mL
¼ cup	dried sweet or sour cherries	50 mL
¼ cup	dried strawberry slices	50 mL
¼ cup	toasted green pumpkin seeds	50 mL

1. In a sealable plastic bag or bags, combine cranberries, raisins, apricots, pineapple, peanuts, cashews, cherries, strawberries and pumpkin seeds. Seal and store at room temperature for up to 1 month.

Sesame Teriyaki Veggie Trail Mix

**Makes about
2 cups (500 mL)**

This colorful homemade mix is sure to satisfy the munchies when you're on the trail.

Tips

Small pieces of vegetables work well for this recipe, so use chopped or sliced vegetables that are similar in size.

Use a thin teriyaki sauce (the consistency of soy sauce) for this recipe. Those with thickeners, such as cornstarch, won't dry properly.

- Leather sheet or parchment paper

1 1/2 cups	mixed dried vegetables (bell peppers, peas, carrots, green beans)	375 mL
1/2 cup	chopped almonds	125 mL
2 tbsp	sesame seeds	25 mL
2 tbsp	thin teriyaki sauce	25 mL

1. In a bowl, combine vegetables, almonds, sesame seeds and teriyaki sauce; toss to coat evenly.

2. Spread mixture onto leather sheet, spacing vegetables out as much as possible. Dry at 135°F (58°C), stirring and spreading out vegetables once or twice, for 2 to 3 hours or until no longer sticky. Let cool completely on trays. Store in an airtight container at room temperature for up to 1 month.

Jerky 'n' Veg Trail Mix

Protein on the go never tasted so good. Keep a bag of this handy in your pocket for those days of hard trekking or paddling. It's sure to get you through to the next meal break.

Tip
Be sure to drink plenty of water when snacking on dried foods. You need to replace the liquid you'd normally get from fresh foods.

Variation
Use your favorite dried vegetables in place of the peas and red peppers. Mix in dried fruits, if you like. Try pineapple or melon for something different.

½ cup	dried green peas	125 mL
½ cup	dried cooked chickpeas	125 mL
½ cup	dried red bell pepper pieces	125 mL
½ cup	dried tomatoes, chopped	125 mL
½ cup	Cajun Jerky or Maple and Grainy Dijon Jerky, broken into small pieces	125 mL

1. In a sealable plastic bag, combine peas, chickpeas, red peppers, tomatoes and jerky. Seal and store at room temperature for up to 1 month.

Wasabi Tofu and Vegetable Trail Mix

Makes about 2¹/₂ cups (625 mL)

This will perk you up with its hot wasabi flavor and high protein and energy content. If you like it really hot, feel free to add more wasabi.

Tip
Be sure to drink plenty of water when snacking on dried foods to replace the water you'd normally get from fresh foods.

● Leather sheet or parchment paper

¹/₂ cup	dried crumbled tofu	125 mL
¹/₂ cup	dried cooked chickpeas	125 mL
¹/₂ cup	dried cauliflower florets, broken into small pieces	125 mL
¹/₂ cup	dried broccoli florets, broken into small pieces	125 mL
¹/₄ cup	dried carrot slices	50 mL
¹/₄ cup	dried green peas	50 mL
1 tsp	sesame seeds	5 mL
1 tsp	wasabi powder	5 mL
¹/₂ tsp	finely chopped dried gingerroot	2 mL
2 tbsp	freshly squeezed lime juice	25 mL

1. In a bowl, combine tofu, chickpeas, cauliflower, broccoli, carrots, peas, sesame seeds, wasabi powder, ginger and lime juice; toss to coat evenly.

2. Spread mixture onto leather sheet, spacing vegetables out as much as possible. Dry at 135°F (58°C), stirring and spreading out vegetables once or twice, for 2 to 3 hours or until no longer sticky. Let cool completely on trays. Store in an airtight container at room temperature for up to 1 month.

Tomato Herb Popcorn Seasoning

**Makes about
4 cups (1 L)**

Whether you have a campfire corn popper, use the microwave at the camp recreation center or buy the nifty type in the foil pan, popcorn is a camp snack tradition. This seasoning will make it even better.

Tip

Be sure the mini chopper bowl, blade and lid are completely dry before chopping the leather mixture. Any bit of moisture will prevent it from processing properly.

Prep at Home

1	2-inch (5 cm) square Tomato Paste Leather	1
¼ tsp	crumbled dried basil	1 mL
¼ tsp	crumbled dried oregano	1 mL
¼ tsp	crumbled dried parsley	1 mL
¼ tsp	salt	1 mL

To Serve

4 cups	hot popped popcorn	1 L
1 tbsp	melted butter	15 mL

Prep at Home

1. Tear leather into small pieces. In a mini chopper, pulse leather, basil, oregano, parsley and salt until very finely chopped, then process until as fine a powder as possible. Transfer to a sealable plastic bag, seal and store at room temperature for up to 1 month.

To Serve

1. In a bowl, combine hot popcorn, butter and seasoning; toss to coat evenly.

Anytime Salsa

Just Add Water

With your own dried vegetables, you can make delicious salsa anytime, no matter where you are. It's super with chips for dipping or to add a zesty flavor to recipes.

Tips

If you like a fiery salsa, increase the chile pepper slices to ½ to ¾ tsp (2 to 3 mL) or season with hot pepper sauce to taste when serving.

If you want to pack a big batch of this for your trip, use a blender or a regular food processor fitted with a metal blade to chop the dried vegetables. For each ½ cup (125 mL) portion, use about ¼ cup (50 mL) dried vegetable mixture for each ½ cup (125 mL) water.

Prep at Home

2 tbsp	dried tomatoes	25 mL
1 tbsp	dried red bell pepper pieces	15 mL
1 tbsp	dried green bell pepper pieces	15 mL
1 tsp	dried onion pieces	5 mL
¼ tsp	dried hot chile pepper slices (or to taste)	1 mL
¼ tsp	crumbled dried oregano	1 mL
¼ tsp	finely chopped dried lime zest (optional)	1 mL
⅛ tsp	salt	0.5 mL

To Serve

½ cup	water	125 mL

Prep at Home

1. In a mini chopper, pulse tomatoes, red and green bell peppers, onions, hot peppers, oregano, lime zest (if using) and salt until vegetables are finely chopped. Transfer to a sealable plastic bag, seal and store at room temperature for up to 1 month.

To Serve

1. In a saucepan, combine vegetable mixture and water. Bring to a boil over high heat. Remove from heat, cover and let stand for 30 minutes or until vegetables are soft and liquid is absorbed.

> **Fresh Addition**
> Stir in 1 tbsp (15 mL) freshly squeezed lime juice or red wine vinegar when you remove the vegetable mixture from the heat.

Just-Add-Water Hummus

Just Add Water

No Heat Required

Why buy a mix when it's so easy to make your own and you can control exactly what ingredients go into it? Hummus is indispensable as a flavor and protein booster with crackers or veggies as a snack, spread on a sandwich or even stirred into soup to thicken it.

Tips

With dried ingredients, it is tricky to get the tangy flavor that is one of the true characteristics of hummus. You can add a pinch of citric acid powder (available at pharmacies and health food stores) with the lemon zest to add tang or add 1 tbsp (15 mL) fresh lemon juice in place of an equal amount of water.

Make a big batch of the dry mix, using a regular food processor or a blender to grind the ingredients. Use about 2$\frac{1}{2}$ tbsp (32 mL) dry mix for each serving.

Prep at Home

1	small dried garlic slice (or $\frac{1}{2}$-inch/ 1 cm square dried roasted garlic)	1
$\frac{1}{4}$ cup	dried cooked chickpeas	50 mL
2 tsp	sesame seeds	10 mL
$\frac{1}{4}$ tsp	finely chopped dried lemon zest	1 mL
$\frac{1}{8}$ tsp	salt	0.5 mL
$\frac{1}{8}$ tsp	freshly ground black pepper	0.5 mL
Pinch	ground cumin (optional)	Pinch

To Serve

$\frac{1}{4}$ cup	water	50 mL

Prep at Home

1. In a mini chopper, pulse garlic, chickpeas, sesame seeds, lemon zest, salt, pepper and cumin (if using) until chickpeas are powdery, with as few small chunks as possible. Transfer to a sealable plastic bag, seal and store at room temperature for up to 1 month.

To Serve

1. In sealable bag or a bowl, combine chickpea mixture and water. Seal or cover and let stand, mashing or stirring occasionally, for 30 minutes or until chickpeas are soft and liquid is absorbed.

Variations

Add 1 tbsp (15 mL) dried red bell pepper pieces with the chickpeas.

Give the hummus a spicy kick by adding a pinch (or more) of hot pepper flakes.

Power-Packed Cereal Squares

Makes 24 squares

These squares are packed with much more energy, protein and nutrients than fluffy crispy rice squares but are just as easy to make and are super-tasty.

Tip

Use a high-energy flake cereal for these squares to maximize the nutritional boost. We like a multigrain cereal, such as Just Right, Vector, Weetabix GrainShop High Fiber Crisp or Ultima Organic High Fiber.

- 13- by 9-inch (33 by 23 cm) metal baking pan, lined with greased foil or parchment paper, leaving a 2-inch (5 cm) overhang

6 cups	ready-to-eat multigrain flake cereal	1.5 L
1 cup	chopped toasted nuts	250 mL
3/4 cup	raisins	175 mL
3/4 cup	chopped dried apples	175 mL
1/2 cup	roasted salted sunflower seeds	125 mL
1 cup	packed brown sugar	250 mL
1/2 cup	instant skim milk powder	125 mL
1/2 cup	corn syrup	125 mL
2 tbsp	butter	25 mL
1 tsp	vanilla extract	5 mL

1. In a large bowl, combine cereal, nuts, raisins, apples and sunflower seeds. Set aside.

2. In a saucepan, whisk together brown sugar and milk powder; whisk in corn syrup. Bring to a boil over medium heat, stirring until sugar is dissolved. Remove from heat and let bubbles subside. Add butter and vanilla; stir until butter is melted. Pour over cereal mixture and toss with a heatproof spatula until evenly coated.

3. Press firmly into prepared pan. Let cool completely in pan on a wire rack. Using foil overhang as handles, remove from pan and transfer to a cutting board. Peel off foil and cut into squares. Store in an airtight container at room temperature for up to 5 days or in the refrigerator for up to 2 weeks.

Multigrain Fruit and Nut Granola Bars

Making your own granola bars is cost-effective, and they're much more nutritious than most store-bought ones. You can vary the flavor by adding other dried fruits in place of or along with the bananas and blueberries — try cherries or chopped mango or strawberry slices.

Tip

For longer storage, wrap bars individually in plastic wrap, then overwrap in foil or place in a freezer bag or an airtight container and freeze for up to 2 months.

- Preheat oven to 350°F (180°C)
- 8-inch (20 cm) square metal baking pan, lined with foil or parchment paper, leaving a 2-inch (5 cm) overhang

1 cup	quick-cooking rolled oats	250 mL
1/2 cup	spelt or barley flakes	125 mL
1/4 cup	natural wheat bran	50 mL
1/2 cup	finely chopped dried banana slices	125 mL
1/4 cup	dried blueberries or chopped dried cherries	50 mL
1/4 cup	ground flax seeds	50 mL
1/4 cup	chopped toasted nuts or sunflower seeds	50 mL
1/4 cup	packed brown sugar	50 mL
1	egg	1
1/3 cup	liquid honey	75 mL
1/4 cup	butter, melted	50 mL
1 tsp	vanilla extract	5 mL

1. In a large bowl, combine oats, spelt flakes, wheat bran, bananas, blueberries, flax seeds and nuts. Set aside.

2. In another bowl, whisk together brown sugar, egg, honey, butter and vanilla. Pour over dry ingredients and stir until evenly coated.

3. Press batter into prepared pan. Bake in preheated oven for about 30 minutes or until golden brown. Let cool in pan on a wire rack for 15 minutes. Using foil overhang as handles, transfer to a cutting board. Cut into bars and let cool on board until firm. Store in an airtight container at room temperature for up to 5 days or in the refrigerator for up to 2 weeks.

"Bird Seed" Squares

The funny name for these squares comes from Jay's friend Kirby, who claims they look like bird seed. He sure doesn't complain when he eats them every chance he gets, though! They're full of protein, energy and vitamins and make a great start to the day or a snack any time.

Tips

Use your favorite flake cereal for these squares, or use a mixture, such as corn, wheat and bran flakes. Keep in mind, bran flakes alone would be quite dense. We like a multigrain cereal called Weetabix High Fiber Crisp (GrainShop) or Ultima Organic High Fiber.

Use any mixture of dried fruits you like. For the best texture, choose those that are soft and pliable. If using dry, crisp fruit, steam it lightly over simmering water and pat dry before adding in step 2.

These are best if kept refrigerated, or at least cool, so they're not the best choice for backpacking in hot weather. If you're bringing a cooler or trekking in cool weather, they are terrific to tote along.

- 8-inch (20 cm) square baking pan or dish, lined with greased foil with a 2-inch (5 cm) overhang

3 cups	ready-to-eat flake cereal (see tip, at left)	750 mL
1/4 cup	roasted sunflower seeds or green pumpkin seeds	50 mL
1/4 cup	chopped toasted pecans or almonds (see tip, page 168)	50 mL
2 tbsp	flax seeds	25 mL
1 tbsp	sesame seeds	15 mL
1/2 cup	corn syrup	125 mL
1/2 cup	smooth peanut butter	125 mL
3/4 cup	chopped dried fruit (see tip, at left)	175 mL
1 tbsp	butter	15 mL

1. In a large bowl, combine cereal, sunflower seeds, pecans, flax seeds and sesame seeds.

2. In a saucepan, over medium heat, combine corn syrup and peanut butter. Heat, stirring often, until peanut butter is melted. Remove from heat and add fruit and butter. Stir until butter is melted. Pour over cereal mixture and stir until evenly coated.

3. Press into prepared pan. Refrigerate for about 1 hour or until firm and set. Using foil overhang as handles, remove from pan and transfer to a cutting board. Cut into squares. Squares can be refrigerated in an airtight container or individually wrapped for up to 2 weeks.

Chewy Chocolate Fruit Bars

Makes 24 bars

Jennifer was determined to create a chocolaty treat that doesn't require refrigeration. These are more like a candy, and you only need a small piece to get that sweet chocolate and carbohydrate kick.

Tips

You'll need about 8 graham crackers to make $\frac{1}{2}$ cup (125 mL) crumbs. Break crackers into chunks and pulse in a food processor fitted with a metal blade until fine.

Use any mixture of dried fruits you like. For the best texture, choose those that are soft and pliable.

Variation

Add $\frac{1}{2}$ cup (125 mL) finely chopped or ground peanuts with the graham crumbs.

- 8-inch (20 cm) square metal cake pan, lined with parchment paper, leaving a 2-inch (5 cm) overhang

$\frac{1}{4}$ cup	brown sugar	50 mL
$\frac{1}{4}$ cup	instant skim milk powder	50 mL
$\frac{1}{4}$ cup	unsweetened cocoa powder	50 mL
$\frac{1}{4}$ cup	corn syrup	50 mL
$\frac{1}{4}$ cup	butter, cut into cubes	50 mL
1 cup	chopped dried fruit	250 mL
1 tsp	vanilla extract	5 mL
$\frac{1}{2}$ cup	graham cracker crumbs	125 mL

1. In a medium saucepan, whisk together brown sugar, milk powder and cocoa powder. Whisk in 2 tbsp (25 mL) water, corn syrup and butter. Heat over medium heat, stirring often, until sugar dissolves and mixture comes to a boil. Reduce heat and boil, stirring constantly, for 2 minutes or until slightly thickened and syrupy. Remove from heat.

2. Stir in fruit and vanilla until evenly coated. Stir in graham crumbs and pour into prepared pan. Using a greased heatproof spatula, press firmly into pan. Let cool in pan on a wire rack until firm.

3. Using paper overhang as handles, remove from pan and transfer to a cutting board. Cut into bars, dipping knife in hot water and wiping dry between cuts as necessary. Store in an airtight container or wrapped individually at room temperature for up to 2 weeks.

Apple Cinnamon Oat Crisps

These crispy snacks, made with the fantastic flavor of apple and cinnamon and a touch of brown sugar, can be enjoyed at home or on the go.

Tip

Use a clean plastic ruler, the straight edge of a dough scraper or an offset spatula to spread the mixture evenly on the sheets.

- Leather sheets or parchment paper

1 cup	steel-cut oats	250 mL
$\frac{1}{2}$ tsp	salt	2 mL
3 cups	water	750 mL
2	apples, chopped	2
$\frac{1}{4}$ cup	packed brown sugar or liquid honey	50 mL
$\frac{3}{4}$ tsp	ground cinnamon	3 mL

1. In a saucepan, combine oats, salt and water. Bring to a boil over high heat. Reduce heat to low and cook, stirring often, for about 30 minutes or until oats are tender and thick. Measure out 3 cups (750 mL) and transfer to a shallow dish; let cool. Reserve any extra for another use.

2. In a food processor, combine apples, sugar and cinnamon; pulse until very finely chopped. Add oats and pulse until mixture is fairly smooth and a paste consistency.

3. Spread out to $\frac{1}{4}$-inch (0.5 cm) thickness, as evenly as possible, on leather sheets, leaving it slightly thicker around the edges. Dry at 130°F (55°C) for 5 to 8 hours or until top is very firm and it is easy to lift from the sheet. Flip onto a cutting board and cut into $1\frac{1}{2}$-inch (4 cm) square pieces.

4. Transfer pieces to mesh drying trays, moist side down, and dry for about 2 hours or until firm and crisp. Let cool completely on trays or on wire racks. Serve immediately or store in a cookie tin at room temperature for up to 2 months.

Brown Rice, Cinnamon and Raisin Crisps

Makes about 120 small crisps

These are a not-too-sweet, biscotti-like snack. Doing the second "baking" in the dehydrator rather than the oven prevents the crisps from getting overbaked, while drying them to a perfect crispiness. They're terrific topped with soft cheese or pâté, spread with nut butter or on their own.

Variations

For savory crisps, replace the cinnamon with ½ tsp (2 mL) crumbled dried rosemary and add ½ tsp (2 mL) freshly ground black pepper.

Add ½ cup (125 mL) roasted salted sunflower seeds with the raisins in either the sweet or the savory version.

- Preheat oven to 350°F (180°C)
- Baking sheet, lined with parchment paper

1	egg	1
1 cup	cooked brown rice, cooled	250 mL
¼ cup	packed brown sugar or liquid honey	50 mL
1¾ cups	whole wheat flour	425 mL
1 tsp	ground cinnamon	5 mL
½ tsp	baking powder	2 mL
½ tsp	salt	2 mL
1 cup	raisins	250 mL

1. In a food processor, purée egg, rice and sugar until fairly smooth. Add flour, cinnamon, baking powder and salt; pulse until combined and a crumbly dough forms. Add raisins and pulse just until evenly distributed and slightly chopped.

2. Divide dough in half and squeeze each half into a log about 10 inches (25 cm) long. Place on prepared baking sheet, leaving at least 3 inches (7.5 cm) between logs. Press down until logs are about ¾ inch (2 cm) thick. Bake in preheated oven for about 30 minutes or until firm and a tester inserted in the center comes out clean. Let cool on pan on a rack for 10 minutes.

3. Transfer logs to a cutting board. Using a serrated knife and a gentle sawing motion, cut crosswise into slices about ⅛ inch (0.25 cm) thick.

4. Place slices on mesh drying trays. Dry at 155°F (68°C) for 2 to 4 hours or until firm and very crisp. Let cool completely on trays or on wire racks. Serve immediately or store in a cookie tin at room temperature for up to 2 months.

Double Pumpkin Biscotti Crisps

These are a little sweeter than crackers but not as sweet as cookies and make a nice snack between meals. They keep very well and are sturdy, so they are perfect for packing to enjoy along the trail.

- Preheat oven to 350°F (180°C)
- Large baking sheet, lined with parchment paper

1¼ cups	whole wheat flour	300 mL
1 cup	all-purpose flour	250 mL
1 tsp	baking powder	5 mL
1 tsp	salt	5 mL
1 tsp	ground cinnamon	5 mL
1 tsp	ground ginger	5 mL
⅔ cup	packed brown sugar	150 mL
1	egg	1
¾ cup	pumpkin purée (not pie filling)	175 mL
¼ cup	butter, melted	50 mL
2 tsp	vanilla extract	10 mL
½ cup	green pumpkin seeds	125 mL

1. In a large bowl, whisk together whole wheat flour, all-purpose flour, baking powder, salt, cinnamon and ginger.

2. In a separate bowl, whisk together brown sugar, egg, pumpkin, butter and vanilla. Stir in flour mixture until evenly moistened. Stir in pumpkin seeds.

3. Divide dough in half. Spoon each half onto prepared baking sheet in a rough log shape about 14 inches (35 cm) long, leaving at least 3 inches (7.5 cm) between logs. With floured hands, form each portion into a smooth log 14 inches (35 cm) long by 2 inches (5 cm) wide.

4. Bake in preheated oven for about 40 minutes or until golden and firm. Let cool on pan on a wire rack for 15 minutes. Reduce oven temperature to 300°F (150°C).

5. Transfer logs to a cutting board. Using a serrated knife and a gentle sawing motion, cut crosswise on a slight diagonal into slices about ½ inch (1 cm) thick. Return slices to unlined baking sheet, cut side down. Bake for about 45 minutes, flipping over halfway through, until very dry and firm. Let cool completely on wire racks. Store in a cookie tin at room temperature for up to 1 month.

Apricot Hazelnut Grain Crisps

**Makes about
120 small crisps**

Whole grains mixed with
dried apricots and flavorful
hazelnuts create satisfying
and nutritious crisps that
are great for munching on
their own, as a base for
cheese or jam, or along
with fresh fruit.

● Baking sheet, lined with parchment paper

⅓ cup	quinoa	75 mL
½ cup	dried apricot slices (see tip, at right)	125 mL
¼ cup	packed brown sugar or liquid honey	50 mL
1	egg	1
1¼ cups	whole wheat flour	300 mL
½ cup	cornmeal, preferably stone-ground	125 mL
½ tsp	ground ginger or cinnamon	2 mL
½ tsp	baking powder	2 mL
½ tsp	salt	2 mL
¾ cup	hazelnuts, toasted and skins removed (see tip, at right)	175 mL

1. In a small saucepan, bring ⅔ cup (150 mL) water to a boil over high heat. Gradually stir in quinoa; cover, reduce heat to low and simmer for 15 minutes or until grains are tender and liquid is almost absorbed. Stir in apricots, cover and let stand for 5 minutes or until apricots are slightly softened. Transfer to a shallow dish and let cool to room temperature.

2. Preheat oven to 350°F (180°C).

3. In a food processor, purée quinoa mixture, brown sugar and egg until it starts to form a paste. Add flour, cornmeal, ginger, baking powder and salt; pulse until combined and a crumbly dough forms. Add hazelnuts and pulse just until evenly distributed and slightly chopped.

4. Divide dough in half and, with moistened hands, squeeze each half into a log about 10 inches (25 cm) long. Place on prepared baking sheet, leaving at least 3 inches (7.5 cm) between logs. Press down until logs are about ¾ inch (2 cm) thick. Bake for about 30 minutes or until firm and a tester inserted in the center comes out clean. Let cool on pan on a wire rack for 10 minutes.

Tips

If using commercially dried apricots that are soft, chop them into small pieces and add them to the food processor with the hazelnuts rather than with the quinoa.

To toast hazelnuts, spread out on a baking sheet and bake in a 350°F (180°C) oven for about 8 minutes or until toasted, fragrant and skins start to split. Transfer to a clean towel and let cool slightly. Rub off as much of the skins as possible with the towel (a little bit left on the nuts is fine).

5. Transfer logs to a cutting board. Using a serrated knife and a gentle sawing motion, cut crosswise into slices about $\frac{1}{8}$ inch (0.25 cm) thick.

6. Place slices on mesh drying trays. Dry at 155°F (68°C) for 2 to 4 hours or until firm and very crisp. Let cool completely on trays or on wire racks. Serve immediately or store in an airtight container at room temperature for up to 1 month.

Oat and Grain Hard Tack

Hard tack was the
ubiquitous cracker sent
as rations for sailors
and soldiers. The main
advantage was that it
didn't spoil and provided
carbohydrates — taste
wasn't a consideration.
This version has a good
flavor and adds nutrition
by using a variety of grains,
but do heed the name: the
biscuits are hard and need
to be softened in liquid.
Crumble them into soup
or stews, or soak them in
water and mash up for a
simple cereal.

Tip

If you prefer, you can use
your dehydrator to dry out
the biscuits. Cut as directed
in step 4 and place squares
on mesh drying trays. Dry
at 155°F (68°C) for 3 to
4 hours or until very firm
and dry. Let cool completely
on trays or on wire racks.

- Preheat oven to 400°F (200°C)
- Baking sheet, lined with parchment paper

1 cup	large-flake (old-fashioned) rolled oats	250 mL
1/2 cup	barley flakes	125 mL
1 1/2 cups	whole wheat flour	375 mL
1/4 cup	millet	50 mL
1/4 cup	instant skim milk powder (optional)	50 mL
2 tbsp	ground flax seeds	25 mL
2 tbsp	packed brown sugar	25 mL
1 tsp	salt	5 mL
3/4 cup	water	175 mL
1 tbsp	vegetable oil	15 mL

1. In a food processor fitted with a metal blade, process
   oats and barley flakes until finely ground and slightly
   powdery. Add whole wheat flour, millet, milk powder
   (if using), flax seeds, brown sugar and salt; pulse to
   combine. Add water and oil; pulse until dough starts
   to form a ball.

2. Turn out onto prepared baking sheet and knead
   slightly to smooth dough. With floured hands or a
   rolling pin, press into a rectangle about 11 by 8 inches
   (28 by 20 cm) and slightly less than 1/2 inch (1 cm)
   thick. Using a fork, prick dough all over.

3. Bake in preheated oven for about 20 minutes or
   until golden and firm. Let cool on pan on a wire rack
   for 5 minutes. Reduce oven temperature to 250°F
   (120°C).

4. Transfer to a cutting board. Using a sharp knife, cut
   into 2-inch (5 cm) squares. Return biscuits to unlined
   baking sheet. Bake for 1 to 1 1/2 hours or until very dry
   and firm. Let cool completely on wire racks. Store in a
   cookie tin at room temperature for up to 2 months.

Wild Rice, Cranberry and Cashew Chews

The nuttiness of wild rice and cashews and the tang of cranberries and apples complement each other well in these decidedly different, toothsome snacks.

Tip
You'll need about $1/2$ cup (125 mL) raw wild rice to get 2 cups (500 mL) cooked.

Variation
Use almonds, brazil nuts, walnuts or pecans in place of the cashews. To enhance the flavor, toast nuts in a dry skillet over medium heat, stirring constantly, for about 3 minutes or until fragrant.

- Leather sheets or parchment paper

2 cups	cooked wild rice, cooled	500 mL
1 cup	cranberries (fresh or frozen and thawed)	250 mL
1 cup	chopped apple	250 mL
$1/4$ cup	roasted salted cashews	50 mL
2 tbsp	liquid honey	25 mL
1 tbsp	unsweetened apple juice or cranberry juice (approx.)	15 mL

1. In a food processor or in a tall cup (to use an immersion blender), pulse rice, cranberries, apple, cashews and honey until finely chopped. Add just enough apple juice to make a thick, fairly smooth paste.

2. Drop by heaping teaspoonfuls (5 mL), at least 1 inch (2.5 cm) apart, onto leather sheets. Using a moistened spatula, press to $1/4$-inch (0.5 cm) thickness. Dry at 130°F (55°C) for 3 to 4 hours or until tops are firm and edges are easy to lift.

3. Lift carefully and transfer to mesh drying trays, moist side down. Dry for 2 to 3 hours or until firm inside and out but still slightly flexible. Lift from mesh trays to loosen and let cool completely on trays or on wire racks. Serve immediately or store in an airtight container at room temperature for up to 1 month.

Peanut Banana Chews

Makes about 70 pieces

A portable snack with the classic flavors of peanut and banana is sure to satisfy you, whether you're on the trail or on the road.

Tips

Use ripe bananas (with brown spots) for the best flavor and texture.

For an extra treat, spread melted chocolate on the bottom side of one chew and sandwich with another.

- Leather sheets or parchment paper

1½ cups	roasted salted peanuts	375 mL
3	bananas	3
1 tbsp	packed brown sugar	15 mL

1. In a food processor, pulse peanuts until finely chopped. Add bananas and brown sugar; purée until fairly smooth.

2. Drop by heaping teaspoonfuls (5 mL) onto leather sheets, at least 2 inches (5 cm) apart. Using a spatula, spread to ⅛-inch (0.25 cm) thickness. Dry at 130°F (55°C) for 4 to 5 hours or until tops are firm and edges are easy to lift.

3. Lift carefully and transfer to mesh drying trays, moist side down. Dry for 3 to 4 hours or until firm but still slightly flexible, with no sign of moisture inside. Lift from mesh trays to loosen and let cool completely on trays or on wire racks. Serve immediately or store in an airtight container at room temperature for up to 1 month.

Fruit and Nut Chews

**Makes about
30 chews**

When you need a hit of
energy and protein, these
all-natural sweet treats
will do the trick. Starting
with dried fruit and
reconstituting it before
drying may sound like a
strange technique, but it
creates a better texture
for these chewy snacks
than if you started with
fresh fruit.

Variation
Instead of making individual
drops, you can spread the
fruit mixture onto leather
sheets to ¼-inch (0.5 cm)
thickness, spreading as
evenly as possible and
leaving it slightly thicker
around the edges. Dry at
130°F (55°C) for about
5 hours. When top is very
firm and edges are easy to
lift, carefully flip over and
continue drying for 3 to
5 hours or until evenly firm
but still flexible. Let cool
on a wire rack, then cut into
squares or rectangles and
wrap as directed.

- Preheat oven to 375°F (190°C)

1 cup	pecan halves	250 mL
1 cup	almonds or walnut halves	250 mL
1 cup	dates	250 mL
½ cup	dried apricot or peach slices	125 mL
½ cup	raisins or dried plums	125 mL
⅓ cup	unsweetened apple juice or orange juice	75 mL
2 tbsp	liquid honey	25 mL

1. Spread pecans and almonds on a baking sheet.
   Bake in preheated oven for about 8 minutes or until
   toasted and fragrant. Transfer to a bowl and let cool
   completely.

2. Meanwhile, in a small saucepan, combine dates,
   apricots, raisins, apple juice and honey. Bring to a
   simmer over medium heat, stirring occasionally. Cover,
   reduce heat to low and simmer gently, stirring often,
   for about 5 minutes or until fruit is plump and liquid
   is almost completely absorbed. Uncover and let cool
   to room temperature.

3. In a food processor fitted with a metal blade, process
   nuts until finely chopped, but not ground. Add fruit
   mixture and pulse until finely chopped and mixture
   starts to form a ball.

4. Scoop out a level tablespoonful (15 mL) of fruit
   mixture and roll into a ball. Press into a circle about
   ¼ inch (0.5 cm) thick. Place on mesh drying trays.
   Repeat with remaining mixture, placing drops at least
   ½ inch (1 cm) apart.

5. Dry at 130°F (55°C) for 8 to 10 hours or until evenly
   firm. Let cool completely on trays or on wire racks.
   Wrap individually, or in twos or threes, in plastic wrap,
   then in a sealable bag or an airtight container. Store at
   room temperature for up to 1 month.

Lemon Pecan Biscotti

These thin, crispy biscotti, bursting with lemon flavor, are nice to snack on with coffee, tea or fruit drinks, or just while you're hiking along.

Tip

When traveling with these biscotti, it's best to pack them in a rigid container to prevent them from breaking. A plastic container is fine for a few days of storage, but a cookie tin keeps them crisper for longer storage.

- Preheat oven to 325°F (160°C)
- Baking sheets, one lined with parchment paper

2³⁄₄ cups	all-purpose flour	675 mL
1¹⁄₂ tsp	baking powder	7 mL
¹⁄₄ tsp	salt	1 mL
1 cup	granulated sugar	250 mL
¹⁄₂ cup	butter, melted	125 mL
3	eggs	3
2 tbsp	grated lemon zest	25 mL
1 tsp	vanilla extract	5 mL
1 cup	chopped pecans	250 mL

1. In a bowl, combine flour, baking powder and salt.

2. In a large bowl, whisk together sugar and butter until blended. Whisk in eggs, one at a time, until well blended. Whisk in lemon zest and vanilla. Using a wooden spoon, stir in flour mixture in three additions. Stir until a soft dough forms. Stir in pecans.

3. Divide dough into thirds. Spoon each third onto prepared baking sheet in a rough log shape about 12 inches (30 cm) long, leaving at least 3 inches (7.5 cm) between logs. With lightly floured hands, form each portion into a smooth log 12 inches (30 cm) long by 2 inches (5 cm) wide.

4. Bake in preheated oven for about 30 minutes or until firm and starting to turn golden. Let cool on pan on a wire rack for 10 minutes. Reduce oven temperature to 300°F (150°C), or to 275°F (140°C) if using dark baking sheets.

5. Transfer logs to a cutting board. Using a serrated knife and a gentle sawing motion, cut crosswise on a slight diagonal into slices about ¹⁄₄ inch (0.5 cm) thick. Return slices to unlined baking sheets, cut side down. Bake, in batches as necessary, for about 15 minutes, rotating pans halfway through, until cookies are dry and crisp but not browned. Let cool on pans on wire racks. Store in a cookie tin at room temperature for up to 2 weeks or freeze for up to 3 months.

Chocolate Biscotti

Chocolate is a tricky thing to pack along if the weather is hot. The beauty of chocolate biscotti is that they won't melt on even the hottest days and will definitely satisfy any chocolate craving.

Tip

These logs spread to about double the width during the first baking, so if you don't have a large baking sheet, place each half of dough on a separate parchment-lined baking sheet and bake one sheet at a time.

Variation

Add 1 cup (250 mL) chopped toasted almonds or dried cherries to dough.

- Preheat oven to 350°F (180°C)
- Large baking sheets, one lined with parchment paper

3 oz	bittersweet (dark) chocolate, chopped	90 g
3½ cups	all-purpose flour	875 mL
½ cup	unsweetened cocoa powder	125 mL
1 tsp	baking powder	5 mL
½ tsp	baking soda	2 mL
½ tsp	salt	2 mL
2 cups	granulated sugar	500 mL
¾ cup	butter, softened	175 mL
3	eggs	3
2 tsp	vanilla extract	10 mL

1. In a heatproof bowl set over a saucepan of hot (not boiling) water, melt chocolate, stirring until smooth. Let cool to room temperature, stirring often.

2. In a large bowl, whisk together flour, cocoa, baking powder, baking soda and salt.

3. In a separate large bowl, using an electric mixer, cream sugar and butter until light and fluffy. Beat in eggs and vanilla. Beat in melted chocolate. Using a wooden spoon, stir in flour mixture in three additions. Stir until a soft dough forms.

4. Divide dough in half. Spoon each half onto prepared baking sheet in a rough log shape about 14 inches (35 cm) long, leaving at least 4 inches (10 cm) between logs. With lightly floured hands, form each portion into a smooth log 14 inches (35 cm) long by 2½ inches (6 cm) wide.

5. Bake in preheated oven for 35 minutes or until firm. Let cool on pan on a wire rack for 15 minutes. Reduce oven temperature to 300°F (150°C)

6. Transfer logs to a cutting board. Using a serrated knife and a gentle sawing motion, cut crosswise on a slight diagonal into slices about ½ inch (1 cm) thick. Return slices to unlined baking sheets, standing up if possible. Bake for about 45 minutes, flipping over halfway through if placed cut side down, until very dry and firm. Let cool on pans on wire racks. Store in a cookie tin at room temperature for up to 2 weeks or freeze for up to 3 months.

Cinnamon Crisps

Makes about 48 crisps

These thin, crispy cookies have a warmly spiced flavor, but are neither too bold nor too sweet. The rectangles are a little different from traditional ice box cookie logs. They look nice and can be packed efficiently for traveling.

Tips

The key to good spice flavor is to make sure your spices are fresh and pungent. If you can't detect the aroma when you open a jar or package of a spice (without getting very close), it is time to buy fresh and discard the stale spice. It will improve the flavor of your baked goods dramatically.

You can freeze the wrapped dough logs in a freezer bag or an airtight container for up to 3 months. Let thaw in the refrigerator for at least 6 hours or overnight, then slice and bake as directed.

● Large baking sheets, lined with parchment paper

1½ cups	all-purpose flour	375 mL
½ cup	whole wheat flour	125 mL
1½ tsp	ground cinnamon	7 mL
1 tsp	baking powder	5 mL
¼ tsp	salt	1 mL
¼ tsp	ground nutmeg	1 mL
1 cup	packed brown sugar	250 mL
½ cup	butter, softened	125 mL
1	egg	1
2 tsp	vanilla extract	10 mL

1. In a bowl, combine all-purpose flour, whole wheat flour, cinnamon, baking powder, salt and nutmeg.

2. In a large bowl, using an electric mixer, cream brown sugar and butter until light and fluffy. Beat in egg and vanilla. Using a wooden spoon, stir in flour mixture in three additions. Stir until a soft dough forms.

3. Divide dough in half. Place one half on a sheet of parchment paper or plastic wrap and shape into a rectangle about 7 by 2 by 1 inches (18 by 5 by 1 cm), squaring off sides often with a ruler or a long knife. Wrap rectangle log and refrigerate until firm, about 1 hour. Repeat with remaining dough.

4. Preheat oven to 350°F (180°C).

5. Using a sharp knife, cut logs into ¼-inch (0.5 cm) thick slices, periodically flipping log onto another side as necessary to maintain the rectangle shape while cutting. Place slices at least 1 inch (2.5 cm) apart on prepared baking sheets.

6. Bake for about 15 minutes, rotating pans halfway through if necessary, until edges brown slightly and are crisp. Let cool on pans on wire racks for 2 minutes. Transfer to racks to cool completely. Store in a cookie tin at room temperature for up to 2 weeks or freeze for up to 3 months.

Desserts

Fruit-Studded Bannock on a Stick

Just Add Water

Bannock is a traditional bread baked over a wood fire. This slightly sweet fruit version makes a nice simple dessert or snack.

- Four ½-inch (1 cm) thick sticks, at least 2 feet (60 cm) long
- Four 8-inch (20 cm) pieces of foil

Prep at Home

½ cup	all-purpose flour	125 mL
1 tbsp	instant skim milk powder	15 mL
1 tbsp	granulated sugar	15 mL
½ tsp	baking powder	2 mL
¼ tsp	ground cinnamon (optional)	1 mL
⅛ tsp	salt	0.5 mL
1 tbsp	cold shortening or butter	15 mL
¼ cup	chopped dried fruit (apples, pears, peaches, cherries, berries)	50 mL

To Serve

¼ cup	water	50 mL

Prep at Home

1. In a bowl, combine flour, milk powder, sugar, baking powder, cinnamon (if using) and salt. Using a pastry blender or two knives, cut in shortening until fine crumbs form. Transfer to a sealable plastic bag. Place fruit in another bag. Seal both bags and store at room temperature for up to 1 month (or in the refrigerator if butter was used).

To Serve

1. Prepare campfire.

2. In a bowl, combine fruit and water. Let stand for 10 minutes or until fruit starts to soften.

3. Shake flour mixture in bag to mix and pour into fruit mixture. Using a fork, stir just until a soft dough forms. Gather with your hands and lightly knead in the bowl just until dough holds together.

4. Wrap a square of foil around one end of each stick, covering at least 4 inches (10 cm). Divide dough in quarters and squeeze one piece around the foil-wrapped section of each stick, making sure dough is about $\frac{1}{2}$ inch (1 cm) thick on all sides of the stick.

5. Cook bannock on sticks over the fire, holding it over a medium-hot area if possible and turning often, until golden brown and firm.

Banana Peanut Butter S'mores

A camping trip wouldn't be the same without at least one feast on s'mores. This version takes it up a notch with the addition of dried bananas and peanut butter. Look out: other campers will be sneaking over to see what all the oohing and aahing is about.

Variation

Replace the peanut butter with almond butter or another nut butter, or omit it.

- Four 12-inch (30 cm) squares of foil
- Grill rack or flat rocks to place close to fire

8	graham crackers	8
1/4 cup	peanut butter	50 mL
1/4 cup	dried banana slices	50 mL
4	1-inch (2.5 cm) pieces thin chocolate bar (or 1/4 cup/50 mL chocolate chips)	4
4	large marshmallows, cut in half lengthwise	4

1. Prepare campfire and place grill rack over fire, if using.

2. Place one cracker in the center of each square of foil. Spread crackers with half the peanut butter and top each with one-quarter of the banana slices and 1 piece of chocolate. Place 2 marshmallow halves, cut side down, on top of the chocolate. Spread the remaining peanut butter on one side of the remaining graham crackers and place on top to sandwich. Wrap sandwiches tightly with foil.

3. Place on grill rack or on flat rocks close to the fire. Heat for about 10 minutes or until heated through and chocolate is melted. Let stand for 2 minutes before unwrapping.

Oatmeal Raisin Pan Cookies

Makes 4 cookies

You don't need an oven to create amazing oatmeal cookies. These can be made in just a few minutes, just about anywhere.

Tips

Parchment paper might sound a little fussy for camping, but it does allow you to "bake" in a skillet without adding oil, which would create a fried product rather than a tender baked one. The parchment, if not charred, can be wiped off, allowed to dry and folded up to use again.

If you have a camp oven, these can be baked as directed in the oven instructions.

The oil does help make more tender cookies, but if you don't have any, just add 1 tsp (5 mL) extra water.

- Parchment paper to fit inside skillet

Prep at Home

3 tbsp	quick-cooking rolled oats	45 mL
2 tbsp	whole wheat flour	25 mL
1 tbsp	packed brown sugar	15 mL
1 tsp	powdered eggs	5 mL
1/4 tsp	baking powder	1 mL
1/8 tsp	ground cinnamon	0.5 mL
1/8 tsp	salt	0.5 mL
2 tbsp	raisins	25 mL

To Serve

1 tbsp	water (approx.)	15 mL
1 tsp	vegetable oil	5 mL

Prep at Home

1. In a sealable plastic bag, combine oats, flour, brown sugar, eggs, baking powder, cinnamon and salt, mashing up any lumps of brown sugar. Add raisins. Seal bag and store at room temperature for up to 1 month.

To Serve

1. With the dull side of a knife, draw a circle on the parchment paper the size of the inside bottom of your skillet. Rub a little water over both sides of parchment paper to make it more flexible and prevent burning.

2. Heat skillet over medium heat until fairly warm.

3. Add 1 tbsp (15 mL) water and oil to oat mixture in bag and gently squeeze until a dough forms, being careful not to mash the raisins too much. Spoon one-quarter of the dough into a mound inside the circle on the parchment paper. Repeat with remaining dough, leaving as much space as possible between cookies within the circle. Flatten mounds slightly.

4. Place parchment in the skillet, reduce heat to low and cook for 2 to 3 minutes or until cookies are golden brown on the bottom. Flip over and cook for 2 minutes or until second side is golden and tops are firm when touched. Serve warm or let cool on a plate.

Campfire Apple Crumble

Just Add Water

Apple crumble is always a terrific dessert. Made over a campfire and topped with sweet cookies, it is even better than terrific!

Tip
You can find maple sugar granules at farmers' markets and specialty food stores.

Variation
Substitute dried pears for the apples and ground ginger for the cinnamon.

● Shallow flameproof metal or foil baking pan (for campfire cooking) or saucepan (for camp stove cooking)

Prep at Home

½ cup	dried apple slices	125 mL
1 tbsp	packed brown sugar or maple sugar granules	15 mL
½ tsp	finely chopped dried lemon zest (optional)	2 mL
¼ tsp	ground cinnamon	1 mL
½ cup	crumbled oatmeal or ginger cookies	125 mL

To Serve

¾ cup	water	175 mL

Prep at Home

1. In a sealable plastic bag, combine apples, brown sugar, lemon zest (if using) and cinnamon. Place cookie crumbs in another bag. Seal both bags and store at room temperature for up to 1 month.

To Serve

1. In baking pan or saucepan, combine apple mixture and water. Let stand for 15 minutes or until apples start to soften.

2. Simmer over a campfire or over low heat on a stove, stirring occasionally, for about 10 minutes or until apples are plump and hot. Sprinkle with cookie crumbs. Serve hot or warm.

Pear Cherry Ginger Crumble

Makes 2 servings

Just Add Water

Just because you're on the trail or at a camp doesn't mean you can't have a mouth-watering dessert fit for company!

Tip

Using fruit juice instead of water adds more flavor and gives the topping a better texture, but water does work well.

- Saucepan (for camp stove cooking) or shallow flameproof metal or foil baking pan (for campfire cooking)

Prep at Home

1/2 cup	dried pear slices	125 mL
2 tbsp	dried cherries	25 mL
1 tbsp	packed brown sugar	15 mL
1/4 tsp	finely chopped dried gingerroot (or 1/8 tsp/0.5 mL ground ginger)	1 mL
1/4 cup	crumbled ginger cookies	50 mL
1/4 cup	quick-cooking rolled oats	50 mL

To Serve

1 cup	water or fruit juice, divided	250 mL

Prep at Home

1. In a sealable plastic bag, combine pears, cherries, brown sugar and ginger. Place cookie crumbs and oats in another bag. Seal both bags and store at room temperature for up to 1 month.

To Serve

1. In saucepan or baking pan, combine pear mixture and all but 2 tbsp (25 mL) of the water. Let stand for 10 minutes or until pears start to soften.

2. Bring to a simmer on a stove over low heat or over a campfire. Simmer, stirring occasionally, for about 10 minutes or until fruit is plump and hot.

3. Add remaining water to cookie crumb mixture in bag and toss to combine. Sprinkle over fruit mixture and simmer for 5 minutes or until topping is hot. Serve hot or warm.

Mixed Fruit Cobbler

Just Add Water

Cobbler, with its sweet dumpling topping and bubbling fruit bottom, is a warming dessert that will cap off a great day just perfectly.

Tips

This works best in a saucepan that is 5 to 8 inches (12.5 to 20 cm) in diameter, to allow enough room for the dumplings to cook properly.

If you don't have a lid for your saucepan, pack a few pieces of foil to use as a lid when necessary. Roll the foil around a paper towel tube or other cylinder to prevent the cracking that happens with folding. Foil can often be wiped off, allowed to dry and reused several times.

Variation

Add 2 tbsp (25 mL) chopped toasted pecans, almonds or walnuts with the flour in the topping.

Prep at Home

½ cup	mixed dried fruit slices or pieces (such as peaches, apples, pears, berries, apricots, raisins, cherries)	125 mL
1 tsp	vanilla sugar (see tip, page 234)	5 mL
½ tsp	finely chopped dried orange zest (optional)	2 mL

Topping

⅔ cup	all-purpose flour or whole wheat flour	150 mL
2 tbsp	instant skim milk powder or buttermilk powder	25 mL
2 tbsp	vanilla sugar	25 mL
¼ tsp	baking powder	1 mL
⅛ tsp	salt	0.5 mL
⅛ tsp	ground cinnamon, ginger or nutmeg	0.5 mL

To Serve

1 cup	water, divided	250 mL

Prep at Home

1. In a sealable plastic bag, combine fruit, vanilla sugar and orange zest (if using). Seal and store at room temperature for up to 1 month.

2. *For the topping:* In another bag, combine flour, milk powder, vanilla sugar, baking powder, salt and cinnamon. Seal and store at room temperature for up to 1 month.

To Serve

1. In a saucepan, combine fruit mixture and ⅔ cup (150 mL) of the water. Let stand for 15 minutes or until fruit starts to soften.

2. Add remaining water to topping mixture in bag and knead gently until a very soft dough forms.

3. Bring fruit mixture to a boil over medium heat. Drop topping by spoonfuls over fruit mixture. Reduce heat to low, cover and simmer for 5 to 10 minutes or until dumplings are puffed and a tester inserted in a dumpling comes out clean. Uncover and simmer for about 2 minutes or until dumplings look dry. Let cool for at least 5 to 10 minutes. Serve hot or warm.

Fudgy Skillet Brownies

Makes 4 brownies

Brownies are one of those things: if you're a fan, you just *have* to have one when the craving hits. This version is closer to a rich and chocolaty pancake, but can be whipped up in no time at all over a camp stove.

Tip
If you have a camp oven, these can be baked as directed in the oven instructions.

Variations
If you prefer, you can use vegetable oil instead of butter. Skip step 1 and simply add the water and oil to the flour mixture in bag and gently squeeze until evenly moistened.

If the weather is cool or you have a cooler, add 2 tbsp (25 mL) chopped bittersweet (dark) chocolate or chocolate chips with the flour mixture, or pack separately, sprinkle over top of the hot baked brownie and let stand until melted.

● Parchment paper to fit inside skillet (see tip, page 221)

Prep at Home

¼ cup	all-purpose flour	50 mL
3 tbsp	vanilla sugar (see tip, page 234) or granulated sugar	45 mL
2 tbsp	unsweetened cocoa powder	25 mL
2 tsp	powdered eggs	10 mL
⅛ tsp	baking powder	0.5 mL
⅛ tsp	salt	0.5 mL

To Serve

3 tbsp	water	45 mL
1 tbsp	butter	15 mL

Prep at Home

1. In a sealable plastic bag, combine flour, vanilla sugar, cocoa, eggs, baking powder and salt, mashing to break up any lumps of cocoa. Seal and store at room temperature for up to 1 month. Pack an extra sealable plastic bag (optional).

To Serve

1. In a saucepan, heat water over high heat just until warm enough to melt butter. Add butter and stir until melted (or place butter in extra sealable plastic bag, pour in warm water and knead until butter is melted). Let water cool to lukewarm.

2. Heat a skillet over medium heat until fairly warm.

3. Add flour mixture to butter mixture and stir (or gently squeeze in bag) until evenly moistened.

4. Rub a little water over both sides of parchment paper to make it more flexible and prevent burning. Place parchment in skillet. Pour batter onto the paper and spread evenly. Cover, reduce heat to low and cook for 5 to 10 minutes or until top looks dry and springs back when lightly touched. Slide parchment onto a plate or heatproof surface and let cool slightly. Serve warm or cool, cut into wedges.

Skillet Carrot Pineapple Cakes

These do take a little time to prepare, but if you soak the carrot mixture before you prepare your main course, you can cook the cakes when you're ready to enjoy them. Or make them before dinner and hide them until dessert time!

Tip
Use kitchen scissors to cut the pineapple rings into very small pieces, wiping the blades with a hot cloth when they get sticky.

Variations
Add 2 tbsp (25 mL) chopped toasted pecans, almonds or walnuts to the flour mixture.

Add ½ tsp (2 mL) minced dried gingerroot to the carrot mixture.

• Parchment paper to fit inside skillet (see tip, page 221)

Prep at Home

2 tbsp	dried grated carrots	25 mL
1 tbsp	finely chopped dried pineapple rings	15 mL
¼ cup	all-purpose flour	50 mL
1½ tbsp	packed brown sugar or vanilla sugar (see tip, page 234)	22 mL
1 tsp	powdered eggs	5 mL
½ tsp	baking powder	2 mL
¼ tsp	ground cinnamon	1 mL
⅛ tsp	salt	0.5 mL

To Serve

¼ cup	water (approx.)	50 mL
2 tsp	butter or vegetable oil	10 mL

Prep at Home
1. In a sealable plastic bag, combine carrots and pineapple. In another bag, combine flour, brown sugar, eggs, baking powder, cinnamon and salt, mashing to break up any lumps of brown sugar. Seal both bags and store at room temperature for up to 1 month.

To Serve
1. In a saucepan, bring water to a boil over high heat. Add carrot mixture and butter; remove from heat (or pour boiling water into the carrot mixture in the sealable bag and add the butter). Cover (or seal) and let stand for about 30 minutes or until carrots are soft and water has cooled.

2. Heat a skillet over medium heat until fairly warm.

3. Add flour mixture to carrot mixture and stir (or gently squeeze in bag) until evenly moistened.

4. Rub a little water over both sides of parchment paper to make it more flexible and prevent burning. Place parchment in skillet. Spoon one-third of the batter onto the paper in a mound. Repeat with remaining batter, leaving as much space as possible between cakes. Spread mounds slightly. Cover, reduce heat to low and cook for 5 to 10 minutes or until cakes are golden brown on the bottom and tops look dry and spring back when lightly touched. Slide parchment out onto a plate or heatproof surface and let cool. Serve warm or let cool completely.

No-Bake Blueberry Cheesecakes

Makes 1 serving

Just Add Water

These might be a little different from any other cheesecakes you've made, but they give the same sweet and fruity dessert satisfaction.

Tip
If you have a cooler or refrigerator, the prepared cheesecake can be covered and chilled for up to 1 day.

Prep at Home

¼ cup	dried blueberries	50 mL
¼ cup	powdered dried cottage cheese	50 mL
1 tbsp	granulated sugar	15 mL
Pinch	finely chopped dried lemon zest	Pinch
2 tbsp	graham cracker crumbs	25 mL

To Serve

½ cup	water	125 mL

Prep at Home
1. In a sealable plastic bag, combine blueberries, cottage cheese, sugar and lemon zest. Place graham crumbs in another bag. Seal both bags and store at room temperature for up to 2 weeks or refrigerate for up to 3 months.

To Serve
1. In a saucepan, bring water to a boil. Stir in blueberry mixture, remove from heat, cover and let stand for about 30 minutes, stirring occasionally, until mixture is thick and cooled to room temperature. Scrape into a bowl, if desired, and serve sprinkled with graham crumbs.

Pumpkin Pie Pudding

Makes 1 serving

Just Add Water

Jennifer was on a camping trip in Oregon during Canadian Thanksgiving (in mid-October), and there wasn't a pumpkin pie to be found. She improvised by making a pudding with canned pumpkin and creating a water bath to cook over the campfire. It did cook — eventually. This version is much, much easier and much less smoky tasting (definitely a plus!).

Tips

If the leather is pliable, you can tear or crumble it by hand; if it's crisp, you can tear it into pieces and pulse it in a mini chopper or spice grinder.

If you don't have pumpkin pie spice, use ⅛ tsp (0.5 mL) each ground cinnamon and ginger and a pinch of ground nutmeg.

Prep at Home

¼ cup	crumbled Roasted Pumpkin Leather or Roasted Winter Squash Leather	50 mL
1 tbsp	packed brown sugar	15 mL
1 tbsp	instant skim milk powder	15 mL
1 tsp	cornstarch	5 mL
¼ tsp	pumpkin pie spice	1 mL

To Serve

⅔ cup	water	150 mL

Prep at Home

1. Tear leather into very small pieces. In a sealable plastic bag, combine leather, brown sugar, milk powder, cornstarch and pumpkin pie spice. Seal and store at room temperature for up to 1 month.

To Serve

1. In a saucepan, stir pumpkin mixture to make sure it's evenly blended. Gradually stir in water. Let stand for 15 minutes or until pumpkin starts to soften.

2. Bring to a boil over medium heat, stirring often. Reduce heat and boil gently, stirring constantly, for about 2 minutes or until thickened. Serve hot or let cool.

Apple Spice Rice Pudding

Just Add Water

Rice pudding is one of Jennifer's all-time favorite desserts. The addition of dried apples and warm spices makes it even better.

Variation
Replace the apples with 1 tbsp (15 mL) each finely chopped dried peaches and dried cherries.

Prep at Home

⅓ cup	dried cooked long-grain white or brown rice	75 mL
2 tbsp	finely chopped dried apples	25 mL
2 tbsp	instant skim milk powder	25 mL
1 tbsp	packed brown sugar	15 mL
1 tsp	powdered eggs (optional)	5 mL
¼ tsp	ground cinnamon	1 mL
Pinch	ground nutmeg or ginger	Pinch
Pinch	salt	Pinch

To Serve

1 cup	water	250 mL

Prep at Home
1. In a mini chopper or small food processor, process rice until finely chopped and about one-quarter is powdery. Transfer to a sealable plastic bag and add apples, milk powder, brown sugar, eggs (if using), cinnamon, nutmeg and salt. Seal and store at room temperature for up to 1 month.

To Serve
1. In a saucepan, combine rice mixture and water. Cover and let stand for 20 minutes or until rice starts to soften.

2. Uncover and bring to a boil over medium heat, stirring often. Reduce heat and simmer, stirring often, for about 5 minutes or until rice is tender and pudding is creamy and thickened.

Raspberry Chocolate Pudding

Makes 1 serving

Just Add Water

Chocolate is always a good choice for dessert, and when it's cooked into an easy pudding, spiked with raspberries and served warm, you might be tempted to eat dessert first!

Prep at Home

2 tbsp	skim milk powder	25 mL
1 tbsp	granulated sugar	15 mL
1 tbsp	unsweetened cocoa powder	15 mL
1 tsp	cornstarch	5 mL
2 tbsp	dried raspberries	25 mL

To Serve

$\frac{1}{2}$ cup	water	125 mL

Prep at Home

1. In a sealable plastic bag, combine milk powder, sugar, cocoa and cornstarch, mashing to break up any lumps of cocoa. Add raspberries. Seal and store at room temperature for up to 1 month.

To Serve

1. In a small saucepan, stir raspberry mixture to make sure it's evenly blended. Gradually stir in water. Bring to a boil over medium heat, stirring often. Reduce heat and boil gently, stirring constantly, for about 2 minutes or until thickened. Serve hot or let cool.

> **Fresh Addition**
> Add $\frac{1}{4}$ tsp (1 mL) vanilla extract after removing the pudding from the heat.

Banana Coconut Pudding

Makes 1 serving

Just Add Water

Cook up this easy pudding to bring a tropical flavor to your dessert. It's perfect after a meal of curry or any Asian dish.

Tip

Use kitchen scissors to cut the banana slices into very small pieces, wiping the blades with a hot cloth when they get sticky.

Prep at Home

2 tbsp	instant skim milk powder	25 mL
1 tbsp	packed brown sugar	15 mL
1 tbsp	finely chopped dried coconut slices or store-bought shredded coconut	15 mL
1 tbsp	finely chopped dried banana slices	15 mL
2 tsp	cornstarch	10 mL
1 tsp	powdered eggs (optional)	5 mL

To Serve

$\frac{1}{2}$ cup	water	125 mL

Prep at Home

1. In a sealable plastic bag, combine milk powder, brown sugar, coconut, bananas, cornstarch and eggs (if using). Seal and store at room temperature for up to 1 month.

To Serve

1. Pour banana mixture into a small saucepan and stir to make sure it's evenly blended. Gradually stir in water. Bring to a boil over medium heat, stirring often. Reduce heat and boil gently, stirring constantly, for about 2 minutes or until thickened (it will thicken more upon cooling). Serve hot or let cool.

Fresh Addition

Add $\frac{1}{4}$ tsp (1 mL) vanilla extract or 1 tsp (5 mL) rum after removing the pudding from the heat.

Chocolate Toffee Bread Pudding

Just Add Water

Bread pudding is perfect comfort food, and after a long, hard day of trekking, this is sure to warm your body and soul.

Tip
Toffee bits are available in bags in the baking section at supermarkets, usually where the chocolate chips are displayed.

Variation
If the weather is cool or you have a cooler, add 1 tbsp (15 mL) chopped bittersweet (dark) chocolate or chocolate chips with the toffee bits.

- Saucepan (for camp stove cooking) or shallow flameproof metal or foil baking pan with foil to cover (for campfire cooking)

Prep at Home

2 tbsp	instant skim milk powder	25 mL
2 tbsp	powdered eggs	25 mL
1 tbsp	granulated sugar or vanilla sugar (see tip, page 234)	15 mL
1 tbsp	unsweetened cocoa powder	15 mL
1/2 cup	coarse dried bread crumbs	125 mL
1 tbsp	toffee bits	15 mL

To Serve

1/3 cup	water	75 mL

Prep at Home
1. In a sealable plastic bag, combine milk powder, eggs, sugar and cocoa, mashing to break up any lumps of cocoa. Place bread crumbs and toffee bits in another bag. Seal both bags and store at room temperature for up to 1 month.

To Serve
1. Add water to cocoa mixture in sealable bag and mash until blended. Add bread crumb mixture and gently mix. Let stand for 5 minutes or until bread starts to soften.

2. Transfer bread mixture to saucepan or baking pan. Cover with lid or foil and simmer on a stove over low heat or over a campfire for 5 to 10 minutes or until heated through and set. Serve hot or warm.

Warm Peaches with Ginger

Makes 1 serving

Just Add Water

Peaches and ginger are a delightful combination, whether served in a bowl on their own or with cookies, over cake or on biscuits.

Tips

You can find maple sugar granules at farmers' markets and specialty food stores.

If you have a spice grinder, use it to finely chop or powder the dried gingerroot slices, chopping 1 to 2 tbsp (15 to 25 mL) at a time and storing it in an airtight container. Alternatively, use a sharp knife, though it's a little more work.

Prep at Home

1/3 cup	dried peach slices	75 mL
1 tsp	packed brown sugar or maple sugar granules	5 mL
1/4 tsp	minced dried gingerroot	1 mL

To Serve

1/3 cup	water	75 mL

Prep at Home

1. In a sealable plastic bag, combine peaches, brown sugar and ginger. Seal and store at room temperature for up to 1 month.

To Serve

1. In a small saucepan, combine peach mixture and water. Let stand for 15 minutes or until peaches start to soften.

2. Bring just to a simmer over medium heat, stirring often. Serve hot or let cool.

Tropical Fruit Compote

Just Add Water

A little taste of the tropics is just the thing to warm you up at the campsite on a chilly evening.

Tip

To make vanilla sugar:
In a food processor, mini chopper or blender, combine 1 cup (250 mL) granulated sugar and half a vanilla bean, cut into thirds; process until vanilla is very finely chopped. Transfer to an airtight container and let stand for at least 1 week or for up to 3 months. Sift through a fine-mesh sieve to remove any large pieces of vanilla. Return to airtight container for up to 1 year from the date you made it.

Prep at Home

1/3 cup	chopped mixed dried tropical fruit (pineapple, papaya, mango, kiwifruit, melon)	75 mL
2 tsp	vanilla sugar (see tip, at left)	10 mL

To Serve

1/2 cup	water	125 mL

Prep at Home

1. In a sealable plastic bag, combine fruit and vanilla sugar. Seal and store at room temperature for up to 1 month.

To Serve

1. In a small saucepan, combine fruit mixture and water. Let stand for 15 minutes or until fruit starts to soften.

2. Bring just to a simmer over medium heat, stirring often. Serve hot or let cool.

Fresh Addition

Replace the water with fruit juice and add a splash of rum after removing the compote from the heat.

Foil-Baked Apples

Makes 1 serving

Baked apples are a classic comfort-food dessert that never goes out of style. Take them to the campfire and you'll be feeling the comfort with just one bite.

Tip

For the best taste and texture, use cooking apples that hold their flavor, such as Granny Smith, Northern Spy, Empire, McIntosh or Ida Red.

- One 12-inch (30 cm) square of foil
- Grill rack or flat rocks to place close to fire

Prep at Home

1 tbsp	raisins or dried cranberries	15 mL
2 tsp	vanilla sugar (see tip, page 234) or maple sugar granules	10 mL
1/4 tsp	finely chopped dried orange or lemon zest	1 mL
1/8 tsp	ground cinnamon	0.5 mL

To Serve

1	apple	1

Prep at Home

1. In a sealable plastic bag, combine raisins, sugar, orange zest and cinnamon. Seal bag and store at room temperature for up to 1 month.

To Serve

1. Prepare campfire and place grill rack, if using, over fire.

2. Using a paring knife, and starting at the stem end, cut out the apple core, almost but not all the way through to the bottom. Fill the cavity with the raisin mixture. Place in the center of the square of foil, with the bottom down, wrap the edges up and seal, keeping seams on top of the apple.

3. Place wrapped apple on grill rack or on flat rocks close to fire. Heat for about 30 minutes, rotating occasionally if on the side of the fire, until you can hear sizzling. Open a seam at the top of the foil and insert a fork to check that the apple is tender. If not, reseal foil and bake longer.

Chocolate Banana Nut "Quesadillas"

Makes 1 serving

Flour tortillas can be used to wrap all sorts of things. Here, they're used for a sweet treat filled with delicious combination of gooey chocolate, bananas and nuts.

Tips

Use kitchen scissors to cut the banana slices into very small pieces, wiping the blades with a hot cloth when they get sticky.

If the weather is warm and you won't have a cooler, substitute 2 tbsp (25 mL) chocolate hazelnut spread or dark chocolate spread for the chocolate chips. You might want to double-bag the gooey mixture, just in case!

No-Heat Option

Instead of chocolate chips, use chocolate hazelnut spread or dark chocolate spread and spread the mixture over the center of the tortilla, leaving a 1-inch (2.5 cm) border. Fold up the bottom, then roll up into a cylinder to enclose the filling.

Prep at Home

2 tbsp	semisweet chocolate chips or chopped chocolate	25 mL
1 tbsp	finely chopped nuts, preferably toasted	15 mL
1 tbsp	finely chopped dried banana slices	15 mL

To Serve

1	small flour tortilla	1

Prep at Home

1. In a sealable plastic bag, combine chocolate chips, nuts and bananas. Seal and store at a cool room temperature for up to 1 month.

To Serve

1. Heat a skillet over medium-low heat until warm.

2. Sprinkle chocolate mixture over half the tortilla, leaving a 1-inch (2.5 cm) border. Fold tortilla over to enclose filling. Place in the dry skillet and heat, flipping once, until slightly toasted on both sides and chocolate is melted.

Campfire Banana Boats

Jennifer's friend Leanne was very excited to share her banana boat expertise with us for this book. Leanne and her family pack the ingredients for every camping trip — it's a tradition. Now you can make it your tradition too.

Tip

Keeping packed bananas from bruising does require some care. Pack them into a rigid container and pack napkins or paper towels around them. Leave the lid of the container loose to prevent the bananas from spoiling. The napkins or paper towels will come in handy when you're eating your banana boats!

- One 12-inch (30 cm) square of foil
- Grill rack or flat rocks to place close to fire

Prep at Home

8	miniature marshmallows	8
1 tbsp	semisweet chocolate chips	15 mL
1 tbsp	finely chopped dried fruit (optional)	15 mL

To Serve

1	banana (unpeeled)	1

Prep at Home

1. In a sealable plastic bag, combine marshmallows, chocolate chips and fruit (if using). Seal bag and store at room temperature for up to 1 month.

To Serve

1. Prepare campfire and place grill rack, if using, over fire.

2. Using a knife, slit the inner curved side of the banana lengthwise, almost but not all the way through. Place on a diagonal in the center of the square of foil and squeeze ends gently to open slit. Place marshmallow mixture along the length of the cut. Wrap edges up over banana and seal, keeping seams on top of the banana.

3. Place wrapped banana on grill rack or on flat rocks close to fire. Heat for about 15 minutes, rotating occasionally if on the side of the fire, until banana is warmed and chocolate is melted.

Berry Sauce

**Makes
1 to 2 servings**

Just Add Water

If you happen to pick up some ice cream or a cake to eat at your campsite, add this berry sauce to turn it into a fancy dessert. It's also delicious served over pancakes for breakfast.

Variation

Berry Cherry Sauce: Use ¼ cup (50 mL) mixed dried berries and 1 tbsp (15 mL) dried cherries.

Prep at Home

⅓ cup	mixed dried berries	75 mL
1 tbsp	vanilla sugar (see tip, page 234)	15 mL
½ tsp	minced dried orange or lemon zest	2 mL

To Serve

½ cup	water	125 mL

Prep at Home

1. In a sealable plastic bag, combine berries, vanilla sugar and orange zest. Seal and store at room temperature for up to 1 month.

To Serve

1. In a small saucepan, combine fruit mixture and water. Let stand for about 15 minutes or until berries start to soften.

2. Bring just to a simmer over medium heat, stirring often. If desired, mash berries slightly for a thicker sauce. Serve hot or let cool.

Beverages

Strawberry Vanilla Protein Drink

Makes 1 serving

Fruit leathers dissolve nicely in water to make a flavorful fruit drink on the trail. The protein powder and milk powder provide extra nutrition, along with the all-important hydration.

Variation

Strawberry Banana Protein Drink: Use Strawberry Banana Leather in place of the Strawberry Apple Leather.

Prep at Home

1	4-inch (10 cm) square Strawberry Apple Leather	1
1/4 cup	vanilla-flavored protein powder (see tip, below left)	50 mL
2 tbsp	instant skim milk powder (optional)	25 mL

To Serve

1 cup	water, divided	250 mL

Prep at Home

1. Tear leather into very small pieces. In a sealable plastic bag, combine leather, protein powder and milk powder (if using). Seal and store at room temperature for up to 1 month.

To Serve

1. Add about 1/4 cup (50 mL) of the water to the leather mixture in the plastic bag. Seal bag and shake to mix well, mashing leather pieces with your fingers until dissolved. Pour into a cup or bottle with the remaining water and stir or shake to blend.

Chocolate Banana Protein Drink

Makes 1 serving

Chocolate and banana add a surprising creaminess to this power-packed drink.

Tips

This recipe is based on a protein powder that calls for 1/4 cup (50 mL) per 1 cup (250 mL) of liquid. If the directions are different for your protein powder, adjust the amount accordingly.

It is easiest to make individual servings of this drink in small plastic bags, rather than making a multiple batch, so you can shake it directly in the bag and mash the leather to help it dissolve.

Prep at Home

1	4-inch (10 cm) square Banana Chocolate Leather	1
1/4 cup	vanilla-flavored protein powder (see tip, at left)	50 mL
2 tbsp	instant skim milk powder (optional)	25 mL
1 tsp	unsweetened cocoa powder	5 mL

To Serve

1 cup	water, divided	250 mL

Prep at Home

1. Tear leather into very small pieces. In a sealable plastic bag, combine leather, protein powder, milk powder (if using) and cocoa. Seal and store at room temperature for up to 1 month.

To Serve

1. Add about 1/4 cup (50 mL) of the water to the leather mixture in the plastic bag. Seal bag and shake to mix well, mashing leather pieces and cocoa with your fingers until dissolved. Pour into a cup or bottle with the remaining water and stir or shake to blend.

Chocolate Almond Shake

Makes 1 serving

Almonds add protein and a terrific flavor, especially when combined with rich chocolate in this easy-to-make milkshake.

Tips

For extra flavor, toast the ground almonds in a dry skillet over medium heat, stirring constantly, for about 2 minutes or until golden and fragrant. Immediately transfer to a bowl and let cool completely before mixing in the bag.

Prep at Home

¼ cup	instant skim milk powder	50 mL
2 tbsp	ground almonds	25 mL
1 tbsp	vanilla sugar (see tip, page 234) or granulated sugar	15 mL
1 tbsp	unsweetened cocoa powder	15 mL

To Serve

1 cup	water, divided	250 mL

Prep at Home

1. In a sealable plastic bag, combine milk powder, almonds, vanilla sugar and cocoa. Seal and store at room temperature for up to 1 month.

To Serve

1. Add about ¼ cup (50 mL) of the water to the milk powder mixture in the plastic bag. Seal bag and shake to mix well, mashing any lumps of cocoa with your fingers until cocoa and sugar are dissolved. Pour into a cup or bottle with the remaining water and stir or shake to blend.

Antiox Berry Shake

Makes 1 serving

Berries contain antioxidants and terrific flavor, too. The flax seeds add omega-3s and a terrific thick texture to this shake.

Tip

This recipe doesn't work with commercially dried berries, as they have sugar and often oil added to them and won't grind to a powder.

Prep at Home

¼ cup	instant skim milk powder	50 mL
2 tbsp	dried blueberries	25 mL
2 tbsp	crumbled dried raspberries	25 mL
1 tbsp	dried cranberries	15 mL
1 tbsp	ground flax seeds	15 mL
1 tbsp	granulated sugar	15 mL

To Serve

1 cup	water, divided	250 mL

Prep at Home

1. In a mini chopper, process milk powder, blueberries, raspberries, cranberries, flax seeds and sugar until berries are finely ground. Transfer to a sealable plastic bag, seal and store at room temperature for up to 1 month.

To Serve

1. Add about ¼ cup (50 mL) of the water to the milk powder mixture in the plastic bag. Seal bag and shake to mix well, mashing any lumps with your fingers until sugar is dissolved. Pour into a cup or bottle with the remaining water and stir or shake to blend.

Green Power Drink

Makes 1 serving

When you need some get-up-and-go, this drink will certainly do it. We're warning you: it's ugly, but it tastes surprisingly delicious.

Tips

Instead of using a mini chopper, you can mash the spinach leather to a powder using a mortar and pestle, then just combine it in the bag with the other ingredients.

Use kitchen scissors to cut the strawberry banana leather into very small pieces, wiping the blades with a hot cloth when they get sticky.

Prep at Home

1	2-inch (5 cm) square Spinach Leather	1
¼ cup	instant skim milk powder or vanilla-flavored protein powder	50 mL
1 tsp	ground flax seeds	5 mL
1	4-inch (5 cm) square Strawberry Banana Leather or Strawberry Apple Leather	1

To Serve

1 cup	water, divided	250 mL

Prep at Home

1. In a mini chopper, process spinach leather, milk powder, flax seeds and sugar until spinach leather is finely ground. Transfer to a sealable plastic bag. Tear strawberry banana leather into small pieces and add to bag. Seal and store at room temperature for up to 1 month.

To Serve

1. Add about ¼ cup (50 mL) of the water to the leather mixture in the plastic bag. Seal bag and shake to mix well, mashing leather pieces with your fingers until dissolved. Pour into a cup or bottle with the remaining water and stir or shake to blend.

Homemade Hot Cocoa Mix

Makes 4 servings

Making your own hot cocoa mix means you know exactly what ingredients you're using, and it's much more economical than the packaged variety. You can adjust the sweetness to your own taste, too.

Tip

Plain sugar will work just fine, but the vanilla sugar brings out the rich chocolate flavor from the cocoa.

Prep at Home

1 cup	instant skim milk powder	250 mL
¼ cup	vanilla sugar (see tip, page 234) or granulated sugar	50 mL
¼ cup	unsweetened cocoa powder	50 mL
Pinch	salt	Pinch

To Serve

1 cup	water per serving, divided	250 mL

Prep at Home

1. In a sealable plastic bag, combine milk powder, vanilla sugar, cocoa and salt, mashing up any lumps of cocoa. Seal and store at room temperature for up to 1 month.

To Serve

1. For each serving, in a heatproof mug or bottle, combine a slightly heaping ⅓ cup (75 mL) mix with a little of the water, stirring to moisten. In a saucepan, bring the remaining water to a boil over high heat. Pour into mug, stirring to blend.

Hot Cocoa with a Kick

It sounds surprising, but the kick from hot pepper goes beautifully with chocolate, and it's sure to warm you up extra quickly.

Fresh Addition

If you have cream or milk, use it to replace half the water for a rich hot cocoa with a kick.

Prep at Home

1 cup	instant skim milk powder	250 mL
1/3 cup	packed brown sugar	75 mL
1/4 cup	unsweetened cocoa powder	50 mL
1/4 tsp	cayenne pepper or minced dried jalapeño peppers	1 mL
Pinch	salt	Pinch

To Serve

1 cup	water per serving, divided	250 mL

Prep at Home

1. In a sealable plastic bag, combine milk powder, brown sugar, cocoa, cayenne pepper and salt, mashing up any lumps of cocoa. Seal and store at room temperature for up to 1 month.

To Serve

1. For each serving, in a heatproof mug or bottle, combine a slightly heaping 1/3 cup (75 mL) mix with a little of the water, stirring to moisten. In a saucepan, bring the remaining water to a boil over high heat. Pour into mug, stirring to blend.

Chocolate Malted Milk

This nutritious drink will give you sustenance and satisfaction any time of day.

No-Heat Option

You can make this a cold drink. Just mix a little of the water with the mix in a cup or bottle, then gradually add the remaining water, stirring or shaking to blend well. It may not be as smooth, but it will still taste delicious.

Prep at Home

1/2 cup	instant skim milk powder	125 mL
1/2 cup	malted milk powder, such as Ovaltine	125 mL
1/4 cup	unsweetened cocoa powder	50 mL
3 tbsp	granulated sugar	45 mL

To Serve

1 cup	water per serving, divided	250 mL

Prep at Home

1. In a sealable plastic bag, combine skim milk powder, malted milk powder, cocoa and sugar, mashing up any lumps of cocoa. Seal and store at room temperature for up to 1 month.

To Serve

1. For each serving, in a heatproof mug or bottle, combine a slightly heaping 1/3 cup (75 mL) mix with a little of the water, stirring to moisten. In a saucepan, bring the remaining water to a boil over high heat. Pour into mug, stirring to blend.

Mexican Coffee

Makes 4 servings

The touch of cinnamon and vanilla adds a depth to the coffee that is particularly welcome when you're drinking instant instead of freshly ground.

Variation

If you have a camp stove coffee maker or a cone and filters, use freshly ground coffee in place of the instant, combine it with the cinnamon at home and pack the vanilla sugar separately. Brew as directed and sweeten brewed coffee in your mug with the sugar.

Prep at Home

6 tbsp	instant coffee granules (see tip, below left)	90 mL
2 tbsp	vanilla sugar (see tip, page 234) or granulated sugar	25 mL
1/4 tsp	ground cinnamon	1 mL

To Serve

1 cup	water per serving	250 mL

Prep at Home

1. In a sealable plastic bag, combine instant coffee granules, vanilla sugar and cinnamon. Seal and store at room temperature for up to 1 month.

To Serve

1. For each serving, place 2 tbsp (25 mL) mix in a heatproof mug or bottle. In a saucepan, bring water to a boil over high heat. Pour into mug, stirring to blend.

Mochaccino Mix

Makes 4 servings

A little chocolate, a little sweetness and coffee combine into perfect bliss as a pick-me-up. Make a big batch of this mix to brew up a cup any time.

Tip

The amount of instant coffee in this recipe is based on directions that specify 1 tbsp (15 mL) per 6-oz (175 mL) cup. Depending on the variety you use, the directions may vary. For this recipe, use six times the amount specified for one 6-oz (175 mL) cup.

Prep at Home

6 tbsp	instant coffee granules (see tip, at left)	90 mL
1/4 cup	instant skim milk powder	50 mL
2 tbsp	unsweetened cocoa powder	25 mL
2 tbsp	vanilla sugar (see tip, page 234) or granulated sugar	25 mL

To Serve

1 cup	water per serving, divided	250 mL

Prep at Home

1. In a sealable plastic bag, combine instant coffee granules, milk powder, cocoa and sugar. Seal and store at room temperature for up to 1 month.

To Serve

1. For each serving, in a heatproof mug or bottle, combine 2 heaping tbsp (25 mL) mix with a little of the water, stirring to moisten. In a saucepan, bring the remaining water to a boil over high heat. Pour into mug, stirring to blend.

Vanilla Chai Mix

Makes 6 servings

The warming spices and comforting sweetness in this spin on the traditional Indian drink are sure to ward off the chill at the end of even the coldest hike.

Tip

Do not let the water boil; keep it at as low a simmer as possible to prevent the tea from being bitter.

Prep at Home

½ cup	instant skim milk powder	125 mL
¼ cup	vanilla sugar (see tip, page 234)	50 mL
½ tsp	ground cinnamon	2 mL
¼ tsp	ground ginger	1 mL
⅛ tsp	each ground cardamom and cloves	0.5 mL
6	bags black tea	6

To Serve

1 cup	water per serving	250 mL

Prep at Home

1. In a sealable plastic bag, combine milk powder, vanilla sugar, cinnamon, ginger, cardamom and cloves; add tea bags. Seal and store at room temperature for up to 1 month.

To Serve

1. In a saucepan, for each serving, combine 1 of the tea bags, 2 slightly heaping tbsp (25 mL) mix and water. Bring just to a simmer over medium heat. Reduce heat to low and simmer for about 5 minutes or until flavors are blended and tea is desired strength. Discard tea bag and pour tea into heatproof mugs.

Spiced Apple Cider

Makes 1 serving

You can buy powdered apple cider mix, but it's often made with artificial ingredients. This version uses leather made from pure applesauce and real spices, and you can control the sugar or leave it out completely.

Variation

For an extra-warming effect, add a splash of brandy or rum to your hot cider after removing the saucepan from the heat.

Prep at Home

1	4-inch (10 cm) square Apple Cinnamon Leather	1
½ tsp	packed brown sugar (or to taste)	2 mL
Pinch	ground ginger	Pinch
Pinch	ground nutmeg	Pinch

To Serve

1 cup	water, divided	250 mL

Prep at Home

1. Tear leather into very small pieces. In a sealable plastic bag, combine leather, brown sugar, ginger and nutmeg. Seal and store at room temperature for up to 1 month.

To Serve

1. Add about 2 tbsp (25 mL) of the water to the leather mixture in the plastic bag. Seal bag and mash leather pieces with your fingers until dissolved. Pour into a saucepan and add the remaining water. Bring to a boil over medium heat. Pour into a heatproof mug.

Ginger Lemon Tea

Makes 1 serving

This is the simplest of infusions, yet it makes an amazingly soothing hot drink.

Tip

When preparing the zest to dehydrate, be sure you don't get any of the white pith with the zest, as it will taste bitter. If some is attached to the zest when you peel off a strip, place the strip on a cutting board, pith side up, and scrape off the white pith with the dull side of a knife.

Prep at Home

2	dried lemon zest strips	2
1	dried ginger slice	1

To Serve

1 cup	water	250 mL

Prep at Home

1. In a sealable plastic bag, combine lemon zest and ginger. Seal and store at room temperature for up to 1 month.

To Serve

1. In a saucepan, combine lemon zest mixture and water. Bring to a simmer over medium heat. Reduce heat and simmer for 2 to 3 minutes or until flavorful. If desired, discard lemon and ginger (or leave them in so they continue to steep as you drink). Pour tea into a heatproof mug.

Citrus-Spiked Sun Tea

Makes 4 servings

Citrus adds oomph to black or green tea and gives it a fresh flavor. Steeping it in the sun lets the flavor shine without any bitterness.

Tip

When you decant the tea, you might get a few bits in your cup. If you really don't like bits, strain into the mug through a fine-mesh strainer or place the mix in a paper tea filter or a tea ball before steeping.

Prep at Home

1 tbsp	loose black or green tea leaves	15 mL
1 tsp	finely chopped dried orange zest (see tip, above left)	5 mL
1/2 tsp	finely chopped dried lemon zest	2 mL

To Serve

1 cup	water per serving	250 mL

Prep at Home

1. In a sealable plastic bag, combine tea, orange zest and lemon zest. Seal and store at room temperature for up to 1 month.

To Serve

1. For each serving, in a sealable bag or a clear bottle, combine 1 tsp (5 mL) of the tea mixture and water. Seal or cover and let steep in the sun for at least 30 minutes or for up to 4 hours, or until desired strength. Decant into a cup, leaving leaves in bag or bottle.

Mint Green Sun Tea

Makes 4 servings

Take advantage of the sun's warmth to gently steep this tea: set it on a rock while you prepare your camp, and let the flavor bloom. The combination of mint and green tea is a classic and tastes good at room (outdoor) temperature or heated.

Tip

For a hot tea, decant the steeped tea into a saucepan and heat over medium heat until steaming.

Prep at Home

1 tbsp	loose green tea leaves	15 mL
1 tsp	crumbled dried mint	5 mL

To Serve

1 cup	water per serving	250 mL

Prep at Home

1. In a sealable plastic bag, combine green tea and mint. Seal and store at room temperature for up to 1 month.

To Serve

1. For each serving, in a sealable bag or a clear bottle, combine 1 tsp (5 mL) of the tea mixture and water. Seal or cover and let steep in the sun for at least 30 minutes or for up to 4 hours, or until desired strength. Decant into a cup, leaving leaves in bag or bottle.

Tropical Fruit Infusion

Makes 1 serving

When you're trekking or paddling, you need to make sure you stay hydrated. Adding a burst of tropical flavor to your water makes drinking it much more enjoyable. Fruit leather keeps it all-natural and gives you a little fiber, too.

Tip

You don't need to sweeten this drink, but a touch of sugar does help to enhance the fruit flavors.

Prep at Home

1	4-inch (10 cm) square Tropical Fruit Leather	1
$\frac{1}{2}$ tsp	vanilla sugar (see tip, page 234) or packed brown sugar (or to taste)	2 mL

To Serve

1 cup	water, divided	250 mL

Prep at Home

1. Tear leather into very small pieces. In a sealable plastic bag, combine leather and vanilla sugar. Seal and store at room temperature for up to 1 month.

To Serve

1. Add about 2 tbsp (25 mL) of the water to the leather mixture in the plastic bag. Seal bag and mash leather pieces with your fingers until dissolved. Pour into a saucepan and add the remaining water. Bring to a boil over medium heat. Pour into a heatproof mug.

Berry Splash

Adding dried berries and a touch of citrus to your water gives it a refreshing flavor and helps quench your thirst.

Tips

This recipe doesn't work with commercially dried berries, as they have sugar and often oil added to them and won't grind to a powder.

You can make this without sugar if you prefer; however, the sugar does enhance the berry flavor.

Prep at Home

1 tbsp	dried blueberries	15 mL
1 tbsp	crumbled dried raspberries	15 mL
1 tsp	dried cranberries	5 mL
Pinch	finely chopped dried lemon or orange zest	Pinch
1 tsp	granulated sugar (optional)	5 mL

To Serve

1 cup	water, divided	250 mL

Prep at Home

1. In a mini chopper, process blueberries, raspberries, cranberries, lemon zest and sugar (if using) until berries are finely ground. Transfer to a sealable plastic bag, seal and store at room temperature for up to 1 month.

To Serve

1. Add about 2 tbsp (250 mL) of the water to the berry mixture in the plastic bag. Seal bag and mash with your fingers until sugar is dissolved. Pour into a cup or bottle with the remaining water and stir or shake to blend.

Strawberry Lemonade

A fresh lemon flavor with a touch of strawberry is sure to perk you up on a hot day. This is so much more natural and refreshing than commercial powdered mixes.

Tip

Citric acid powder is available at pharmacies and health food stores, and adds the tang that is missing when you use dried lemon zest rather than fresh lemon juice. A little goes a long way, so be judicious with your pinch.

Prep at Home

1½ tbsp	crumbled dried lemon zest (see tip, page 246)	22 mL
1½ tbsp	dried strawberry slices, torn if large	22 mL
1 tsp	granulated sugar	5 mL
Pinch	citric acid powder (see tip, at left)	Pinch

To Serve

1 cup	water per serving	250 mL

Prep at Home

1. In a mini chopper, process lemon zest, strawberries, sugar and citric acid powder until berries are as finely chopped as possible. Transfer to a sealable plastic bag, seal and store at room temperature for up to 1 month.

To Serve

1. For each serving, in a cup or bottle, combine about 1½ tsp (7 mL) of the berry mixture and water. Let steep for at least 15 minutes, until berries are softened, or overnight.

Library and Archives Canada Cataloguing in Publication

MacKenzie, Jennifer
The complete trail food cookbook : over 300 recipes for campers,
canoeists and backpackers / Jennifer MacKenzie, Jay Nutt, Don Mercer.

Includes index.
ISBN 978-0-7788-0259-4 (bound) -- ISBN 978-0-7788-0236-5 (pbk.).

1. Outdoor cookery. I. Nutt, Jay, 1966- II. Mercer, Don, 1949- III. Title.

TX823.M285 2010   641.5'78   C2009-906693-9

Index